Objective-C
Object-Oriented
Programming Techniques

Objective-C
Object-Oriented
Programming Techniques

Lewis J. Pinson

Richard S. Wiener

University of Colorado at Colorado Springs

ADDISON-WESLEY PUBLISHING COMPANY
Reading, Massachusetts • Menlo Park, California • New York
Don Mills, Ontario • Wokingham, England • Amsterdam • Bonn
Sydney • Singapore •Tokyo • Madrid • San Juan • Milan • Paris

Many of the designations used by manufacturers and sellers to distinguish their products are claimed as trademarks. Where those designations appear in this book, and Addison-Wesley was aware of a trademark claim, the designations have been printed in initial caps or all caps.

The programs and applications presented in this book have been included for their instructional value. They have been tested with care, but are not guaranteed for any particular purpose. The publisher does not offer any warranties or representations, nor does it accept any liabilities with respect to the programs or applications.

Trademarked products cited in text:
Objective-C and ICpak are trademarks of the Stepstone Corporation.
NeXT, Application Kit, Interface Builder, NextStep, Workspace Manager, and Window Server are trademarks of NeXT Computer, Inc.
UNIX is a registered trademark of AT&T
OS/2 and MS-DOS are trademarks of Microsoft, Inc.
Macintosh is a registered trademark and Apple Macintosh is a trademark of Apple Computer, Inc.
Prograph is a registered trademark of TGS Systems, Inc., Halifax, Nova Scotia, Canada.
Display Postscript and Postscript are registered trademarks of Adobe Systems, Inc.

Library of Congress Cataloging-in-Publication Data
Pinson, Lewis J.
    Objective C : object-oriented programming techniques / Lewis J.
Pinson, Richard S. Wiener.
      p.   cm.
    Includes index.
    ISBN 0-201-50828-1
    1. Object-oriented programming (Computer science)   2. C (Computer
program language)   I. Wiener, Richard, 1941– . II. Title.
QA76.64.P57   1991
005.26'2--dc20   90-25807
                                                                 CIP

1 2 3 4 5 6 7 8 9 10 MA 9594939291

CONTENTS

This book has three primary goals. The first goal is to present the basic concepts of object-oriented design and object-oriented programming. The second goal is to provide a description of the Objective-C language, including a discussion of predefined classes. The third goal is to illustrate the general principles by presenting several small-to-medium-sized applications using Objective-C.

This book is intended for computer science students, programmers, and other software development professionals. It may be used for a course on the Objective-C language or a course on Object-Oriented Programming.

The Objective-C presented in this book comes in two flavors: the Stepstone version and the NeXT version. Each of these implementations of Objective-C are outstanding. Although the actual language details are almost identical in these two versions, there are substantial differences in the supporting class libraries. Even the superclass, Object, is different in the two versions. The Stepstone version of Objective-C is featured in Chapters 4 and 5. The NeXT version of Objective-C is featured in Chapters 7 and 8. Chapter 3 presents information and comparisons of both the Stepstone and NeXT implementations, with particular focus on class Object. By presenting these two flavors of Objective-C, we hope to provide a greater richness of examples and a better demonstration of the importance and power of supporting class libraries.

Chapter 1 begins with a discussion of the object-oriented paradigm and object-oriented problem solving. Chapter 2 presents details of an approach to the object-oriented design of software systems. Specification and design are presented for a medium-sized example that has a rich hierarchy of classes. The concept of reusability is discussed in terms of the object-oriented paradigm and in terms of the chosen design for the example.

Chapter 3 presents a precise description of the Objective-C language, contrasting the implementations provided by The Stepstone Corporation (the original developer of Objective-C) and by NeXT Computer, Inc. A discussion is given of class Object, which is the abstract superclass of all classes in Objective-C. Several simple examples of Objective-C software systems illustrate the design and implementation of hierarchies of classes as well as their use.

An important feature of any object-oriented language is the predefined classes that are provided with the system. Chapter 4 describes the sixteen classes provided as part of Stepstone's ICpak 101 foundation library. General comments are given on the purpose of each class.

Chapter 5 illustrates by examples how the Stepstone foundation classes may be used to support problem solutions. The chapter ends with an Objetive-C implementation for the example whose specification and design were presented in Chapter 2. This medium-sized example uses several of the foundation classes in addition to requiring the development of approximately ten new classes. Details of the example are given in Stepstone's version of Objective-C. Porting the solution to the NeXT computer requires implementation of equivalent classes for the foundation classes (these are not currently provided with the NeXT environment). The porting of this example to the NeXT was done easily and is discussed in this chapter.

Two simple design examples are presented in Chapter 6. An informal specification, a design, and limited implementation details are provided.

Chapter 7 discusses the desired features for an object-oriented software development environment. Features of the NeXT computer, including its Interface Builder and Application Kit classes (there are a total of over seventy predefined classes that come with the NeXT), are discussed. Several examples are presented that show how the Application Kit classes may be used directly and from the Interface Builder to assist the development of software systems on the NeXT. These classes make it possible to develop applications that take full advantage of the NeXT's graphic environment.

Chapter 8 presents two case studies that take full advantage of the graphic interface of the NeXT computer. A graphic interface is added to the earlier example described in Chapters 2 and 5. Another example is presented by giving its specification, object-oriented design, and selected implementation details. This last example is a tool for browsing the protocol of Objective-C classes.

An understanding of the C language is helpful in following the detail of code segments, since Objective-C is a superset of the C language.

We wish to thank our editor, Keith Wollman, for his support during this project. Thanks to Steve Jobs and NeXT Computer, Inc. for creating yet another pioneering computer concept. The NeXT is a powerful and user-friendly system, providing the best of two worlds (direct support and access to UNIX as well as a powerful and simple graphic user interface). Thanks to Brad Cox and The Stepstone Corporation for developing the powerful and easy-to-use object-oriented language, Objective-C.

Many of our students have been helpful in identifying errors in concept as well as implementation. We greatly appreciate their assistance. Finally we thank Leigh and Hanne for their love and support.

Lewis J. Pinson
Richard S. Wiener
Colorado Springs, Colorado

Objective-C
Object-Oriented
Programming Techniques

## CHAPTER 1

Basic Principles of Object-Oriented Problem Solving

Work without hope draws nectar in a sieve,
And hope without an object cannot live.

Samuel Taylor Coleridge, *1772–1834*[1]

1.1 PROBLEM SOLVING

Problem solving is something we do throughout our lives in many different contexts. The methods we use for problem solving are learned from others and refined as we gain experience. In the dictionary we find the following definitions:[2]

— *Problem*
A question raised for inquiry, consideration, or solution
— *Solving*
To find a solution for (solve a problem)

Many of the "problems" we solve concern the development of enhanced capabilities in a particular area of activity or intellectual endeavor.

Computer problem solving is problem solving with the aid of computers. It requires the development and application of software designed to assist the solution process. Because the development of software to assist in problem solving is not a precise activity, much effort continues to be expended in trying to improve the process. In fact, a major part of computer problem solving is "solving the problem of how to enhance our ability to do computer problem solving." The techniques described in this book represent one approach to achieve that end. They continue to evolve, to change, and (we hope) to improve.

---

[1] All quotations are taken from the NeXT on-line program *Digital Quotations*, by Kate Smith.

[2] By permission. From *Webster's Ninth New Collegiate Dictionary* © 1990 by Merriam-Webster, Inc., publisher of the Merriam-Webster® dictionaries.

1.2 THE OBJECT-ORIENTED APPROACH

Objects and Organization

The term *object-oriented problem solving* implies that problems are solved through the development and use of relationships among objects. Objects have always been an important part of our learning process. As described in the *Encyclopedia Britannica* under "classification theory" and pointed out by Coad and Yourdon:[3]

> In comprehending the real world, people use three methods of organization:
>
> 1. The differentiation of experience into particular objects and their attributes—e.g., the distinction between a computer (an object) and its processing speed or size (attributes)
> 2. The distinction between whole objects and their component parts—e.g., the computer (whole object) consists of processors, keyboard, disk drives, memory, mouse, operating system, and monitor (component parts—also objects)
> 3. The formation of and distinction between different classes of objects—e.g., the formation of a class for all computer hardware and a class for all computer software and distinguishing between them.

It is not unusual or strange to use objects in computer problem solving. In fact, it is consistent with much of our experience.

Definitions

Among the variety of alternate definitions for the terms in the phrase *object-oriented*, the following are found in *Webster's Ninth New Collegiate Dictionary:*[2]

> — *Object*
> Something mental or physical toward which thought, feeling, or action is directed
> — *Oriented*
> Intellectually or emotionally directed

These definitions coupled with the definitions for problem solving give the following definition for *object-oriented problem solving*:

> — *Object-oriented problem solving*
> The finding of solutions to problems or answers to questions through the intellectual direction of thought and actions toward conceptual or physical objects

---

[3] Peter Coad and Edward Yourdon, *Object-Oriented Analysis*, Yourdon Press, 1990.

In plain English, we define objects, their attributes, and what we want to do with them, including how various objects interact with each other. In computer problem solving, objects are implemented in software. A software object may represent a physical object in the problem space (e.g., a processor, an automobile, a person, or an image sensor), or it may represent a conceptual object (e.g., a bank account, a processing algorithm, an idea, or an action). Software objects may be connected to the physical objects they represent, such as hardware components of a computer.

A Simple Example of Object-Oriented Problem Solving

We illustrate the use of objects in a problem solution with a simple example (Example 1.1).

Example 1.1 _____
A tale of two cities

Problem statement: Given the names of two cities whose longitude and latitude are known, compute the distance between the two cities in kilometers. Display the names and attributes of the two cities and the distance between them. The problem space is depicted in Figure 1.1.

Figure 1.1 _____
Objects in the problem space

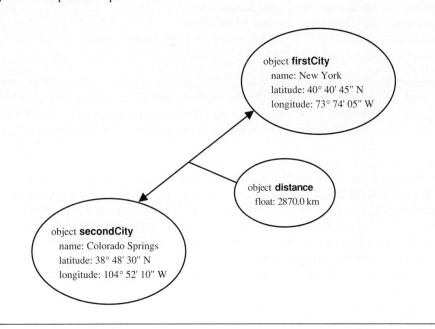

Primary objects in a solution: The following primary objects are identified as part of this problem and are used in a solution:

— firstCity
  the first of the specified two cities
— secondCity
  the second of the specified two cities
— distance
  the distance in kilometers between firstCity and secondCity.

A solution: A high-level, object-oriented solution to the problem is given by the following expressions:

— firstCity display.
— secondCity display.
— secondCity computeAndDisplayDistanceFrom: firstCity.

When executed, the above solution gives the following output:

```
Name:      New York
Latitude:  40 degrees 40 minutes 45 seconds N
Longitude: 73 degrees 74 minutes 05 seconds W
Name:      Colorado Springs
Latitude:  38 degrees 48 minutes 30 seconds N
Longitude: 104 degrees 52 minutes 10 seconds W
The distance of Colorado Springs from New York is 2870.0 kilometers
```

Comments on the Solution in Example 1.1. The solution consists of three simple expressions (it is assumed that objects firstCity and secondCity have been created with the appropriate attributes). Each expression consists of an object followed by the message it receives. The last message includes a parameter object that follows the message. Expressions are terminated with a period in the above example. The goal of this example is to show how simple a high-level, object-oriented solution can be.

Clearly much of the detail of this problem solution is hidden in the implementation of the computeAndDisplayDistanceFrom: message that is sent to object secondCity with object firstCity as a parameter. Object-oriented problem solving is very compatible with this high-level, top-down approach. The fundamental concept is to identify objects, their attributes, and what can be done by those objects, that is, the messages to which they respond and how they respond. We can analyze the above example in more detail by listing attributes of the primary objects, identifying supporting objects, and listing key messages.

Attributes of the Primary Objects.
  • For objects firstCity and secondCity
    ○ name
      A string of characters that is the name of the city

- ○ latitude, longitude
  Earth coordinates giving representations in degrees, minutes, and seconds of the latitude and longitude for the city
- For object distance
- ○ float
  A floating-point number that is the distance in kilometers

Supporting Objects in a Solution. Supporting objects include those represented by the attributes of the primary objects as well as those implied by certain actions taken on the primary objects. For this example the following supporting objects are identified:

- string (name)
  An object that is an ordered collection of characters used to represent the attribute name for city objects. Its implementation depends on another supporting object to represent characters.
- character
  An object that is the basic building block for string objects.[4]
- earthCoordinate (latitude, longitude)
  An object characterized by three attributes that are the degrees, minutes, and seconds of an earth coordinate. Both latitude and longitude are implemented as this supporting object type. The attributes of earthCoordinate (also objects) are represented as numbers (either integer or floating-point).
- float
  A floating-point number used to represent distance and attributes of earth coordinates. As an alternative, depending on required accuracy, the attributes of earth coordinates may be represented by integers.
- displayObject
  The object upon which information is displayed. Typically this is the display screen (a hardware object).

Actions to Which the Objects Must Respond (and Their Response to Each). The following messages and actions are required for the indicated objects:

- For objects firstCity and secondCity
- ○ computeAndDisplayDistanceFrom: aCity
  Compute the distance of the receiver city object from the parameter object aCity; then display with appropriate comments (strings). Respond with a distance in kilometers.
- ○ display
  Display on the displayObject the attributes for the receiver city object. These attributes include the name, latitude, and longitude. The response is to perform the display and return the receiver object.

---

[4] Here we are treating every data item as an object for consistency of thinking.

- For object distance (implemented as supporting object float)
  - ◦ display
    Display the magnitude of the receiver object on the displayObject. The response is to perform the display and return the receiver object.
  - ◦ arithmetic operations
    Normal operations such as addition, subtraction, multiplication, and division are required. Special operations such as squaring and square root are required by this example. In each case the response is to return a temporary float that is the result of the operation.

This refinement of details for the objects is a necessary step in the development of a final solution. The above approach, outlined briefly, leads to a complete solution in terms of primary and supporting objects, their attributes, and operations on those objects. In the next section we formalize our definition for object-oriented problem solving by examining the five key components of the object-oriented paradigm.

1.3 THE OBJECT-ORIENTED PARADIGM

In this section we present the five key components of the object-oriented paradigm and show how these components are applied to a software solution. The five components provide a consistent thread that is woven through the analysis, design, and implementation of object-oriented software systems.

Key Components: Object, Message, Class, Instance, and Method

The five key components of the object-oriented paradigm are object, message, class, instance, and method. We have already seen how objects and messages are used in solving simple problems such as the one illustrated in Example 1.1. The other three components—class, instance, and method—provide ways to avoid duplication of effort and to develop necessary details for a problem solution.

In describing the objects in Example 1.1, we found multiple objects of a given kind; for example, firstCity and secondCity were the same kind of object. Each had the same list of attributes (name, latitude, longitude) whose values could be different. Each could respond to the same set of messages. The supporting objects latitude and longitude were also the same kind of object, with the same set of attributes (degrees, minutes, seconds) and the same set of messages to which each could respond.

In developing a problem solution, we wish to describe a kind of object only once, giving a list of its attributes and a list of the messages to which that kind of object can respond. This description is given within a *class*. A class has a name that represents the kind of object it describes (e.g., class name City for objects firstCity and secondCity). Individual objects are *instances* of a class (firstCity and secondCity are instances of class City). Each instance has the attributes of its class and can respond to messages in the class description. Values for the attributes are unique to each instance. Objects are instances of a class.

It is valid to think of a class as a template for creating objects. All instances of a given class will have a list of attributes and messages to which they respond that are given in the class description. The values of the attributes are unique to each instance and may be different.

In Example 1.1, the high-level solution hid much of the detail in the implementation of a message, computeAndDisplayDistanceFrom:. The implementation details that show how an object responds to a message are given in a *method*. Every message in the class description for a kind of object has a method. The methods for each message are also given in the class description.

The following definitions and relationships among the five key components are given to formalize the properties discussed above.

— *Object*
>   An object is an encapsulated abstraction that has internal state as given by a list of attributes whose values are unique to the object. The object also knows the list of messages to which it can respond and how it will respond to each. *Encapsulation* and *abstraction* are defined in Section 1.4.

— *Message*
>   A message is represented by an identifier, special symbol, or combination of identifiers that implies an action to be taken by an object. Messages may be simple or may include parameters that affect how the receiving object responds. The way an object responds to a message may also be affected by the values of its attributes.

— *Class*
>   A class is a template for creating an object. It includes in its description a name for the kind of object, a list of attributes (and their kinds), and a list of messages with corresponding methods to which an object of the class can respond. Among the messages in the class description are those used to create instances of the class. These instance-creation messages are usually sent to the class name. The exact mechanism for creating instances of a class is dependent on the object-oriented language being used.

— *Instance*
>   An instance is an object with properties defined in its class description. Properties that are unique to an instance are the values of its attributes.

— *Method*
>   A method is a list of detailed instructions that define how an object responds to a particular message. A method typically consists of expressions that send more messages to objects. Every message in a class must have a corresponding method.

In summary, *object*s are *instance*s of *classe*s that respond to *message*s according to *method*s and attributes, as given in the class description. Values of the attributes of an object are unique to the object and dynamic in nature. Values of attributes also affect the way an object responds to a message. Having defined this basic structure for the object-oriented paradigm, we next examine how to solve problems by using it.

Applying the Object-Oriented Paradigm

Object-oriented problem solving consists of performing the following major operations:

- Define and develop descriptions for classes representing objects that are part of a problem solution. The class description must provide a way to create new instances of the class. It must also include all the messages and methods to which instances of the class can respond.
- Create the objects and develop a sequence of expressions (messages sent to objects) that effect a solution to the problem.

  Example 1.2 illustrates these major operations.

Example 1.2 _____
Hello NeXT world

Problem statement: Send the character string "Hello NeXT World" to the printer.

Primary objects in a solution: There are two primary objects in a solution to this simple problem. They are aString (represented by class String) and aPrinter (represented by class Printer).[5] Object aPrinter is a software object that represents and is attached to an actual printer (hardware object).

We proceed by defining limited class descriptions for these two primary objects.

```
class name:          String
instance variables:  characters
instance creation:   new: aStringLiteral
instance methods:    print
        ...details of printing characters...

       ... other methods ...
```

```
class name:          Printer
instance variables:  ... hardware dependent, details not given ...
instance creation:   new
instance methods:    printString: aString
            ... generate hardware commands ...

       ... other methods ...
```

Creation of objects and development of expressions for a solution:
```
aPrinter = Printer new.
aString = String new: "Hello NeXT World".
aPrinter printString: aString.
```

_____

[5] Here and for the remainder of the book we adopt the convention that class names begin with uppercase characters and instance names begin with lowercase characters. Further, we choose instance names to reflect the class to which they belong where possible.

Supporting character objects are implicit in the solution since strings are sequences of characters. They are created and accessed by methods in class String. An alternate way to print the string is to use the expression aString print instead of aPrinterprintString: aString. This implies that the method for print sends the message printString: to the printer object.

This seems like a lot of effort just to send a string to the printer. In practice some shortcuts are taken that make the problem simpler. For example, the software object aPrinter would be created one time only and attached to a specific hardware printer. This operation may even be done behind the scene, so that it is transparent to the user. Additionally, most object-oriented languages provide some kind of support for string literals. With these features in place, the above example reduces to

"Hello NeXT World" print.

1.4 FOUR ESSENTIAL PROPERTIES

There are four essential properties supported by the object-oriented paradigm: abstraction, encapsulation, inheritance, and polymorphism. Together they represent a powerful set of features that may be applied to problem solving. Through proper application of these features, one may build a framework for solving new problems using components (classes) developed for previous problem solutions. This approach has a number of advantages, including

1. the amount of effort required to develop a new problem solution is less since it builds on existing solutions, and
2. chances for logical errors in the problem solution are reduced by using existing, tested components.

In the following sections we describe these four properties and how they support object-oriented problem solving.

Abstraction

— *Abstraction*
An abstraction has conceptual rather than concrete existence. It represents ideas, concepts, and general properties without attention to details. For computer software, this means without attention to implementation details, thus avoiding the necessity of dealing with language syntax or even the choice of a language. The only concern is that a particular language support abstraction.

Abstraction is most important in the early phases of a problem solution, where an attempt is made to understand the problem space and the techniques required for a solution. Although one must eventually deal with details, abstraction makes it possible to defer those details and to organize them in a manageable way through the use of layered abstractions. A *layered abstraction* is one that has varying levels of detail. At the highest level there is very little detail. High-level abstractions are expressed in terms of a small number of lower-level abstractions. The partitioning continues at each level until all details have been included.

In object-oriented problem solving, both objects and messages are abstractions. Each represents a conceptual component of the problem solution with the potential for several underlying layers of additional abstractions. We partition complex objects into simpler objects and high-level messages into lower-level messages.

Encapsulation

— *Encapsulation*
Encapsulation is the act or process of encapsulating. The result of encapsulating is an entity with distinct borders, a well-defined interface, and a protected internal representation. For computer software, an encapsulation is a software component. The integrity of the software component as an encapsulation is dependent on features of the underlying computer language in which the component is implemented.

Encapsulation is an important concept for the development of problem solutions that are less susceptible to errors. A problem is partitioned into a number of components. Each component is encapsulated to interact with the other components only in carefully prescribed ways, as defined by its interface.

In object-oriented problem solving the unit of encapsulation is the object. We speak of objects as being *encapsulated abstractions*.

Inheritance and Multiple Inheritance

— *Inheritance*
Inheritance is the act of acquiring a possession, condition, or trait from past generations. In computer problem solving we talk of software components inheriting properties that describe other software components. In object-oriented problem solving one kind of object inherits properties that characterize another kind of object. Since the properties of objects are given by class descriptions, this implies a hierarchy of classes, where one class is a subclass of another, parent class. Objects that are instances of the subclass have properties given within the subclass description as well as inherited properties given within the parent class and all ancestor classes.

Inheritance provides the potential for building new solutions to problems by adding incremental capability to existing problem solutions through subclassing. If done properly, subclassing is a powerful tool for solving problems.

Instances of a subclass represent a specialization of instances described by a parent class. The subclass instance has all the attributes given by the parent class, plus additional attributes given in the subclass. The subclass instance responds to the same set of messages as given in the parent class, plus additional messages given in the subclass description.

Response by the subclass instance to messages in the parent class may be different from the response of a parent class instance to that same message. It is not valid to consider subclass objects as having fewer attributes than objects described by their parent classes. We illustrate inheritance and subclassing in Example 1.3.

Example 1.3 _____
A simple inheritance example

Consider the following objects: aCar, aJetPlane, aGlider. Create a set of classes to represent these objects.

These objects are all related by the fact that each is a kind of vehicle. Further, the jet and glider are both airborne vehicles. In establishing a potential hierarchy of classes, there are many options depending on how general we wish to be. If the three objects are part of a one-time problem solution, we may wish to represent them by three independent classes. If we wish to solve the problem with the added goal of developing reusable software components, then a more general approach is required.

The one-time-solution approach provides three classes at the same hierarchical level, as shown in Figure 1.2. Attributes for each class are given in parentheses. Another approach that takes advantage of the similarities in the three objects is represented in Figure 1.3. A superclass (or parent class) representing all vehicles is created, with the other three classes as subclasses. This provides the benefit that the three attributes shared by all vehicles (weight, cost, topSpeed) need be given only one time in class Vehicle. They are inherited and therefore part of the attribute list for the subclasses. In addition, the class description for Vehicle would include methods for all messages to which every vehicle can respond. This approach avoids duplication of functionality and data.

A still more general approach that seeks to develop reusable and more general classes is shown in Figure 1.4. The decision to use the more general approach depends on the degree of interest in the family of vehicles. If we expect to be solving other problems with vehicles, then the more general approach is justified. Each level in the hierarchy of classes in Figure 1.4 adds detail to represent a more specific kind of vehicle. It also opens

Figure 1.2 _____
Classes for a one-time solution

```
Car ( weight, cost, topSpeed, driveWheels )
JetPlane ( weight, cost, topSpeed, wingSpan, totalThrust )
Glider ( weight, cost, topSpeed, wingSpan )
```

Figure 1.3 _____
Classes that use inheritance

```
Vehicle ( weight, cost, topSpeed)
    Car (driveWheels)
    JetPlane (wingSpan, totalThrust)
    Glider (wingSpan)
```

Figure 1.4 _____
Reusable classes for a more general solution

```
Vehicle( weight, cost, topSpeed)
    LandVehicle (numberOfWheels)
        Car (driveWheels)
    AirVehicle (maxAltitude)
        Plane (wingSpan)
            JetPlane (totalThrust)
            Glider ( )
```

_____

up the possibility for easily expanding the hierarchy to represent new kinds of vehicles by adding new classes at the appropriate place in the hierarchy. For example, we could add class Bicycle as a subclass of LandVehicle.

_____

Example 1.3 illustrates that the design of classes to represent objects in a software solution is not an exact science. It also shows that no particular hierarchy of classes is the only, or even best, solution. In Section 1.5 we examine options for the development of class hierarchies in terms of the reusability of software components.

Inheritance may be singular (each class inherits from only one parent class), as shown in Example 1.3, or multiple (each class can have more than one parent class). Multiple inheritance adds flexibility to the process of developing class hierarchies for a problem solution and the potential for additional software reuse. On the negative side, multiple inheritance adds complexity to the class hierarchy and increases the probability of conceptual errors in the construction of a class hierarchy. A simple example of multiple inheritance is given in Example 1.4.

Example 1.4 _____
A simple example of multiple inheritance

Consider the following objects aSeaPlane, aBoat, aPlane. Create a set of classes to represent these objects.

These objects are again related by the fact that each is a kind of vehicle. Further, the seaplane has properties of both a boat and a plane. Using the basic structure of classes for vehicles developed in Figure 1.4 and multiple inheritance, we may add new classes to represent a boat and a seaplane as shown in Figure 1.5.

_____

We discover one of the complexities of multiple inheritance by examining the attributes of an instance of class SeaPlane. Through its two inheritance chains, a seaplane object is characterized by powerType, wingSpan, maxAltitude, and two copies of weight, cost, and topSpeed. Clearly a seaplane has only one cost and weight; however, it has a top speed in the air and a different top speed in the water. If multiple inheritance is to be useful, some mechanism must be provided in the supporting software environment for controlling the inheritance of one or multiple copies of attributes given in ancestor classes.

Figure 1.5 _____

Vehicle classes with multiple inheritance

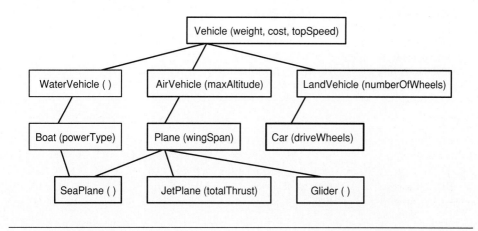

Polymorphism

— *Polymorphism*

Polymorphism is defined as the quality or state of being able to assume different forms. In object-oriented problem solving, polymorphism may apply to either objects or operations on those objects. The more common usage is *operation polymorphism*, which is represented by sending the same message, print, to different objects and having each respond in its own way. Object polymorphism is sometimes represented by objectA posing as objectB. In effect objectA takes on the features of objectB. Its major use is in redefining a class object by letting a subclass object pose as the class. Another way of looking at object polymorphism is given by Example 1.4. The seaplane object is both a boat and a plane. It takes on different conceptual forms depending on whether it is in the air or in the water. The concept of polymorphism is illustrated in Figure 1.6 for operation and object polymorphism.

Operation polymorphism is illustrated in the first column in Figure 1.6 by sending the same message, print, to four different objects. Each must know how to respond in its own way to the message. The second column in Figure 1.6 illustrates how the subclass NewString may pose as its parent class, String. This is object polymorphism from the viewpoint that class String takes on a different form, given by class NewString. The third column in Figure 1.6 shows how the object aSeaPlane can be considered to be other objects. This example of polymorphism is more semantic than anything else. It relies on the fact that SeaPlane is a subclass of both Plane and Boat. In essence the object aSeaPlane is a SeaPlane and is also a special case of each of its parent classes.

Figure 1.6 _____

Operation polymorphism and two kinds of object polymorphism

Operation	Class object	Object
aString print.	class String	aSeaPlane
aNumber print.	class NewString	isa SeaPlane
aCollection print.	NewString poseAs:String	isa Plane
anImage print.	String isa NewString	isa Boat

Figure 1.7a _____

Overloading of message identifiers and operators

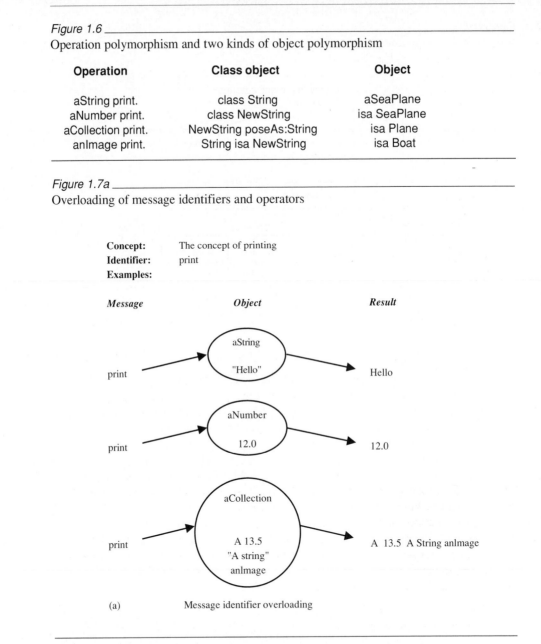

Concept: The concept of printing
Identifier: print
Examples:

Message	*Object*	*Result*

print → aString "Hello" → Hello

print → aNumber 12.0 → 12.0

print → aCollection A 13.5 "A string" anImage → A 13.5 A String anImage

(a)   Message identifier overloading

Polymorphism may be examined further in terms of its supporting properties. A first property of polymorphism is the overloading of message identifiers and operators. Polymorphism is further supported by the binding of a particular method to a message identifier during the execution of a software system. This *late binding*, or *dynamic binding*, is an important feature of the object-oriented approach to problem solving. These two properties are examined in more detail in Figures 1.7 and 1.8.

Figure 1.7b _____

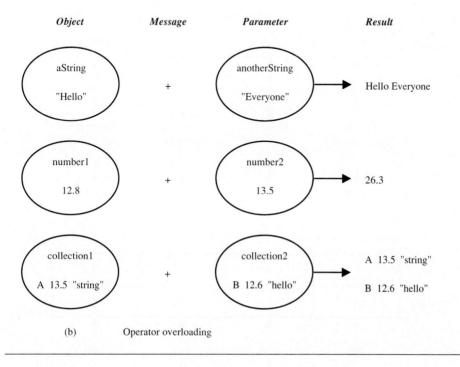

Concept:	Addition or concatenation, adding to	
Operator:	+ anObject	"requires a parameter"
Meaning:	add an Object to the receiver	
Examples:		

(b)   Operator overloading

Message Identifier and Operator Overloading. Message identifiers and operators invoke a specific operation on an object. They are chosen to be meaningful and consistent with our way of thinking about the particular operation; that is, they are chosen to represent the concept of the operation. Figure 1.7 illustrates how the concept of an operation is kept consistent by choosing a single message identifier and how the details of the implementation of that concept may vary for different objects. Part (*a*) of Figure 1.7 shows identifier overloading, and part (*b*) shows operator overloading.

Late Binding. Late binding is important in problem solutions when a specific operation is to be performed on an object whose class changes dynamically during execution of a software system. More specifically, the operation is performed on an object placeholder, and the kind of object occupying the placeholder changes. Object placeholders may be as simple as a temporary object or as complicated as collections of many objects. Late binding is an important implementation issue for object-oriented languages and supports an essential concept in problem solving.

Late binding is illustrated in Figure 1.8 for a collection of four objects. The content of the collection changes during execution of the software. At various stages in the

Figure 1.8 _____

Late binding of methods to messages

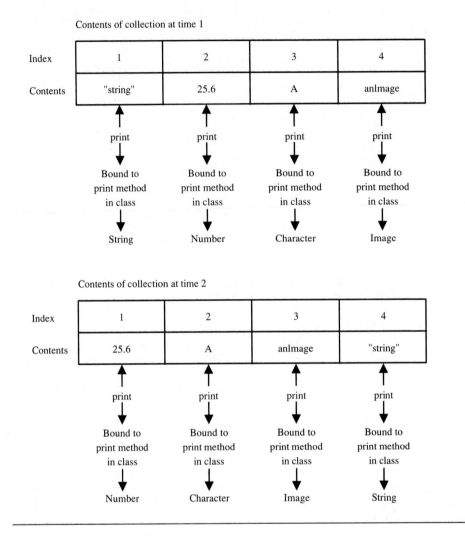

execution of the software system, the message print is sent sequentially to each element in the collection. The specific method for printing must be bound dynamically to the message print depending on the class of the object occupying each element of the collection. This cannot be done statically, since the order of the objects changes dynamically. Support for dynamic binding is an important and essential feature of the object-oriented paradigm.

1.5 REUSABLE SOFTWARE COMPONENTS

In this section we look at some of the characteristics of reusable software components. Of particular interest is how the object-oriented approach to problem solving supports the development of software components with high reusability.

Why Reinvent the Wheel?

Why should we continue to reinvent the wheel? Maybe to build a better wheel, or a new kind of wheel. Even this ancient object has not escaped the processes of refinement and redefinition. Making a better wheel implies refinement of an existing object and involves implementation enhancements such as better materials or better workmanship. Building a new kind of wheel implies creating a new or better design or perhaps adapting the concept of a wheel to a new application. The only attributes shared by all wheels are that they are round and they tend to roll. We will undoubtedly continue to reinvent the wheel.

If we don't have a single best solution for wheels how can we expect to have a single best solution for computer software? Within the wide range of kinds of wheels there is some standardization and a lot of reusability. Refinement of a particular kind of wheel does not eliminate its reusability; it just makes the wheel perform the same job a little better. The design of a new kind of wheel does not eliminate the reusability of other kinds of wheels. Two kinds of wheels are typically independent of each other unless they must work together at some interface. We seek this same rationality for software components.

Since the unit of encapsulation in the object-oriented approach to problem solving is the object, reusable software components must contain as a minimum all the detail for a kind of object. This includes detail given in the class description for the object plus all the detail inherited from parent classes. From another point of view, the very act of subclassing is an example of reusability. The protocol of the parent classes is inherited and used by the subclass.[6]

Better Design of Class Hierarchies

One approach to promoting reusability is to design a hierarchy of base classes to which subclasses can logically be added. A poor choice at any level in the inheritance chain can bring a sudden halt to any additional subclassing in that chain. Classes that are at high levels in the inheritance chain tend to be more general, and those at lower levels tend to be more specific. If a very specific class is added at a high level in the hierarchy, it has the effect of allowing no subclassing below it. Keeping this in mind, the most reusable software components are those representing the most general kinds of objects. This principle is inherent in the more general study of classification theory and is observed in available hierarchies of classes for a variety of object-oriented languages.

---

[6]Protocol is defined as a set of conventions governing the treatment and especially the formatting of data in an electronic communications system.

Figure 1.9 _____
Two possible hierarchies of vehicle classes

Vehicle	Vehicle
LandVehicle	EngineDriven
EngineDriven	LandVehicle
WindDriven	AirVehicle
PeopleDriven	WaterVehicle
AirVehicle	WindDriven
EngineDriven	LandVehicle
WindDriven	AirVehicle
PeopleDriven	WaterVehicle
WaterVehicle	PeopleDriven
EngineDriven	LandVehicle
WindDriven	AirVehicle
PeopleDriven	WaterVehicle
(a) Operating medium / drive power	(b) Drive power / operating medium

Another approach to promoting reusability is to identify kinds of objects that are part of the solution to a large group of problems. Their very nature makes them reusable. Examples in computer problem solving include numbers and strings. Although strings have high reusability, they are not general in nature. They are ordered collections of characters, very specific. This is illustrated by the Smalltalk language, which places the class for strings five levels deep in a hierarchy of classes, for example, Object—Collection—SequenceableCollection—ArrayedCollection—String.[7] Not only is the class for strings reusable; it is part of a hierarchy of parent classes with high reusability.

Reusability can be enhanced or inhibited by the choice of criteria for subclassing at each level in a hierarchy. The first-level subclasses for vehicles in Example 1.4 were based on the medium in which the vehicle operates: LandVehicle, AirVehicle, WaterVehicle. An alternative criterion for the first-level classification of vehicles is based on the driving force that makes the vehicle move: EngineDriven, WindDriven, PeopleDriven. If all six classifications of vehicles are to be included in a hierarchy of vehicle classes, there are two possible choices, depending on which criterion is used for the first-level partitioning. Figure 1.9 shows the two possible hierarchies. In Figure 1.9 (*a*) the first-level criterion is operating medium and the second-level criterion is drive power. In Figure 1.9 (*b*) the order of the criteria is reversed.

One thing that is obvious from Figure 1.9 is the duplication of subclasses at level 2 for either choice.[8] One way to avoid this costly duplication of subclasses is to incorporate

_____

[7] Adele Goldberg and Glenn Robson, *Smalltalk-80: The Language and Its Implementation*, Addison-Wesley, 1983.

[8] Although it causes no conceptual misunderstanding here, duplicate class names are not a good idea. They are not allowed in object-oriented languages.

Figure 1.10 _____

Avoiding redundant subclasses in a hierarchy

Vehicle (drivePower)   Vehicle (operatingMedium)
    LandVehicle   EngineDriven
    AirVehicle   WindDriven
    WaterVehicle   PeopleDriven

(a) Operating medium   (b) Drive power

_____

Figure 1.11 _____

Two possible hierarchies for specific vehicle classes

Vehicle   Vehicle
    LandVehicle   EngineDriven
        Car (EngineDriven)   Car (LandVehicle)
            Plane (AirVehicle)
                JetPlane
            Boat (WaterVehicle)
    AirVehicle   WindDriven
        Plane   (EngineDriven)   Glider (AirVehicle)
            JetPlane
        Glider   (WindDriven)
    WaterVehicle   PeopleDriven
        Boat (EngineDriven)

(a) Operating medium / drive power   (b) Drive power / operating medium

_____

the feature represented by the subclasses into an attribute of the parent class, Vehicle, as illustrated in Figure 1.10. In part (*a*) of Figure 1.10, the criterion for drive power is represented by the instance variable drivePower added to class Vehicle. In part (*b*) of Figure 1.10, the criterion for operating medium is represented by the instance variable operatingMedium added to class Vehicle.

The problem with the class hierarchies in Figure 1.10 is that some subclassing opportunities have been eliminated by including an important criterion for classification as an instance variable in the parent class Vehicle. An alternative approach to reducing the redundancy in Figure 1.9 without eliminating subclassing opportunities is to realize that all potential subclasses in Figure 1.9 do not have the same importance. For example, there are very few wind-driven land vehicles and people-driven air vehicles. Figure 1.11 shows how the vehicle objects given in Example 1.3 map into the class hierarchies of Figure 1.10.

One point to be made when comparing the two approaches for vehicle classification is that most vehicles tend to be engine-driven. The class hierarchy in Figure 1.11 (*b*) will be heavily weighted with classes under subclass EngineDriven. Further, it groups together kinds of vehicles that have significant differences in attributes. While it's difficult to argue that the classification given in Figure 1.11 (*a*) is the best possible, it is obviously better than the classification scheme in Figure 1.11 (*b*).

The point to remember is that the choice of criteria for partitioning into subclasses at each level of a class hierarchy is extremely important. It is not an exact science, and no one partitioning scheme will always be best. Wise choices for partitioning significantly enhance the reusability of the classes in a hierarchy.

1.6 CONTAINERSHIP, COMPOSITION, AND OBJECT DEPENDENCIES

In the last section we discussed the dependence of objects on properties inherited through a hierarchy of classes. Another kind of dependence is illustrated by the situation where the attributes of a particular kind of object are other objects. The relationship is often referred to as *containership*, or *composition*. One object is said to contain other objects or be composed of other objects. The concept of containership is not new, nor is it unique to software objects. An object such as a room contains other objects—furniture, carpet, and so on. A piece of furniture is composed of wood, metal, and other materials. The concept of containership implies that an object is a repository for other objects that may not be functionally related to the container object. In contrast, composition implies that an object is composed of other functionally related objects. Recognition and correct application of the concepts of containership and composition is important in building a valid hierarchy of classes with appropriate attributes for each class.

A result of building classes that contain objects of other classes is a horizontal dependency among the classes in a hierarchy. Inheritance produces a vertical dependency. Figure 1.12 illustrates how inheritance, composition, and containership are developed for a particular class. In the figure, class X depends on classes Object, Y, and Z through inheritance. It depends on classes A and B through direct containership or composition and inherited containership or composition.[9] It depends on class C through containership or composition combined with inheritance. Finally it depends on class D through multiple containership or composition.

Containership and composition in conjunction with inheritance complicate the issue of reusable software components. We stated earlier that if an object is to be a reusable software component, it must provide details of its own class protocol plus all the inherited protocol from parent classes. With the added flexibility of each class in the hierarchy being able to contain other objects, "all the detail" implies knowledge of the class for each contained object and all its parent classes and all the detail of the classes and parent classes of their contained objects, and so on. The classes in a set may become so interconnected and dependent on each other that the only reusable software component is the entire set of classes.

---

[9]This example does not provide sufficient information for determining which attributes are contained or which attributes are composite parts of the object represented by each class.

Figure 1.12 _____

Dependencies of a class on inheritance, composition, and containership

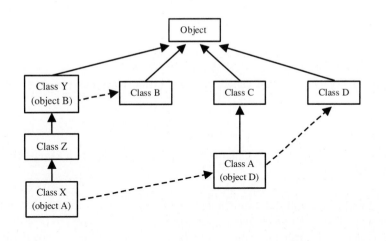

1.7 DELEGATION AND TARGETS

This section deals with attributes in two related categories: delegates and targets. It is not correct to say that these objects are contained within the object of which they are attributes; their purpose is to support another kind of dependency that requires inter-object communication and transfer of control.

Delegation: Sharing Responsibility

The concept of delegation has been used to explain inheritance. Subclass objects are sometimes described as *delegates* of the parent class because they add new functionality to that represented by the parent class. Specialization is delegated to a subclass object. Another quite different way of looking at delegation is to consider that subclass objects delegate responsibility for certain actions to protocol defined in their parent classes. In this case the parent class is a delegate for the subclass object.

   Delegation has also been described in the literature to represent the sharing of responsibilities without reference to classes or inheritance. Our discussion of delegation begins with the following definition:

   — *Delegate*
      An object that acts on behalf of another object

Any object may declare another object as its delegate and pass responsibility to that delegate for handling a specified set of events. The process of delegation, as we will use it, is independent of inheritance, except that it may be used to eliminate the need for subclassing. In that spirit, the delegate of an object adds protocol that would normally have been defined in a subclass. An object has only one delegate.

Since delegates are objects, they have a class description. The class for a delegate is typically in a different hierarchy chain from the one that includes the class of the object of which it is a delegate. Further, the delegate will generally have roles other than being a delegate. Its duties as a delegate are handled with a specific set of messages in its class protocol. An object may be a delegate for one or more client objects.

The mechanism for creating a delegate for a client object is to

1. define an instance variable called delegate in the class description for the client object,

2. provide messages in the client object's class description to set or answer the delegate object, and

3. define a set of messages to which the client object responds by passing responsibility to its delegate.

Response by a delegate object requires that its class description implement certain specific messages. The client object message must have a default action in case the delegate object does not implement the required messages. The client object should first verify that its delegate implements a message before attempting to send it.

Example 1.5 illustrates the concept of a delegate and its relationship to its client. In the example a single client object has a delegate. The class of the delegate does implement a method, change, to handle an event for the client (causing the message clientWill-Change to be sent to the client object). If an object is the delegate for more than one client, then some mechanism (such as a client code) must be provided to assist the delegate in determining which client sent a message.

Example 1.5 _____

A delegate and its client

Class Descriptions for the client and its delegate

class Client   class Delegate
   instance variables   *instance variables*
    delegate   ....
    ....
   methods for delegate   *methods as delegate*
    setDelegate: aDelegate   ....

    clientWillChange   change
      delegate respondsTo: change
        ifTrue - delegate change
        ifFalse - default action

The objects for the client and its delegate

aClient = Client new
aDelegate = Delegate new
aClient setDelegate: aDelegate

Sequence of expressions illustrating role of delegate

aClient clientWillChange	"Sent by an external event"
aDelegate change	"Sent by client object to its delegate"

A delegate is represented by an instance variable in the class description of the client object that is different from other instance variables that represent attributes of the object. Attributes describe properties of the client objects whereas the delegate shares responsibility with the client object. Further, there is no requirement that the client object always have a delegate; it can go to the default action for responding to messages that its delegate would have handled.

Delegates may be used for responding to events such as the following requests:

- Open or close a file for a variety of client applications
- Edit or change the contents of a window
- Resize a window for an application
- Activate or deactivate an application
- Take any action for which flexibility of response is desired without adding multiple subclasses to represent all the possible repsonses.

A client object will give its delegate a chance to respond to a set of messages for which the delegate may assume responsibility. If the delegate does not respond, the client object will respond with a default action. The kinds of messages that are sent to delegates fall in the following categories:

- Notification messages that tell the delegate about an action that was taken or is about to be taken by the client object
- Action messages to which the client object could respond but to which the delegate gets the first chance to respond
- Messages from other applications or processes requesting something of the client object
- Announcements of events from the system that require action by the client object but are passed to the delegate.

Not all kinds of objects require or need a delegate. Delegates are most useful for adding special constraints to actions that the client object could perform.

Targets: Specific Actions

Targets are objects that receive action messages from their client objects in much the same way that delegates receive messages from their clients. The target object is sent a message in response to some action taken on the client object. Targets differ from delegates in the sense that a target is the *receiver* of an action from its client, and the delegate *acts in place* of its client. A definition for target follows.

— *Target*
Something to be affected by an action

Targets also differ from delegates in allowing the user to select the message to be sent to the target in response to the client action. Messages sent to delegates are determined by the protocol of the client object's class. Messages sent to targets may be selected by the user from any available message in the protocol of the target object's class.

Targets are the preferred way to invoke specialized algorithms as a result of client actions. Most objects in a user interface will have targets and corresponding response messages.

1.8 PERSISTENT OBJECTS AND ARCHIVING

Definitions for *persistent* and for *archiving* are given in *Webster's Ninth New Collegiate Dictionary* (by permission, from *Webster's Ninth New Collegiate Dictionary* © 1990 by Merriam-Webster, Inc., publisher of the Merriam-Webster® dictionaries) as follows:

— *Persistent*
Existing for a long or longer than usual time; continuing without change in function or structure

— *Archiving*
To file or collect as if in an archive

In terms of object-oriented problem solving, a persistent object is one that exists after a software system has terminated execution. It persists beyond the execution of any particular part of the software system. A persistent object retains all its state data and their values. Archiving is the process of saving an object so that all its attributes are retained. The archiving may be to a file or to memory or to a port. The thread of commonality is typically a stream that is attached to a file, memory, or a port. Archiving methods then deal directly with the stream.

In archiving an object that is an instance of a class several levels deep in a hierarchy, care must be taken to include representations for all inherited attributes as well as those given in the object's own class. A usual way of implementing archiving methods in a class is to first call the archiving method in the parent class and then add details for the current class. It may also be desirable to archive information about the class hierarchy and the version number for the software environment.

Several interesting options develop when archiving objects that have a delegate or target in their list of instance variables. These instance variables represent objects that are external to the archived object and may or may not need to be included in the archiving process. Other instance variables represent attributes of an object and are always important in archiving the object.

Archiving as well as the concepts represented by delegates and targets are treated differently in various object-oriented languages. The examples given in later chapters show how Objective-C implements these concepts.

## CHAPTER 2

Methods for
Object-Oriented Design

*It is to be noted that when any part of this
paper appears dull there is a design in it.*

Sir Richard Steele, *1672–1729*

The development of any software system begins with a statement of the problem and an analysis of its requirements. Design and implementation follow analysis. Testing should be initiated at the very beginning and continued throughout the entire development process. The real power of the object-oriented approach to problem solving is that analysis methods map directly into design methods, which map directly into implementation methods. In going from analysis to design to implementation, we add refinement and detail to the same set of concepts and the same model.

The fundamental component of an object-oriented software system is the object. Thus a key step in the design of such a software system is to define the objects. Objects are characterized by their attributes and the messages to which they respond, which leads to another key step—defining the attributes and messages for each kind of object. The objects in a software system have relationships among themselves that are represented by their dependencies; therefore, a third key step in designing a software system is to identify a structure that accurately depicts these relationships. The implementation of these three key steps really boils down to *defining and developing hierarchies of classes.*

Various design methods share these three steps, although they may differ in their approaches or in their criteria for structuring the hierarchy of classes. Tools for verifying the design, such as preconditions and postconditions, may be part of a design method. A particular design method may give rise to a number of different designs, depending on the extent to which generality and reusability have been goals of the design. In Section 2.1 we give a list of steps that represent one approach to an object-oriented design. In the following sections the steps are illustrated with an example. Section 2.6 shows how different object-oriented designs may emerge for the solution to a problem.

2.1 MAPPING A PROBLEM SPECIFICATION TO AN OBJECT-ORIENTED SOLUTION

The beginning of any software system is a statement of need from the customer. It starts as an idea for solving a problem. The idea may be well-formulated or very rough at first. The statement of need should spell out as clearly as possible exactly what the problem is and what the solution is to provide. It should also describe the framework within which the proposed problem solution is to function. After discussion and refinement of the goals for the software system, a precise definition of the problem and its proposed solution can be developed. The result is a specification document. After the specification comes the design.

The Steps in an Object-Oriented Design

The problem definition and specification is the starting point for applying the following steps in an object-oriented design.

1. *Identify the primary objects.*
   The primary objects are those that are essential parts of the problem and its solution. These objects may or may not be unique to the current problem solution. The primary objects may be at varying levels of abstraction, from the system level down to the component level.

2. *Identify attributes of the primary objects.*
   Attributes include descriptive features of the objects, such as size, shape, color, and value. In a pure, object-oriented sense, these descriptive attributes are objects as well. Attributes can also be contained or composite objects; for example, an automobile contains an engine. Attributes may also serve as targets or references for the object; for example, a fish needs to know the ocean in which it lives. The attributes of the primary objects are supporting objects.

3. *Identify the supporting objects and their attributes.*
   This is an iterative step with steps 1 and 2. The goal is to eventually identify all objects and their attributes. Supporting objects are attributes for the primary objects. In addition there are other supporting objects that represent standard parts of a computer system, such as the display screen, printer, keyboard, and mouse. Objects representing typical data structures, such as stacks, strings, arrays, and others, may also be part of a solution.

4. *Develop an initial hierarchy of classes.*
   The purpose of this step is to develop a structure among the objects in the problem solution. Commonality of features is represented through classing and subclassing. Additional dependencies are represented through composition, containership, or the designation of targets or delegates. The result is a hierarchy of classes with attributes that represents the structural relation of all primary objects and supporting objects.

5. *Define high-level key messages for the objects.*
   Using functional decomposition, start with the highest-level, most abstract operations to be performed by an object and define messages representing each. For each mes-

sage, define message identifiers, parameters, and the expected response by the object. Decompose the high-level abstractions into lower-level abstractions and define messages for these operations. Continue the process until a high-level proto-type solution can be constructed from the defined messages. Refinements and additional messages are added later as part of the implementation phase.

6. *Develop a high-level prototype solution.*
   Using messages defined for the objects, develop a prototype that is a skeleton of a solution. Without including all details it should represent a complete solution to the problem. This step is best done in conjunction with the previous step to help identify the messages required for an object.

7. *Reevaluate the hierarchy of classes for generality, reusability, and improved organization.*
   This step implies that something was learned about the structure of classes in the solution from the message definition and prototyping steps, or that it's simply time to rethink the organization of the classes. Increased generality and reusability are often achieved by factoring out the more general properties of an object into an abstract superclass. Abstract superclasses represent general features of commonality that are usually not complete. Thus no instances of abstract superclasses are created; only instances of their more specific subclasses are created.

Although the above steps may be accomplished independently of any computer language, it's advantageous to design the classes and the messages using the syntax of an object-oriented language. The final step of going from design to implementation is then even easier. Further, the choice of language will affect some design decisions. For example, a hybrid language includes predefined types in the underlying base language. These types may be used to represent selected objects or attributes. The operations on these types are determined by the language and its supporting libraries.

The design is also affected by the availability of existing classes and their properties in the chosen object-oriented language. An existing rich set of classes often reduces the effort required to complete of a solution by a significant percentage.

Notational Conventions

In lieu of a chosen implementation language, some form of notation must be used to represent classes, attributes, and messages in the design. The notational conventions adopted by a number of object-oriented languages are useful; among them are the following, which we use in developing examples in this chapter.[1]

- Class names begin with uppercase characters.
- Instance names begin with lowercase characters and are chosen either to indicate the class to which they belong or to indicate more specific information about the instance.

---

[1] These conventions also depend on personal preference. They draw from both Smalltalk and Objective-C.

- Attributes are also instances, and their names follow the convention for instances.
- There are three basic types of messages: unary, binary, and keyword. Unary messages take no parameter. Binary messages take exactly one parameter. Most binary messages are represented by operator symbols.[2] Each keyword in keyword messages is identified with a terminating colon. Keyword messages may have one or more parameters. Multiple keywords are used to represent a keyword message that has more than one parameter. Keywords and parameters are interspersed for enhanced readability. For example, the expression

  getPixelAt: aPoint withAccuracy: numBits

  has two keywords, getPixelAt: and withAccuracy:, and two parameters, aPoint and numBits.
- Messages begin with lowercase characters.
- Successive words in multiword identifiers begin with uppercase characters for readability.
- Assignment is indicated by the equal (=) operator.
- In expressions, messages follow the objects receiving them. Expressions are terminated with a period.
- Comments are placed between double quotes; for example, "This is a comment."

Sections 2.2 through 2.5 show the application of the design approach discussed above.

Problem Definition and Specification: An Example

A relatively simple but rich example is used to demonstrate the design steps defined in the section above. We begin here with a detailed description of the problem, a proposed solution, and a software system for the example.

The Problem. The problem is to design and implement a software system that illustrates adaptive learning with varying skill levels. The solution is to be a simulation with user-selectable skill levels and other user-selected parameters that affect the simulation. At least four different skill levels are to be represented. The simulation should be graphic in nature. Meaningful statistics are to be computed for each simulation run. These statistics are to be displayed at the end of each run and archived as an option.

This problem statement is far more general than those normally encountered by a software developer. It is the problem we posed to ourselves to illustrate the design method. The following proposed solution is our answer to this general statement of need.

The Proposed Solution. The simulation is to be called *Swamp Runner.* In *Swamp Runner* we have runners who try to traverse a swamp along a path.

---

[2] Objective-C does not support binary operator overloading.

Figure 2.1 _____

Pictorial representation of the *Swamp Runner* software system

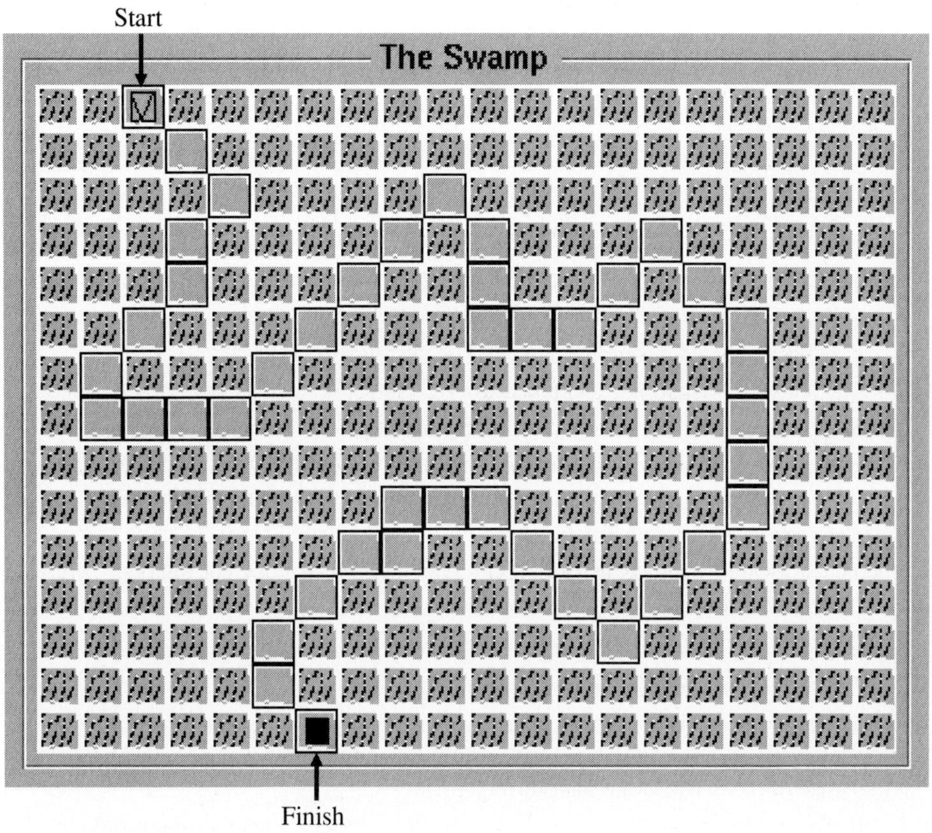

At the beginning of each simulation, a swamp is initialized with user-defined or default parameters. The swamp consists of a two-dimensional array of swamp cells. Initially the swamp cells may be one of two types—quicksand or path. The initialized swamp is displayed with graphic images representing the quicksand and path cells. The path cells represent a single, nonoverlapping path through the swamp, with a beginning position and an end position. An attempt is made to traverse the swamp (staying on the path) by one of four kinds of swamp travelers—aDimwit, aHalfwit, aWit, or aGenius. The four kinds of swamp travelers represent increasing levels of learning skills. Consistent with the graphic simulation, the swamp travelers also have images. Figure 2.1 shows some of the details of the *Swamp Runner* software system.

Informal Specification of the Problem. The operation of the Swamp Runner software system is governed by the following list of informal specifications and rules. They are grouped into the following categories:

1. system-level
2. the simulation
3. the swamp
4. swamp cells
5. swamp travelers
6. statistics
7. swamp archive

1. *System-level specifications: environment and constraints*
   - The software system is to be a simulation that illustrates
     a. Adaptive learning for varying skill levels of swamp travelers
     b. Object-oriented design principles
   - The software system is constrained to
     a. Be implemented in an object-oriented language
     b. Provide a graphic display as the simulation proceeds; may use character or image displays, depending on the supporting environment and language
     c. Accept user-input parameters for controlling the simulation
   - The software system is to be a stand-alone system. It does not interface with other software or hardware systems.

2. *Specifications for the simulation*
   - Features of the *Swamp Runner* simulation include
     a. The swamp—There is only one swamp for any given simulation run. The swamp may be reinitialized for subsequent simulation runs to be of different size or have a different path through it.
     b. The swamp traveler—At any given time, there is one swamp traveler attempting to cross the swamp.
     c. The swamp statistics—For any given simulation run, a number of statistics are computed and displayed. All these statistical parameters are features of the swamp or the swamp traveler and are described in the specifications for those objects.
     d. The swamp archive—As an option, the user may choose to archive the results of selected simulation runs.
   - Initialization of the *Swamp Runner* software system consists of the following operations.
     a. Select options and parameters—Prompt the user to enter the size of the swamp in number of rows and number of columns. Provide default values for these two parameters and maximum acceptable values adjusted to fit the screen for the chosen development environment. Prompt the user to specify a mode of operation. Prompt the user for path generation by the user or by the simulation program.

Mode of operation

Initially only simple modes of operation are provided. The user may choose to run the simulation one time with a selected kind of swamp traveler (aDimwit, aHalfwit, aWit, or aGenius) or run the simulation once for each kind of swamp traveler.

b. Initialize the swamp—Create an initial swamp with number of rows and columns as specified, which has only quicksand cells. Display this initial swamp and proceed to the user-selected method for generating a path through the swamp.

Path generation

Proceed to either an interactive mode for user-generation of the path or an automatic mode for path generation. Create the path with enforced rules for path generation and logic for completion of the path. The path must begin and end with a cell on the border of the swamp. It will have a minimum length that is the smaller of the number of rows or the number of columns in the swamp. The path cannot retrace, cross, or double back on itself.

User-generated path

Enter an interactive mode where the user may toggle a swamp cell between quicksand and path by clicking on the cell using a cursor and mouse. Use rules for path generation to prevent invalid selection of path cells. The first cell must be on the border. As each valid path cell is selected, display its image on the swamp. Clicking an invalid cell causes no change in the swamp. Continue until a completed path is generated.

Automatic path generation

Generate a path using random selection for the direction to move from any given path cell. The starting cell is chosen randomly from the border cells. The next cell is chosen randomly from neighboring cells of the current path cell, subject to constraints that the path must satisfy. Path generation is complete when the next border cell is selected. When completed, display the entire path on the swamp.

∘ A simulation run consists of one or more traversals of the swamp. Based on earlier mode selection by the user,

1. a single kind of swamp traveler traverses the swamp once, or

2. each kind of swamp traveler traverses the swamp once. A traversal is complete when the swamp traveler reaches the last path cell and exits the swamp. The following logic governs a single traversal of the swamp.

   a. Initialize parameters.–Initialize number of attempts to 1 and number of steps to 0.

   b. Move swamp traveler to first path cell.–Increment number of steps and display the swamp traveler image at that location in the swamp.

   c. Select next move for the swamp traveler and move to new swamp cell.– Increment number of steps and display the swamp traveler image at that location in the swamp.

d. If swamp traveler moves to a path cell, repeat step (*c*).

e. If a swamp traveler moves to a quicksand cell, increment number of attempts, redisplay the swamp, and go to step (*b*).

f. A traversal is complete when the swamp traveler moves along the path from beginning to end without stepping in quicksand (moving to a quicksand cell).

g. Display statistics for the traversal and prompt user for desire to archive the traversal.

h. If there are more swamp travelers, repeat steps (*a*) through (*g*) for each.

○ Statistics for a traversal are displayed in a suitable way on the screen. The following statistics are displayed for each traversal of the swamp by a swamp traveler.

a. Length of the path

b. Kind of swamp traveler

c. Number of attempts for traversal

d. Total number of steps for traversal

e. Number of guesses for the genius swamp traveler

○ If the user chooses to archive the traversal, the following objects are archived.

a. The swamp—This object includes all information necessary to recreate the swamp. It knows its size and the path through it.

b. The swamp traveler—This object knows its kind and all details about the number of attempts and number of steps required for its traversal.

3. *Specification for the swamp*

○ The swamp consists of a two-dimensional array of swamp cells. It has a specified number of rows and columns and has a path through it. Swamp cells may be either quicksand or path. Each has a unique image. The swamp is all quicksand until a path is defined. Specific features of the swamp include the following.

a. Number of rows—A user-specified number that is constrained to result in a swamp display that fits on the screen of the chosen hardware/software environment.

b. Number of columns—A user-specified number with the same constraints as the number of rows.

c. Swamp cells—A two-dimensional array of swamp cells that are the swamp. Initially all swamp cells are quicksand cells. After a path is defined, path cells replace the quicksand cells in this two-dimensional array at each path coordinate.

d. The path—A path is defined either by the user or by the software system on initialization of the swamp for a simulation run. The path consists of an ordered collection of coordinate pairs representing the path cells in the swamp.

e. Origin—A two-dimensional coordinate pair representing the upper-left corner of the swamp. This feature is used to display the swamp at a specific location on the screen.

f. Minimum path length—A number that is the smaller of the number of rows or the number of columns.

g. Random—A random number generator used in automatic generation of the path. Within constraints, the next path cell is chosen at random.

h. Border coordinates—A list of the coordinates for all cells on the border of the swamp. This feature is used in selecting an initial path cell and for determining when a swamp traveler has traversed the complete path.

i. Other features—Additional features or data structures may be added to support the logic for selecting a path through the swamp. The need for such additional features is deferred to the design phase.

○ Major operations on the swamp include the following.

a. Initialization—In this step a swamp of quicksand cells is created, with the specified number of rows and columns.

b. Display—Using the origin and the methods for displaying a swamp cell, sequentially display the entire swamp.

c. Path creation—Select a beginning path cell at random from the border cells. Using the logic for selecting a random neighbor cell, subject to the constraints of the path-generation rules, choose more path cells until the path is completed.

d. Display the path—For each path coordinate, display the image for a path cell at the appropriate offset in the swamp.

4. *Specification for the swamp cells*

○ Swamp cells are passive objects that have the following features.

a. Image—The image of a swamp cell will depend on the kind of the swamp cell; it may be a simple character or a graphic image, as dictated by the chosen language and support environment.

b. Coordinate—Each swamp cell knows its coordinate location relative to the origin of the swamp.

○ Operations for swamp cells include the following.

a. Instance creation—Create a swamp cell with the appropriate image (quicksand or path) at a specified coordinate within the swamp.

b. Display—Display a swamp cell image at its coordinate offset on its target swamp.

5. *Specification for the swamp travelers*

○ Features of swamp travelers include the following.

a. Image—Each kind of swamp traveler has an image that represents its level of intelligence. As was true for swamp cells, the image for swamp travelers may be characters or graphic images.

b. Coordinate—At any given time during the simulation, a swamp traveler must know its coordinate location relative to the origin of the swamp.

c. Number of steps—Each swamp traveler keeps track of the total number of steps it took to successfully traverse the swamp.

d. Number of attempts—Most swamp travelers require multiple attempts to cross the swamp.

e. Target swamp—In order to traverse a swamp, the swamp traveler must be aware of the specific swamp it is attempting to traverse. This feature is to be interpreted as a target object of the swamp traveler and not as a contained object.

f. Other features—Additional features or data structures may be defined during the design phase to support the logic by which a swamp traveler makes its next move.

○ Major operations to be performed by the swamp traveler include the following.

a. Display—A swamp traveler must be able to display its image at its coordinate. Its coordinate is the offset within its target swamp.

b. Returning statistics—Each swamp traveler keeps a record of the number of attempts, steps, and guesses (for the genius) required to traverse the swamp.

c. Traversing—A swamp traveler begins its traversal of the swamp in response to an operation called traverse. Swamp travelers begin their traversal of the swamp on the starting path cell. All swamp travelers move from their current swamp cell to a neighboring swamp cell according to rules.

○ The traversal rules are different for each kind of swamp traveler, as described below. These rules represent varying levels of learning ability for each kind of swamp traveler.

a. Dimwit—The dimwit swamp traveler moves randomly at all times and may even move backward, retracing its own steps. It has no memory of previous moves made during failed attempts.

b. Halfwit—The halfwit is smarter than the dimwit, it remembers the quicksand cells already visited from one attempt to another. It never moves to a quicksand cell twice. Path cells in the list are eliminated at the end of each attempt and added to the list as an attempt progresses. The halfwit never backtracks and never repeats past errors, yet its moves are still random (with constraints) at each step.

c. Wit—The wit remembers all successful moves from each attempt and builds a valid path through the swamp. This removes randomness from its moves (up to the last path cell it has previously been on) and eliminates some potential quicksand moves. Once the wit has retraced its path from a previous attempt, it proceeds to move randomly, using the same rules as the halfwit. The wit never backtracks or moves to any quicksand cell twice.

d. Genius—The genius has figured out how to avoid stepping in quicksand. Before each move, the genius guesses the next best move from a knowledge

of previous moves and tests the targeted cell for quicksand. It repeats this
process until the next path cell is found. The genius traverses the swamp in
one attempt. The total number of guesses required by the genius is tallied.

6. *Specification for the swamp statistics*

   ◦ Statistics for any simulation run include details of the swamp and the swamp
     traveler. The swamp traveler has features that represent its performance in
     traversing the swamp. At the end of a traversal, the following features are to
     be displayed.

     a. Length of the path—This is simply the number of path cells in the path.

     b. Kind of swamp traveler—This is a name representing one of the four kinds
        of swamp travelers.

     c. Number of attempts—Display the number of attempts required before suc-
        cessfully traversing the swamp.

     d. Number of steps—This is the total number of moves made by the swamp
        traveler in traversing the swamp, summed cumulatively over all attempts.

   ◦ The genius swamp traveler requires only one attempt for traversal. The num-
     ber of guesses is tallied and reported. The total number of steps required by
     the genius (number of moves) is the number of path cells plus one (we assume
     the traveler wants to get out of the swamp).

7. *Specification for the swamp archive*

   ◦ The swamp archive is intended to allow the archiving of a specific swamp
     simulation run. As such it must archive all essential information for recreating
     the simulation and its results. This requires storage of the following objects
     with all their attributes.

     a. The swamp—This object includes all information necessary to recreate the
        swamp. It knows its size and the path through it.

     b. The swamp traveler—This object knows its kind and all details about the
        number of attempts and number of steps required for a traversal.

From this informal specification we can begin next the steps in the development of
an object-oriented design.

2.2 IDENTIFYING OBJECTS AND ATTRIBUTES

Objects in a software system are identified from a statement and specification of the
problem. The more precise the problem statement and specification, the more complete
will be the initial list of objects. Once the primary objects are identified, their attributes
are next determined. Finally, the supporting objects and their attributes are identified.
Supporting objects may be attributes or supplementary objects that are part of the underlying software system. We illustrate by identifying the objects and attributes in the
Swamp Runner software system.

Primary Objects in the Swamp Runner Software System

A major difference between the specification and the design of an object-oriented software system is the precision with which objects, attributes, operations, and structure are described. The increased precision of the design phase for the *Swamp Runner* software system will be obvious in the choice of identifiers for each component. There is also a change in type style to emphasize components that will eventually become part of the implementation in an object-oriented language.

The following primary objects are identified as being part of the *Swamp Runner* simulation software system. In defining these objects we have encapsulated the entire simulation into an object called aSwampSimulation.

- aSwampSimulation

  This object is a simulation of the Swamp Runner software system. It is the main driver program that groups together all the primary objects in a swamp simulation. It includes as attributes objects representing the swamp, the swamp traveler, and an archive object. Its protocol includes the high-level messages representing the various operational modes of the software system, for example, initialization, selection of a simulation mode, running the simulation, decision to archive, decision to quit.

- theSwamp

  Another primary object is the swamp. The swamp consists of a two-dimensional array of cells that may be one of two types: quicksand or path. The swamp has a size that is given by a number of rows and a number of columns. The swamp knows the path through it.

- aSwampCell

  A swamp cell is the basic building block of the swamp. It knows its coordinates (*x* and *y*) within its swamp, and it has an image. All swamp cells share these attributes. Object aSwampCell is an abstract object; the actual swamp consists of more specialized kinds of swamp cells (subclass objects aPathCell and aQuicksandCell).

- aPathCell

  Object aPathCell is a kind of swamp cell that represents hard ground (a safe path) in the swamp. It has an image that represents its nature.

- aQuicksandCell

  Object aQuicksandCell is a kind of swamp cell that represents quicksand. It has an appropriate image.

- aSwampTraveler

  This object represents all kinds of swamp travelers that may attempt to traverse the swamp. A swamp traveler has an image that represents varying levels of capability. The actual image is different for each specific kind of swamp traveler. Object aSwampTraveler is an abstract object since only its subclass objects are valid swamp travelers. It is represented by an abstract class called Swamp-Traveler; no instance of this abstract class will actually be created. Actual swamp travelers are more specialized objects represented by subclasses of SwampTraveler.

- aDimwit

  A dimwit is not capable of learning. This object is constrained to make moves randomly, never learning from past mistakes. It begins on the starting path cell and moves by picking randomly from its neighboring swamp cells.

- aHalfwit

  A halfwit keeps track of all cells already visited during any attempted traversal and does not step on a cell twice. In addition it remembers from one attempt to another the quicksand cells upon which it has stepped. As the number of attempts increases, it builds an increasing list of cells to avoid and eventually makes smarter moves. At the beginning of each attempt, all path cells already visited are removed from the list of cells visited since they must be traversed again.

- aWit

  A wit has two distinct abilities that enable it to make smarter moves. First, it remembers from one attempt to another the quicksand cells upon which it has stepped (as does the halfwit). It can thus avoid repeating past errors. In addition the wit remembers the sequence of path cells it has successfully traversed from past attempts. This ensures error-free movement up to the last path cell from the previous attempt. Moves beyond this point are again made at random and subject to error, except that quicksand cells already stepped in are avoided.

- aGenius

  A genius has all the capabilities of the other swamp travelers plus the ability to test a neighboring cell to see if it is quicksand or path before making a move. The genius traverses the swamp in one attempt. It keeps track of the number of guesses required for the traversal.

- aSwampArchive

  This object represents specific statistics for simulation runs of the Swamp Runner software system. Its major purpose is to encapsulate all information about a particular simulation run for ease of archiving.

Attributes and Supporting Objects

We continue with the definition of objects and attributes by listing and discussing attributes for each of the primary objects identified. We will see that some of the primary objects are also attributes of other primary objects. Some of the attributes are new kinds of objects that will be represented by class descriptions.

- For primary object aSwampSimulation, the following attributes are defined.

  1. theSwamp—This is the swamp. It is created one time for any given simulation run or sequence of runs. It may have its path changed, but it is still the one and only swamp. It is also one of the primary objects.

2. aSwampTraveler—There is only one swamp traveler at any given time during the simulation. Subsequent runs of the simulation may have different kinds of swamp travelers. This is also one of the primary objects.

3. aSwampArchive—This object is a convenience for keeping track of and archiving the statistical results of any simulation run. Its main purpose is to encapsulate the details of all the statistics that are kept for each simulation run. It is also one of the primary objects.

- For primary object aSwamp, the following attributes are defined.

1. numRows—This is an integer representing the actual number of rows of swamp cells in the swamp. This is a supporting object.[3]

2. numCols—This is an integer representing the actual number of columns of swamp cells in the swamp. This is a supporting object.

3. swampCells—This object is a two-dimensional array of swamp cells that defines the swamp. The swamp contains only quicksand cells until a path is defined. This is a supporting object. It is a two-dimensional array of objects.

4. thePath—The path through the swamp is an ordered collection of coordinates of the path cells. This is a supporting object.

5. origin—This object is a two-dimensional coordinate pair representing the upper-left corner of the swamp with respect to the display screen. It is a supporting object. Additional coordinate objects are used in other parts of the software system.

6. minPathLength—This object is the minimum number of path cells in the path. This is set equal to the smaller of numRows or numCols.

7. random—This object is a random number generator for supporting the random generation of the next swamp coordinate in thePath. This is a supporting object.

8. borderCoords—This is a list of coordinate pairs of all cells on the border of the swamp. One coordinate pair in this list is chosen at random as the starting path location. This supporting object is also useful for detection of the last step in completing the path through the swamp.

9. offsets—Because of their repeated use throughout the path-generation process, a collection of coordinate offsets representing the eight nearest neighbors of a swamp cell are encapsulated into the attribute called offsets. It is a supporting object and is an ordered collection of coordinate pairs.

10. validCoords—This collection of neighbor coordinates is used in selecting the next path cell coordinate. It is initially loaded with all the coordinate pairs in offsets, along with the current path cell coordinate. The logic for generating a valid path is then used to remove all invalid coordinate pairs. The next path coordinate is then selected at random from the remaining elements in validCoords. This object is an ordered collection of coordinate pairs.

---

[3]For consistency with the object-oriented concept, this parameter is treated as an object. In a language like Objective-C, this parameter is normally implemented as the C type, int.

- For primary object aSwampCell, the following attributes are defined. As an abstract object, it represents attributes that are shared by all subclass objects.

  1. coordinate—Each swamp cell knows its two-dimensional coordinate location within the swamp. This is a supporting object.

  2. image—All swamp cells have an image that is different for the various kinds of swamp cells. This is a supporting object. The kind of object it is depends on constraints of the chosen language and environment, as mentioned earlier. It may be a simple character or a sophisticated graphic image.

- For object aQuicksandCell, the following attribute is defined. In addition it inherits the attributes of aSwampCell.

  1. QuicksandImage—All quicksand cells have the same image. Attributes that have the same value for all instances are capitalized.

- For object aPathCell, the following attribute is defined. In addition it inherits the attributes of aSwampCell.

  1. PathImage—All path cells have the same image.

- For primary object aSwampTraveler, the following attributes are defined. It is also an abstract object and represents attributes shared by all its subclass objects.

  1. image—This object is the image for a swamp traveler. The exact image is different for each kind of swamp traveler and is specified in the appropriate subclass object. Images for the swamp traveler have the same constraints and possibilities as images for the swamp cells.

  2. coordinate—Each swamp traveler knows its coordinate offset within the swamp. This is another supporting object of the two-dimensional coordinate variety.

  3. numSteps—For any particular simulation run, this attribute is a running total of all steps required for traversal of the swamp by a swamp traveler. It is a number and a supporting object or type.

  4. numAttempts—This attribute is a running total of all the attempts to cross the swamp for a given swamp traveler.

  5. targetSwamp—The swamp traveler is defined to travel on a target swamp. It must know details of that swamp in making decisions for subsequent moves. This supporting object is also a primary object.

  6. neighborCoords—In making a decision on its next move, a swamp traveler chooses from a set of neighbor coordinates. This supporting object is a list of two-dimensional coordinate pairs. It begins as a list of coordinates for all eight adjacent neighbors (established by accessing offsets from targetSwamp and adding to coordinate for the swamp traveler). The logic for making the next move is then used to selectively remove some of the coordinates from neighborCoords. The logic is dependent on the specific swamp traveler subclass object. A choice for the next move is then made from the remaining coordinates in neighborCoords. This supporting object is an ordered collection of coordinates.

  7. coordsVisited—Each swamp traveler keeps track of coordinate locations in the swamp that it has already visited. Retained knowledge of coordsVisited from one

attempt to another is dependent on the specific swamp traveler subclass object. This supporting object is an ordered collection of coordinates.

- For primary object aDimwit, the following attribute is defined in addition to those inherited from abstract object aSwampTraveler.
  1. DimwitImage—All dimwit objects have the same image.

- Primary object aHalfWit has attributes inherited from abstract object aSwamp-Traveler plus the following.
  1. HalfwitImage—All halfwit objects have the same image.

- For primary object aWit, the following attributes are defined in addition to those inherited from abstract object aSwampTraveler.
  1. pathTraveled—This object is an ordered collection of path cell coordinates that represents the sequence of path cells in the swamp from the beginning path cell through the last path cell visited by a wit. The wit remembers successful path steps from previous attempts.
  2. WitImage—All wit objects have the same image.

- Primary object aGenius has attributes inherited from abstract object aSwamp-Traveler plus the following.
  1. pathTraveled—This supporting object is the same as defined for object aWit.
  2. numGuesses—The genius makes guesses before each move. The smarter the genius, the fewer wrong guesses it makes. This supporting object is a number.
  3. GeniusImage—All geniuses have the same image.

A number of observations may be made from this initial list of attributes for the primary objects in the *Swamp Runner* simulation software system. First, there are a number of supporting objects identified that are used several times. These include

1. image,
2. coordinate,
3. orderedCollection objects of various names,
4. number objects of various names, and
5. random.

Each of these supporting object types may have additional attributes of other types.

A complete list of all objects and attributes in a design for the *Swamp Runner* simulation software system requires that we continue the process of identifying the attributes of supporting objects and their attributes and attributes of their attributes until no new object types are found. Fortunately, this process is shortened by choosing a particular object-oriented language. Some languages come with a set of predefined classes that may represent many of the supporting object types. Object-oriented languages built on a base language will represent some of the supporting objects as types in the base language. For these reasons, we halt the process of finding all the attributes of all the supporting objects, with the justification that it is better done after choosing an implementation language.

2.3 DEVELOPING AN INITIAL HIERARCHY OF CLASSES

From the list of primary and supporting objects (with their attributes), an initial hierarchy of classes is developed for the *Swamp Runner* software system. In constructing the hierarchy, subclasses are required to satisfy the "is a" relationship with their parent classes. For example, aPathCell "is a" special case of aSwampCell. For the swamp traveler classes, we decided to make each smarter class of swamp traveler a special case of the less smart swamp traveler objects. In other words, aGenius "is a" special case of aWit "is a" special case of aHalfwit "is a" special case of aDimwit "is a" special case of aSwampTraveler. This organization is logically satisfactory and allows subclass objects to inherit most of their protocol from superclass objects. The initial hierarchy of classes for the Swamp Runner simulation, showing classes for the primary objects, is given in Figure 2.2. Attributes for each class are listed in parentheses following the class name.

Figure 2.3 shows a hierarchy of classes that represents some of the supporting objects in the software system. In this initial hierarchy of classes, it is assumed that everything is an object, even numbers. The hierarchy of classes shown in Figure 2.3 for the supporting objects is only one possible representation. Object-oriented languages that provide existing classes will probably have different hierarchies for the identified supporting classes in the *Swamp Runner* simulation. Attributes are not given for all the supporting classes, as they will also depend on the chosen language and its set of predefined classes. Additional classes representing attributes of supporting classes or classes that provide user input, menus, and screen display may be part of the software system.

Figure 2.2 _____

Initial hierarchy of classes for primary objects in the *Swamp Runner* simulation

Object
  SwampSimulation (theSwamp aSwampTraveler aSwampArchive)
  Swamp (swampCells numRows numCols thePath origin minPathLength
     borderCoords random offsets validCoords)
  SwampCell (coordinate image)
   QuicksandCell (QuicksandImage)
   PathCell (PathImage)
  SwampTraveler (image coordinate numSteps numAttempts targetSwamp
      neighborCoords coordsVisited)
   Dimwit (DimwitImage)
    Halfwit (HalfwitImage)
     Wit (pathTraveled WitImage)
      Genius (numGuesses GeniusImage)
  SwampArchive (theSwamp aSwampTraveler numTraversals)

Figure 2.3 _____
Potential hierarchy of classes for supporting objects in *Swamp Runner*


```
Object
  Coordinate ( x y )
  Image ( bitmap tiffFile )
  Collection ( )
   OrderedCollection ( )
  Number ( )
   Integer ( )
  Random
```

2.4 IDENTIFYING KEY MESSAGES AND COMMUNICATION REQUIREMENTS AMONG OBJECTS

The next step in an object-oriented design is to identify the key messages to which each primary object should respond. The approach is top-down, with initial messages representing high-level, abstract operations essential to a successful problem solution. This initial list of messages is then decomposed into supporting messages. The process continues until a solution is achieved. Exactly where the process stops during the design phase and where it continues during the implementation phase is not predetermined.

For the *Swamp Runner* simulation software system, we define in the following section a list of key messages with an explanation of the functionality for each. Messages that are indented after a key message are supporting messages for that key method. They represent a further partitioning of the action indicated by the key message. For example, key message initialize for primary object aSwampSimulation is partitioned into four supporting messages: initializeSwamp, selectMode, getSwampRunner, and initializeStat.

Identification of Key Messages for Primary Objects in Swamp Runner

The following list of key messages and explanations is given for primary objects aSwampSimulation, aSwamp, aSwampCell, aSwampTraveler, and aSwampArchive. For subclasses of aSwampCell and aSwampTraveler, some of the key messages will need to be redefined. The expected modifications at subclass levels are indicated for selected messages. Keep in mind that some of these ideas may change as we proceed from design to implementation and verification of concept.

For object aSwampSimulation:

— create

Create a simulation object. No initialization is implied in the creation since separate messages are provided for initialization. This approach is often used when initialization is complex and/or requires user inputs. For the swamp simulation, a number of user inputs are required.

— initialize

The next step after the creation of a swamp simulation object is to initialize it. Initialization for the swamp simulation requires initialization of the swamp, choice of a simulation mode, choice of a swamp runner and other initialization operations. This key message is partitioned into the following four supporting messages.

— initializeSwamp

The swamp simulation object contains an object called theSwamp. Logically, initialization of the swamp is accomplished by sending a message for initialization to theSwamp. The responsibility for details of that initialization is thus passed on to the swamp object.

— selectMode

This operation requires user input. The user's response is requested and constrained to be one of the operational modes provided for the swamp simulation.

— getSwampTraveler

Some modes of the swamp simulation allow the user to specify the kind of swamp traveler. This message prompts the user and accepts the appropriate response.

— initializeStat

This message creates and initializes a SwampArchive object for storing statistics of the run.

— run

Once all parameters have been initialized, the next step is to run the simulation. Logically this message is implemented by sending an appropriate message to the contained object aSwampTraveler, such as traverse.

— stats

After a simulation run is completed, statistics are displayed, and the user is prompted for whether to archive the result. Since contained objects theSwamp and aSwampTraveler have attributes representing all statistics of interest to the simulation, this message is implemented by sending appropriate messages to those contained objects. Again the details for a particular operation are partitioned and passed to another message.

For object aSwamp:

— initialize

Initialization of the swamp consists of prompting the user for number of rows and number of columns, creating the two-dimensional array of quicksand cells and establishing a path through the swamp. We partition the total initialization of the swamp into these three suboperations.

— promptForRowsAndColls

Prompt the user for number of rows and number of columns to be in the swamp. Provide information on expected range of responses, with a maximum value that is enforced.

— setSwampCells

Create the two-dimensional array of quicksand cells and display it on the screen. This establishes values for the attribute swampCells.

— setPath

Based on the user response for either automatic generation or usergeneration of a path, begin generation of a path through the swamp. The first step is to select a border cell. Additional cells in the path are chosen subject to constraints on how the path may be defined. The path is finally complete when all constraints have been met and when it ends on another border cell. Clearly the logic for this message is a good candidate for additional partitioning. We choose to do that partitioning during prototyping or implementation instead of here as part of the design phase.

— display

An obvious message for the swamp object in a graphic simulation is display. This message iterates over the two-dimensional array of swamp cells, swampCells, and sends a message to each swamp cell to display itself on the swamp. Since swamp cells are considered to be passive objects, they must be told the swamp upon which they are to be displayed. A message such as displayOn: aSwamp must be provided in the class for swamp cells if this approach is to work.

— displayPath

It is desirable to be able to display the path through the swamp without redisplaying all swamp cells. This message is implemented by iterating over the attribute thePath and sending the message displayOn: aSwamp to each cell in the path.

— accessing methods

As a general rule, it is often necessary to provide methods for accessing (returning or setting) values for all attributes of an object. For object aSwamp, most attributes are established by initialization methods. There may be a need to return values of attributes swampCells, numRows, numCols, thePath, origin, minPathLength, borderCoords, random, offsets, and validCoords. Decisions on the necessity of these accessing methods are deferred to the prototyping and implementation phases.

For object aSwampCell and its subclass objects:

— createAt: aCoordinate

Swamp cells exist as parts of a swamp, and they have a specific coordinate offset within the swamp. This creation message establishes a value for the coordinate offset. Subclass objects will also establish a default image upon creation. One approach is to define an initialization message that is redefined for subclass objects to assign the appropriate image.

— initialize

This message assigns a specific image to a newly created swamp cell object.

It is redefined in subclasses to do the appropriate assignment. The implementation in the abstract superclass SwampCell may be defined to prevent the creation of an abstract object.

— displayOn: aSwamp

This message is sent by a swamp object to its swamp cells. It displays the image for a swamp cell on the swamp at its coordinate offset.

— accessing methods

Accessing messages may be required for returning or setting each of the attributes of a swamp cell, for example, coordinate and image.

*For object **aSwampTraveler** and its subclass objects:*

— createOn: aTarget

Swamp travelers are created to travel on a particular swamp. One of their attributes is a target swamp. This message creates a swamp traveler on a specific swamp. It then initializes attributes that are common to all kinds of swamp travelers by sending itself the message initialize. Initialization that is specific to subclass objects is handled by a separate, subclass-redefined message called init that is also sent to newly created swamp traveler objects.

— initialize

This message initializes attributes that are common to all swamp travelers. In particular all swamp travelers start with numAttempts initialized to 1, numSteps initialized to 0, coordinate initialized to (0,0) outside the swamp, and empty collections for neighborCoords and coordsVisited.

— init

Each subclass object redefines this message to represent class-specific initialization such as assignment of an appropriate image to a swamp traveler. In addition, the wit initializes pathTraveled to be an empty collection, and the genius initializes numGuesses to be 0.

— traverse

The primary purpose of any swamp traveler is to traverse the swamp on which it is defined. This high-level message starts the traversal process. It is partitioned into two lower-level operations for making the first move and for making all subsequent moves. This partitioning recognizes the fact that some subclass objects use different logic for making the first move.

— makeFirstMove

The usual first move made by a swamp traveler is to simply move to the first path cell in the target swamp. Subclass objects aWit and aGenius use slightly different logic. They move sequentially to all path cells previously visited before using logic to make the next move.

— makeNextMoves

Each swamp traveler picks a neighbor cell for its next move, moves to the cell, and continues until reaching the end of the path. The logic for picking the next neighbor cell is different for each subclass object. This class-dependent action is separated into a single message called choose-

Neighbors. Three supporting messages for makeNextMoves are choose-Neighbors, moveTo: aCoordinate, and atEndOfPath.

atEndOfPath

This message returns a Boolean true if the swamp traveler's coordinate location matches the coordinate of the last cell in thePath of the target-Swamp.

chooseNeighbors

This is an important message because it includes the logic for choosing a valid neighbor coordinate for the next move by a swamp traveler. The logic for choosing this next neighbor is subclass-dependent and must represent the rules for each kind of swamp traveler.

moveTo: aCoordinate

Once a coordinate is chosen for the next move by a swamp traveler, this message does the actual move and changes the display to reflect the move.

— accessing methods

Methods for returning statistical attributes such as numSteps and num-Attempts are required. Most other attributes are either initialized on creation of the swamp traveler object or are for internal use only. Finally, since the real action of the simulation is centered on the swamp traveler (via message traverse), it is unlikely that accessing messages will be required for any other attributes.

For object aSwampArchive:

— accessing methods

The major role of the swamp archive object is to store attributes. Therefore the major messages for a swamp archive object are those that either return or set values for attributes. The attributes for a swamp archive are the-Swamp, theSwampTraveler, and numTraversals.

Refinement of the Key Messages for Swamp Runner

Refinement of the key messages given in the previous section can be continued at the design phase or at the implementation phase. For object-oriented languages that support rapid prototyping, design and implementation can be performed simultaneously. Implementation and verification of concepts is an important design tool along with logical testing for validation of design.

2.5 A PROTOTYPE SOLUTION: THE FIRST LEVEL— EXPRESSIONS THAT WILL EVENTUALLY WORK

Solution prototypes may be developed using a top-down approach, a bottom-up approach, or a combination of the two. A high-level solution to the Swamp Runner problem is given by the following expressions, using a top-down approach:

```
aSwampSimulation = SwampSimulation create.
aSwampSimulation initialize.
aSwampSimulation run.
aSwampSimulation stats.
```

Essentially, we create an instance of SwampSimulation, initialize it, run the simulation, and output the statistics. It's that simple. From this high-level solution, we begin to break down each message into lower-level messages that represent in more detail what happens for each. Many of the messages for the primary objects are determined from this functional decomposition of a prototype solution.

The Second Level of a Prototype Solution

Each operation implied by the three messages sent to object aSwampSimulation is partitioned into more detailed operations, as shown below.

- Partitioning of the initialize message sent to object aSwampSimulation:

```
aSwampSimulation initializeSwamp.
aSwampSimulation selectMode.
aSwampSimulation getSwampRunner.
aSwampSimulation initializeStat.
```

- Partitioning of the run message sent to object aSwampSimulation:

```
aSwampTraveler traverse.
```

- Partitioning of the stats message sent to object aSwampSimulation:

```
theSwamp stats.
aSwampTraveler showStats.
```

The Third Level of a Prototype Solution

Each operation implied by the messages sent to objects aSwampSimulation, theSwamp, and aSwampTraveler at level 2 is partitioned into more detailed operations as shown below. Only two of the more interesting operations are selected for further partitioning at this and subsequent levels; this illustrates the concept without belaboring detail. The chosen messages represent the two major operations to be performed in executing of the *Swamp Runner* simulation:

1. creation of a swamp with a path through it, and
2. traversal of the swamp by a swamp traveler. Comments are added to clarify expressions.

- Partitioning of the initializeSwamp message sent to object aSwampSimulation:

```
theSwamp = Swamp new.      "Create theSwamp"
theSwamp initialize.       "Initialize"
```

- Partitioning of the traverse message sent to object aSwampTraveler:

```
aSwampTraveler makeFirstMove.    "Move to first path cell."
aSwampTraveler makeNextMoves.  "Move until completed traversal."
```

The Fourth Level of a Prototype Solution

At the fourth level of the hierarchy of operations, we give details for message initialize sent to object theSwamp and for messages makeFirstMove and makeNextMoves sent to object aSwampTraveler.

- Partitioning of the initialize message sent to object theSwamp:

```
origin = Coordinate new: 50 and: 20.        "Assign origin to (50,20)"
validCoords = OrderedCollection new.        "Create empty."
thePath = OrderedCollection new.            "Create empty."
random = Random new.                        "Initialize random number generator."
theSwamp setOffsets.                        "Create the offsets collection."
theSwamp promptForRowsAndCols.              "Prompt user for rows & cols."
theSwamp setSwampCells.                     "Create rows x cols quicksand cells."
theSwamp setPath.                           "Create a path in theSwamp."
```

- Partitioning of the makeFirstMove message sent to object aSwampTraveler:

```
coordsVisited = coordsVisited copyEmpty.    "Set to empty."
coord = targetSwamp path first.             "Get first path coord."
aSwampTraveler moveTo: coord.               "Move to first path coord."
```

- Partitioning of the makeNextMoves message sent to object aSwampTraveler:

```
(aSwampTraveler atEndOfPath) whileFalseExecute:
    ( (aSwampTraveler makeNextSuccessfulMove) ifFalseExecute:
        (        targetSwamp displayPath.
                 quicksandCell = swampCells at: coordinate.
                 "the one stepped in"
                 quicksandCell displayOn: targetSwamp.
                 numAttempts = numAttempts + 1.
                 aSwampTraveler makeFirstMove. ) )
```

The swamp traveler makes a move based on rules. If the move is to a path cell, then message makeNextSuccessfulMove returns a Boolean true. If the move is to quicksand, it returns false. If the move is to quicksand, then the swamp display is cleared of all swamp traveler images, the number of attempts is incremented, and the swamp traveler starts over. This block of code is repeated until atEndOfPath returns true.

The Fifth Level of a Prototype Solution

At the fifth level of the hierarchy of operations, we give details for message setPath sent to object theSwamp and for messages atEndOfPath, moveTo: aCoordinate and makeNext-SuccessfulMove sent to object aSwampTraveler.

- Partitioning of the setPath message sent to object theSwamp:

```
"Create path"
(    thePath = thePath copyEmpty.                      "Initialize empty."
     minPathLength = numRows min: numCols.             "Choose smaller"
     currentPathCoord = theSwamp setFirstPathCoord.    "First path coord"
```

```
( currentPathCoord = theSwamp
    setNextPathCoordFrom: currentPathCoord.
  error = currentPathCoord = (0@0).    "No valid path cell found"
  theSwamp pathTerminated or error  ) repeatWhileFalse.
  "Repeat until path complete or error."

error  ) repeatWhileTrue.    "Recreate path until valid."
```

Initialize the path to empty, choose the first path cell, and assign it to currentPath-Coord. Repeat finding the next path cell from the current cell until the path is complete or an error occurs. If an error occurs, start over. Repeat until a valid path is generated.

- Partitioning of the atEndOfPath message sent to object aSwampTraveler:

```
return coordinate == targetSwamp path last.
    "Coordinate of swamp traveler is same as last path cell coord."
```

- Partitioning of the moveTo: aCoordinate message sent to object aSwampTraveler:

```
coordinate = aCoordinate.              "Update location of swamp traveler."
numSteps = numSteps + 1.               "Increment number of steps."
coordsVisited add: aCoordinate.        "Add aCoordinate to those visited."
aSwampTraveler display.      "Display image on swamp at coordinate."
cellVisiting = targetSwamp swampCells at: coordinate.
return cellVisiting class == PathCell.    "True if on path cell"
```

- Partitioning of the makeNextSuccessfulMove message sent to object aSwampTraveler:

```
coordList = aSwampTraveler chooseNeighbors.
    "Use subclass rules to return coords of valid neighbors for move."
index = coordList size * random next
    "Choose a random, in-range index in coordList.
return aSwampTraveler moveTo: (*TIME*coordList at: index ).
    "Return will be a Boolean true if move is to path cell."
```

The Sixth and Other Levels of a Prototype Solution

At the sixth level of the hierarchy of operations, only logic details are given for message setNextPathCoordFrom: currentPathCoord sent to object theSwamp and for message chooseNeighbors sent to object aSwampTraveler.

- Logic for the setNextPathCoordFrom: currentPathCoord message sent to object theSwamp:

```
Create a collection of coords by adding each offset in offsets to coordinate.
Remove coord of previous path cell.
Remove coords not in the swamp.
Remove folded path coordinates.
Return a list of coords for valid moves.
```

• Logic for the chooseNeighbors message sent to object aSwampTraveler:

Create a collection of coords by adding each offset in offsets to coordinate.
Remove all coords that are not in the targetSwamp.
Using logic for each kind of swamp traveler, redefine chooseNeighbors in subclasses
to remove additional coords as required.
Return a collection of coords representing valid moves for the specific swamp traveler.

Each of these steps may be further partitioned as required or desired. The partition-ing is complete when no more details are required for a solution. The question of where to stop partitioning as part of the design and where the partitioning becomes implementa-tion does not always have a clear answer.

We want to emphasize the point that at each level in the partitioning, only a manage-able portion of the solution is presented. Expressions at each level are often simple messages sent to objects that are part of the solution. This partitioning is one way to manage complexity and perhaps enhance reusability at the message level.

2.6 CLASS DESCRIPTIONS:
WHAT ABOUT REUSABILITY, GENERALITY,
AND ROBUSTNESS?

Several variations of a hierarchy of classes representing vehicles were presented in Chap-ter 1. One of the goals in presenting those variations was to show how reusability and generality are enhanced through the definition of abstract classes. An abstract class con-tains protocol that is common to all its subclasses. The common protocol thus needs to be defined only one time. New, specialized kinds of objects may be added easily through subclassing, taking full advantage of inherited protocol from the abstract class. Only new methods specific to a subclass, or methods that should be redefined need be added. The abstract class has a high degree of reusability. The *Swamp Runner* example presented in this chapter makes use of abstract classes to enhance generality and promote reusability. Specifically, classes SwampCell and SwampTraveler are abstract classes. No instances of these classes are ever created; only instances of their subclasses are created.

Reusability is further enhanced through the identification #and use of key messages and methods. A key message is one that is fundamental to other messages that use it and is often identified by the fact that many other messages in a class send the key message as part of their method details. The exact meaning of all these dependent messages is then determined by the specific implementation of the key message. In an abstract class, key messages are often implemented with methods that pass responsibility to a subclass. This operation is so important in supporting the concept of reusability through abstract classes that object-oriented languages with predefined classes typically define a message subclassResponsibility in class Object so that it is available to all classes in the system.

To illustrate how abstract classes and key messages support reusability, we examine the SwampCell and SwampTraveler classes in more detail. Another look at the messages and methods in class SwampCell shows that it contains all the protocol for its subclasses except that the key method initialize must be redefined in PathCell and QuicksandCell. We summarize the role of abstract class SwampCell in Figure 2.4. Even this very simple

Figure 2.4 _____

Properties of SwampCell as an abstract superclass for PathCell and QuicksandCell

SwampCell

   Attributes:

      coordinate—Location within a swamp (2-D)
      image—Image of a swamp cell (a graphic image or character)

   Key messages:

      initialize—Implemented as subclass responsibility; each subclass will assign a
      different graphic image or character to attribute image.

   Other messages:

      createAt: aCoordinate—For creating a swamp cell at a coordinate
       ◦ Create a new instance of a swamp cell.
       ◦ Send the message coordinate: aCoordinate to the new instance.
       ◦ Send the key message initialize to the new instance.
      displayOn: aSwamp—Display the image at its coordinate on aSwamp.
      coordinate—Return the coordinate of the swamp cell.
      coordinate: aCoordinate—Assign coordinate to aCoordinate.
      image—Return the image.
      setImage: anImage—Assign image to be anImage.

QuicksandCell and PathCell

   Attributes inherited from SwampCell:

      coordinate, image

   New attributes:

      QuicksandImage—Image for all quicksand cells (defined in QuicksandCell)
      PathImage—Image for all path cells (defined in PathCell)

   Messages redefined:

      initialize—Implemented to assign the appropriate value for image

   Implementation in class QuicksandCell:

      self setImage: QuicksandImage

   Implementation in class PathCell:

      self setImage: PathImage

_____

hierarchy of three classes capitalizes on reusability through inheritance and the use of an
abstract superclass.

    Another look at the messages and methods in class SwampTraveler shows that it
contains most of the protocol for its subclasses except that the key method init must be

redefined in each subclass to assign the appropriate value for attribute image. Additionally, because the rules for traversal are different for each kind of swamp traveler, a few selected methods are redefined for the subclasses. The overall logic for traversing the swamp is given in SwampTraveler and shared by all the swamp travelers.

Class SwampTraveler defines most of the attributes for all its subclasses. One additional attribute, pathTraveled, is added in class Wit. Another attribute, numGuesses, is added to class Genius. Each subclass also adds an attribute representing the image for any instance of that class.

We summarize the role of abstract class SwampTraveler in Figure 2.5. Note that a different kind of reusability is represented by key method chooseNeighbors. At each subclass level (classes Dimwit and Halfwit), the parent class method is first invoked, followed by additional operations. The subclass method is redefined to add detail, not to replace the parent method. Other methods are redefined to replace the parent method as shown in Figure 2.5.

Figure 2.5 _____

Properties of SwampTraveler as an abstract superclass for Dimwit, Halfwit, Wit, and Genius

SwampTraveler

Attributes:

coordinate—Location within a swamp (2-D)
image—Image of a swamp traveler (a graphic image or character)
targetSwamp—The swamp upon which the swamp traveler moves
numSteps—The number of steps to traverse the swamp
numAttempts—Number of attempts to traverse the swamp
neighborCoords—A collection of neighbor coordinates
coordsVisited—Collection of swamp coordinates already visited

Key messages:

init—Implemented as subclass responsibility; each subclass will assign a
      different graphic image or character to attribute image.
chooseNeighbors—Start with a collection of all neighbor coordinates of a
      swamp traveler and remove those representing invalid moves;
      implementation in SwampTraveler removes coordinates that
      fall outside the swamp.

Other messages:

createOn: aTarget—For creating a swamp traveler on a target swamp
  ° create a new instance of a swamp cell.
  ° send message target: aTarget to the new instance.
  ° send the message initialize to the new instance.
  send the key message init to the new instance.

target: aTarget—Assign targetSwamp to equal aTarget.

initialize—Initialize numSteps, numAttempts, coordinate (0,0),
    neighborCoords, and coordsVisited.

display—Display image at coordinate on targetSwamp.

image: anImage—Assign image to equal anImage.

image—Return the image.

target—Return targetSwamp.

Messages for traversing:

atEndOfPath—Answer true if swamp traveler is at end of path.

traverse—Traverse the swamp.

makeFirstMove—Pick a border coordinate, borderCoord, at random; then
    send the message moveTo: borderCoord

makeNextMoves—Send the message makeNextSuccessfulMove until
    atEndOfPath returns true; provide update of
    numAttempts; update the display.

makeNextSuccessfulMove—Send message chooseNeighbors;
    pick a valid neighborCoord at random;
    send the message moveTo: neighborCoord;
    return true if successful move.

moveTo: aCoordinate—Move the swamp traveler to aCoordinate;
    update numSteps; return true if new location is a path cell;
    return false if new location is a quicksand cell.

Dimwit

Attributes inherited from SwampTraveler:

coordinate, image, targetSwamp, numSteps, numAttempts,
neighborCoords, coordsVisited

New attributes:

DimwitImage—Image for all Dimwit swamp travelers

Messages redefined:

init—Implemented to assign the appropriate value for image, that is,
    image = DimwitImage.

chooseNeighbors—Call parent class method; remove all coordinates of path
    cells except the next path cell from current location. This prevents
    retracing steps on path.

Halfwit

Attributes inherited from SwampTraveler:

coordinate, image, targetSwamp, numSteps, numAttempts,
neighborCoords, coordsVisited

Attributes inherited from Dimwit:

DimwitImage—Inherited but not used; not representative of a halfwit.
         This is a minor flaw in the design.

New attributes:

HalfwitImage—Image for all Halfwit swamp travelers

Messages redefined:

init—Implemented to assign the appropriate value for image, that is,
         image = HalfwitImage.
chooseNeighbors—Call parent class method; remove all coordinates in
         coordsVisited.
makeFirstMove—First remove all path cells in coordsVisited;
         then send message moveTo: firstPathCellCoord.

Wit

Attributes inherited from SwampTraveler:

coordinate, image, targetSwamp, numSteps, numAttempts,
neighborCoords, coordsVisited

Attributes inherited from Dimwit:

DimwitImage—Inherited but not used; not representative of a wit.
         This is a minor flaw in the design.

Attributes inherited from Halfwit:

HalfwitImage—Inherited but not used; not representative of a wit.
         This is a minor flaw in the design.

New attributes:

WitImage—Image for all Wit swamp travelers
pathTraveled—A collection of sequential path cells visited

Messages redefined:

init—Implemented to assign the appropriate value for image and
         initialize pathTraveled, that is,
                  image = WitImage.
                  pathTraveled = OrderedCollection new.
                  pathTraveled add: firstPathCellCoord.
makeFirstMove—First remove all path cells in coordsVisited;
                  then send message moveTo: aCoord for each coordinate in
                  pathTraveled; then send message makeNextMoves.
moveTo: coord—First invoke inherited method; then add coord to
                  pathTraveled if it is a path coordinate.

Genius

Attributes inherited from SwampTraveler:

coordinate, image, targetSwamp, numSteps, numAttempts, neighborCoords, coordsVisited

Attributes inherited from Dimwit:

DimwitImage—Inherited but not used; not representative of a genius.
This is a minor flaw in the design.

Attributes inherited from Halfwit:

HalfwitImage—Inherited but not used; not representative of a genius.
This is a minor flaw in the design.

Attributes inherited from Wit:

WitImage—Inherited but not used; not representative of a genius.
This is a minor flaw in the design.

New attributes:

GeniusImage—Image for all Genius swamp travelers
numGuesses—Running total of guesses for next moves

Messages redefined:

init—Implemented to assign the appropriate value for image, initialize
numGuesses, *and initialize* pathTraveled, *that is,*

        super init.
        image = GeniusImage.
        numGuesses = 0.
makeNextSuccessfulMove—First invoke inherited method for
chooseNeighbors; keep guessing until a path cell is found;
update numGuesses; then move to next path cell.

The *Swamp Runner* simulation illustrates reusability of software components through subclassing and the use of abstract superclasses. Within the software system, attributes and functional abstractions are inherited and reused. Additional reusability of entire classes is illustrated in the *Swamp Runner* simulation through multiple uses of a class called OrderedCollection. Its details are not described in the solution because a class representing ordered collections (with variations on its actual name) is provided as part of several object-oriented language implementations.

In the development of any software solution, one should attempt to define classes with high reusability. Classes with the most reusability are often abstract superclasses with the most generality. More specific classes are typically subclasses at a deeper level in the hierarchy. A framework of high-level abstract classes is a good starting point for the development of reusable software components.

## CHAPTER 3

The Objective-C Language

Poetry is something more philosophical
and more worthy of serious attention than history.

Aristotle, *384–322 B.C.*

3.1 HISTORY AND VERSIONS

Objective-C™ is an object-oriented programming language that is a superset of C. The original version was developed by The Stepstone Corporation (originally called Productivity Products International, Inc.). At the time of this writing, Stepstone continues to support this language, now in version 4.0. In addition, NeXT™ Computer, Inc. has produced a compiled version of Objective-C (also version 4.0—hereafter called Objective-C) that is modeled closely after Stepstone's version. There are only minor differences between the Stepstone implementation and the NeXT implementation.

Objective-C, like other powerful object-oriented languages, is delivered with a class hierarchy—a predefined set of reusable software components. Stepstone has used the term ICPAKS™ to describe its standard class library. More specifically, ICpak 101, modeled after Smalltalk-80's collection classes, includes foundation classes that are derived from an Object class. The class Object is at the root of the tree. Its protocol contains behavior that is common to all objects. The Stepstone foundation classes are described in some detail in Chapter 4 and used in Chapter 5. These reusable software components provide the Objective-C programmer with a great deal of leverage. Because source code is provided with ICpak 101, a programmer can better understand, use, and extend the behaviors built into this library.

The Stepstone implementation of Objective-C uses a translator. The system translates an Objective-C source listing to C and the base C compiler produces an executable image. This process, although not as efficient as direct compilation, allows the user to capture and use the intermediate C code if it is necessary to port this code to a platform that does not have an Objective-C compiler. Stepstone is currently supporting most of the major UNIX™ platforms as well as OS/2™ and MS-DOS™. Stepstone offers a separate package, ICpak 201, of over one hundred classes that support the development of graphical interfaces on UNIX platforms.

The NeXT version of Objective-C, officially released in September 1989, is a compiled version of the language that runs only on the NeXT computer. It is coupled to a powerful Interface Builder™ and is supported by over forty classes called the Application Kit. These classes mainly support the graphic/window/mouse interface of the NeXT computer. There are several classes in the Application Kit designed to support general-purpose Objective-C programming.

The Interface Builder significantly automates the process of developing user applications. It allows the developer to use a graphics editor to configure the windows, buttons, scrollbars, and other graphical components that are relevant to an application. The "look and feel" of this interface is similar to the extremely user friendly interface that is typical of Apple Macintosh™ applications. The Interface Builder generates the skeletal structure of the Objective-C code and allows the programmer to add classes and subclasses to the existing set of Application Kit classes. When finished with the Interface Builder, all the developer must do is flesh out the noninterface portions of the application (easier said than done!). Applications that use the Interface Builder are described in some detail in Chapters 7 and 8.

Objective-C applications that run under an ordinary UNIX shell can also be developed using the NeXT computer. The user can either write directly to a shell or terminal window (opened before the application is run) or directly create windows, menus, buttons, and so on, using the Application Kit classes provided with the system. Unfortunately, the NeXT version of Objective-C does not come with any source code for the Application Kit classes. This makes it more difficult to use and understand each of the subclasses in the system.

The class Object (the root of the class hierarchy) supplied with the Stepstone version differs slightly from that supplied with the NeXT version. This can cause minor difficulty in porting applications from the NeXT to other UNIX platforms that use the Stepstone version of Objective-C. These differences are explored in Chapter 4.

The NeXT version of the code is almost the same as the Stepstone version. In Chapters 4 and 5, which feature ICpak 101, only Stepstone's version of code is presented since ICpak 101 is not available on the NeXT computer at the time of this writing. Chapters 7 and 8 feature code developed on the NeXT computer that utilizes the special features of the NeXT graphical environment. From the Stepstone-based code presented in Chapters 4 and 5 and the NeXT-based code presented in Chapters 6, 7, and 8, the reader should have no difficulty in understanding the minor differences in the two versions as far as basic Objective-C programming is concerned. Some of these differences are summarized at the end of this chapter.

Objective-C was developed to provide the software development community with a language as flexible and readable as Smalltalk while retaining the efficiency of C. In our view, Objective-C satisfies these goals magnificently. In addition to being an outstanding development language and environment, it is, in our view, a wonderful language for exploring the exciting world of object-oriented programming.

3.2 RELATIONSHIP TO THE C LANGUAGE

Objective-C is probably the easiest of all the C-based object-oriented languages to learn. It is derived from the new ANSI C standard. Objective-C adds message-passing and class-definition syntax to ANSI C. That is all. Yet, despite its simplicity, it provides full

Listing 3.1 _____

A C version of incrementing an integer

```
#include <stdio.h>

int increment( int value, int increment_amount )
{
 return value + increment_amount;
}

main()
{
 int my_value = 17;

 printf( "my_value after incrementing by 21 is %d\n", increment( my_value, 21 ) );
}

/* Program output
my_value after incrementing by 21 is 38
*/
```

support for object-oriented programming: encapsulation, inheritance, and polymorphism. Its power as a language derives from its simple yet complete support for object-oriented problem solving.

In this section we provide an appetizer—a brief and early taste of Objective-C, with relatively few details. A simple example is presented in C and in Objective-C. Because of the example's simplicity, we urge the reader to refrain from drawing any conclusions about the potential effectiveness of Objective-C or of object-oriented problem solving.

Listing 3.1 shows a simple C program that defines a function, increment, that increments an integer by a specified value (increment_amount) is shown. In Listing 3.2, the same simple application is rewritten by promoting the simple type, int, to a class, Integer, and performing the increment operation using message-passing syntax. Listing 3.2 demonstrates the relative ease of reading and understanding Objective-C without any formal training and serves as a warmup example. The dashes in Listing 3.2 delimit separate files.

It is assumed that the reader has a working knowledge of ANSI C and can understand the C code in Listing 3.1. It will not be discussed.

In Listing 3.2, the ordinary C type, int, is promoted to a class, Integer. This is entirely unnecessary for the simple application at hand but is done for illustrative purposes. The first file presented is the interface to class Integer. Objective-C uses the double slash, //, as a comment to the end-of-line delimiter. All text between the double slash and the first character of a new line is treated as a comment. The ordinary C comment delimiters, /* and */, are still valid and may be used.

The keyword #import at the top of the interface file works like #include in C except that multiple inclusions are automatically prohibited.

The heading @interface Integer : Object indicates that the newly defined class Integer is a subclass of the root class Object. All of the protocol of Object (instance variables and methods) is available to Integer objects. The heading of each newly defined class in Objective-C must indicate the parent class of the newly defined class.

Listing 3.2 _____
An Objective-C version of incrementing an integer

```
// Interface to simplified Integer class

#import <objc/Object.h>

@interface Integer : Object
{
 int value;
}

// Factory method - Used to create new objects from class Integer
+ new: (int) aValue;

// Initialize
- initialize: (int) aValue;

// Operations
- increment: (int) aValue;

// Display
- print;

@end
------------------------

// Implementation of simplified class Integer

#import "Integer.h"
#import <stdio.h>

@implementation Integer
// Factory method
+ new: (int) aValue
{
 id newInstance = [ super new ];
 [ newInstance initialize: aValue ];
 return newInstance;
}
// Initialize
- initialize: (int) aValue
{
 value = aValue;
 return self;
}

// Operations
- increment: (int) aValue
{
 value += aValue;
 return self;
}
```

```
// Display
- print
{
 printf( "%d\n", value );
 return self;
}

@end
------------------------
```

```
// Main driver program for incrementing integer

#import "Integer.h"
#import <stdio.h>

main()
{
  Integer *myValue = [ Integer new: 17 ];

  [ myValue increment: 21 ];
  printf( "myValue after incrementing by 21 is " );
  [ myValue print ];
}
/* same output as Listing 3.1 */
```

The instance variables of class Integer are given between the opening and closing curly braces. Each instance (object) of class Integer has a potentially unique value for this instance variable, which characterizes the *state* of a particular Integer object.

The message selectors for all the methods of class Integer are declared next. These are preceded by categories given as comments, following the Smalltalk practice of grouping all methods into categories. In Objective-C this classification is purely optional, but we strongly recommend this practice. The first message selector, + new: (int) aValue, indicates that a factory method is declared. Factory methods (they begin with the symbol +) are used to create new objects (instances of a class). In Section 3.4 factory methods are discussed in detail. The other message selectors, - initialize: (int) aValue, - increment: (int) aValue, and - print, are instance methods. These methods (beginning with the symbol -) are used to manipulate instances of class Integer (i.e., they manipulate objects of class Integer). The instance methods define the behavior of Integer objects.

The implementation file begins with the heading @implementation Integer and contains the implementation details of each method. These details are similar to function definitions in ANSI C. The instance variables can be shown in the implementation file, if desired, as follows:

```
@implementation Integer : Object
{
  int value;
}
```

The factory method new, with parameter aValue, declares a local variable, new-Instance, as type id. The id type means "any object," and is a special Objective-C type. The initialization expression [super new] requires some explanation. The rectangular brackets, [ ], are used to indicate message-passing syntax. In general, the format [receivingObject message] is used to send a message to an object. The recipient of the action, receivingObject, is written before the action or the message. Such a message-sending expression may be used wherever a legal C expression would be allowed; this is a fundamental extension to C provided in Objective-C. This message-passing syntax closely resembles Smalltalk's syntax. Having the noun precede the verb (i.e., object precede the action) places the emphasis on the object—the recipient of the action—and may therefore be appropriately called *object-oriented*.

The protocol of class Object contains a factory method, new. This factory method allocates storage for a new object whose size is given by the protocol description given in the interface file—in this case the interface file for class Integer. Since method new is redefined in class Integer, the keyword super indicates that the method new in class Integer's immediate parent class (class Object) should be used instead of a recursive call to the method new in class Integer. The instance method initialize, with parameter aValue, is sent to the newly created Integer object newInstance. A direct assignment of value = aValue in the factory method would be illegal since instance variables are not directly accessible within a factory method. The assignment of value = aValue is accomplished indirectly using the instance method initialize.

The keyword self may be used within a method to refer to the object receiving the message. This keyword is used in the statement return self in the methods initialize, increment, and print. Returning self allows methods to be concatenated. For example,

[[anInteger increment: 5] increment: 12];

first increments the object anInteger by 5 and returns the incremented object (self), which then receives the message increment with parameter 12. The effect is to increment anInteger by 17.

The details of method increment add aValue to the current instance variable value for the object (self) receiving the message.

Finally, the method print uses the printf function from stdio to output the instance variable value to the standard output device (terminal).

The main driver program starts by declaring an object, myValue, to be of class Integer. The variable myValue could just as well been declared, as follows:

id myValue;

The declaration Integer *myValue tells the Objective-C system that myValue belongs to class Integer. This allows the compiler to perform static checking of messages to Integer objects. If an illegal message, such as [myInteger dunkTheBasketBall], were sent to myInteger, the compiler would emit a warning message at compile time indicating that an illegal message was sent to myInteger. If the generic id declaration of myValue given above were used instead, the error would not be flagged at compile time; it would be indicated at run time with a run-time crash. It must be emphasized that in both cases late binding (run-time binding) of the message to the method would be implemented. The important issue of binding is the subject of the Section 3.4.

The initialization expression [Integer new: 17] is used to create a new instance (object) of class Integer, with initial value equal to 17.

The receiver of the factory method new is the class variable Integer, the name of the Integer class. Factory methods, used to create new objects, are always sent to class variables, which in Objective-C are class names.

The object myValue is sent the message increment: 21. Finally, the object myValue is sent the message print.

Listings 3.1 and 3.2 may initially convince you that the plain, short, and simple C solution in Listing 3.1 is superior to the longer and more involved object-oriented solution in Listing 3.2. As indicated before, this example is not constructed to make the point that the object-oriented solution is more appropriate or better than the plain C solution. The point, again, is to introduce the elements of Objective-C and demonstrate how it builds upon the structure of the substrate language, C. Examples that illustrate the real power of the object-oriented paradigm will be presented in later chapters.

3.3 DEFINING CLASSES

Interface Files

An Objective-C interface file defines the instance variables for all objects of the class as well as the message selectors for all methods of the class. In addition, the interface file specifies a parent class. All instance variables of ancestor classes are inherited by and cannot be redefined within a subclass. These instance variables plus the instance variables defined in the given subclass are directly accessible within the implementation file but inaccessible outside of the implementation file. Access methods must be used to set the value of or get the value of these instance variables. Therefore, objects cannot directly access their own instance variables. Requiring the use of access methods guarantees consistency of usage or uniform behavior among the objects of a given class.

All methods of ancestor classes are inherited but can be redefined. Specific methods may be blocked in a subclass by redefining them with empty implementations. The message selectors for a given class define the behavior of all objects of the class.

In designing object-oriented systems, abstract superclasses are often constructed. Such superclasses group instance variables and message selectors that will be used by a cluster of subclasses. Often, many of the methods in such a superclass are not defined; their definitions are given in one or more of the subclasses.

The interface file for a particular class is a separate file from the implementation file for the class. Its file name generally ends with the suffix .h. Interface files begin with the heading @interface and end with the terminator @end. The general format of interface files is as follows:

```
@interface ClassName : ParentClassName
{
  instance variable definitions;
}
```

// Factory methods, if they exist

...

// Instance methods, if they exist

...

@end

An interface file provides the minimum information or protocol that a client needs to know about a given class and in some cases contains the only information that is available about the class. The interface file provides all its subclasses with precise information about the instance variables that they will inherit as well as the methods that they will inherit.

Factory methods all begin with the symbol +, which is followed by a message interface and terminating semicolon. A message interface contains a message selector with named parameters and their types, for example:

+ new: (int) anInt;

The message selector is new:, and the named parameter and its type is (int) anInt.

Instance methods all begin with the symbol -, which is followed by a message interface and a terminating semicolon. Some examples follow:

- put: (int) aValue at: (int) anIndex;

- (int) get: (int) index;

- print: aString;

The absence of a specific return type or argument type, as in methods put (no return type) and print (the parameter aString), means a default type of id. Consider the message selector

- put: (int) aValue at: (int) anIndex;

The actual message selector is put:at:. The parameters are aValue and anIndex. Selectors are only optional. The put:at: selector could be declared as follows:

-put: (int) aValue : (int) anIndex;

Its selector would be, put::.

Factory methods are the equivalent of class methods in Smalltalk; they operate on class variables. In Objective-C, class variables are class names. A class method may be assigned the same name as an instance method. Class methods are generally used in Objective-C to create new instances of the given class; that is why they are called *factory methods*.

Interface files generally must import, using #import, the interface file of their immediate parent. This implies that every interface file imports the interface files of all its ancestor classes.

Implementation Files

An implementation file is structured as follows:

```
@implementation ClassName : ParentClassName
{
    instance variables;
}
// Details of factory methods
...
// Details of instance methods

@end
```

The information between the open and closing curly braces is optional. It is generally our practice in this book to omit this redundant information. An implementation file must import, using #import, its own interface file.

The method details are similar to function definitions in C. As indicated in the previous section, each method of a given subclass has direct access to all its instance variables as well as the instance variables of all its ancestor classes. Direct access means that these instance variables can be mentioned by name.

It is common practice for instance variables and methods to use the same name. For example,

```
@interface Vehicle : Object
{
    int weight;
    ...
}
...
- (int) weight;
...
@end
```

An object, myWeight, might access its own weight as follows:

```
int w = [ myWeight weight ];
```

As indicated earlier, we believe that although it is not absolutely necessary, it is generally desirable to have access to the source code for all the implementation files in the system. This knowledge makes it easier to understand the inherited behaviors of a given subclass as well as the time/space trade-offs that have been designed into the algorithms used in the various subclasses.

Adding Methods to a Class: Categories

Methods can be added to an existing class without access to the source code for the class by establishing a category name within an interface file and defining the methods in an implementation file, using the same category name. The category name serves to inform the compiler that the methods are additions to an existing class and not a new class.

Categories do not support the addition of any new instance variables; they only allow new methods to be added to an existing class. The format for using categories is the following:

#import "ClassName.h"

@interface Classname(CategoryName)
// Method interfaces

...
@end

#import "ClassName.h"

@implementation ClassName(CategoryName)

// Method definitions

...
@end

The methods added under a category cannot override methods defined in the existing class. They can, however, be used to override (redefine) methods in any ancestor class.

Grouping methods into categories allows the Objective-C software developer to

1. Organize related methods together

2. Partition the development of a large class into smaller chunks that several programmers can tackle

3. Allow incremental compilation for large systems

Class Objects

Every object contains its own state variables—a copy of all the instance variables given in the interface file protocol description of the class (See section on Interface Files). Some object-oriented languages, such as Smalltalk, provide another category of variables called *class variables*, which are common to all the objects of the class. If such a variable has its value changed for one object, then its value is simultaneously changed for all objects of the class.

Objective-C currently does not formally support class variables. It does however support class objects, which take the name of the class. In order for all objects of a given class to share data (i.e., to simulate the effect of a class variable), an external variable defined in the implementation file may be used. Generally it is good practice to define this variable to be of storage class static in order to hide it from the linker and thus make it invisible outside of the implementation file. The *Swamp Runner* simulation presented in Chapter 5 illustrates this.

A class object cannot directly access any of its instance variables. That explains why many factory methods invoke the message initialize (or some variant) to set the initial values of one or more instance variables. The following would be illegal:

```
@implementation Integer : Object
{
    int value;
}
```

```
+ new: (int) aValue
{
  id newInstance = [ super new ];
  value = aValue;
  return newInstance;
}
```

The correct version of class method (factory method) new would be the following:

```
+ new: (int) aValue
{
  id newInstance = [ super new ];
  [ newInstance initialize: aValue ];
  return newInstance;
}
- initialize: (int) aValue
{
  value = aValue;
  return self;
}
```

The Use of self and super

The keywords self and super are used extensively in implementing methods. The keyword self refers to the object receiving the message associated with a given method. It is actually a pointer to the object, but this low-level detail is not pertinent to this discussion. Objective-C, like Smalltalk, masks the use of pointers so that the developer can focus on the entities of the problem and not get distracted by the typical, low-level pointer and address management that is so commonplace in ordinary C and assembly language programming. Many well-structured, large Objective-C software systems do not require the use of a single pointer or address operator.

As a general rule, when a method does not specifically return a data type, it returns self. This allows several messages to be concatenated, as demonstrated in Section 3.2.

The keyword super, used in place of self, tells the system to start the search for the method in the parent class. This is useful when a subclass has redefined a parent class method and the intent is to invoke the version of the method defined in the parent class. It must be emphasized that the action given by the parent class method is still applied to the receiving object, just as in the case of using self.

A simple example that illustrates the use of self and super follows.

```
@implementation Person : Object
{
  char name[ 50 ];
}

...
- print
{
  printf( "Name: %s\n", name );
  return self;
}
```

```
...
@end
------------------------

@implementation Student: Person
{
  long id;
}
...
- print
{
  [ super print ];
  printf( "Id: %ld\n", id );
  return self;
}
...
@end
```

Method print in subclass Student sends the message print to super. If print were sent to self, this would represent a recursive call. Instead, the meaning is to apply the method print from class Person to the Student object receiving the message.

Naming Conventions for Classes, Objects, and Instance Variables

Although the Objective-C system does not require it, we strongly recommend the strict use of a few fundamental naming conventions:

- All class names should start with an uppercase letter and use mixed lowercase and uppercase letters for other characters.
- All object names should start with a lowercase letter and use mixed lowercase and uppercase letters for other characters.
- Instance variables should use the same naming conventions as for objects.

These conventions, originating in Smalltalk, have proven helpful in understanding Objective-C code. It can probably be argued that any consistent naming convention would serve the same goal equally well. We adhere closely to these naming conventions throughout this book.

3.4 MESSAGES, DYNAMIC BINDING, AND TYPE CHECKING

The issue of binding can be approached from the low-level viewpoint of a compiler designer. This viewpoint is concerned with the precise mechanism that couples a function call or message to the body of code (method) that implements the function. Technical issues such as constant offsets, dispatch-table lookup and caching, and the like are the central concerns. This is not the viewpoint that will be taken here. We prefer to view the issue of binding from a much higher vantage point—that of a system designer/programmer/application developer. From this vantage point, the consequence of choosing early or late binding profoundly affects the reusability and maintainability of the software components that are developed.

Early binding requires that the compiler know exactly the type of object that is to receive a given message. The message is coupled to an associated method at compile time. This knowledge may lead to greater code efficiency because of the compiler's ability to perform code optimization. In exchange for this potential benefit, the developer (producer) gives up a degree of flexibility in constructing robust, reusable software components. This will be illustrated shortly.

Late binding, also referred to as *run-time* or *dynamic* binding, couples messages to methods at run time. There may be a small performance penalty associated with this type of binding. The benefit of late binding is realized when one or more methods in a superclass are redefined in subclasses. This allows a constant behavior (e.g., print object) to be obtained across a number of disparate objects, which is one of the key benefits of object-oriented problem solving.

Dr. Brad Cox, the inventor of Objective-C, at a conference (SCOOP West in Santa Clara, California, Jan. 1990) presented the following humorous description of early versus late binding. His first slide, depicting early binding, shows a baby born with skis bound to his feet. As this baby matures, he becomes a highly proficient skier, enjoying the benefits of optimization that generally result from early binding. Dr. Cox's second slide shows another baby born with ordinary feet that may be late-bound to shoes, slippers, skis, or any other footwear. Although this baby may not learn to ski as proficiently as the first, she enjoys much greater flexibility in adapting her feet to different environments and footwear. Although these slides somewhat oversimplify the situation, there is nevertheless some truth in this analogy.

Let us closely examine the two approaches to binding, using Objective-C, by constructing two alternative solutions to the same problem. The problem involves building an array of five numeric objects. Each object behaves as either an integer or a floating-point number (a *float*). The first approach features early binding and is implemented in Stepstone's Objective-C, which supports early binding; it builds a single class called Numeric. This class encapsulates the behavior of either an integer or a float. The code for class Numeric is presented in Listings 3.3 and 3.4.

The interface of class Numeric does not contain any factory methods. All objects of class Numeric will be created statically at compile-time. Initial conditions will be established using the instance methods, initializeInt and initializeFloat. Every Numeric object contains an instance variable that indicates whether the object is of integer or float type. This should not cause any difficulty for readers accustomed to using unions within a struct definition in ordinary C to allow variants within a data structure. Every Numeric object may behave as either an integer or a float, depending on how it is initialized.

A short test program is presented in Listing 3.5.

The effects of early binding are evident throughout Listing 3.5. The declaration

Numeric data[5];

allows the compiler to allocate storage for five objects, each of class Numeric.

Listing 3.3 _____
Interface to class Numeric using early binding

```
// Interface to class Numeric - Numeric.h

#import <Primitive.h>

typedef enum { int_type, float_type } numberType;

@interface Numeric : Object
{
 int intValue;
 float floatValue;
 numberType type;
}
// Initialize methods
- initializeInt: (int) anInt;

- initializeFloat: (float) aFloat;

// Increment methods
- incrementByInt: (int) anInt;
- incrementByFloat: (float) aFloat;

// Access methods
- (int) getInt;

- (float) getFloat;

- (numberType) getType;

@end
```
_____

In order to increment each of the five objects by an amount 5, an if else construct must be used to determine whether the receiving object acts like an integer or a float. The same is true when the five objects are printed.

The responsibility for allocating control rests with the **consumer** (client) of class Numeric. In our view and the view of many object-oriented practitioners, this responsibility should rest with the **producer** of class Numeric. The reason we argue for the transfer of responsibility to the producer is related to maintenance. What if one or more additional categories of number type are later added to the software system? If the consumer is responsible for distributing the control of specific messages to allow the different numeric behaviors to be achieved, this burden adds significantly to the cost of maintenance. When the producer assumes this responsibility, the maintenance of the client software system is trivial. This is demonstrated later in this section when some simple maintenance is performed on the early-binding and late-binding solutions.

The solution that utilizes late-binding polymorphism is presented in Listings 3.6–3.10. Listings 3.6 and 3.7 present class Integer; Listings 3.8 and 3.9 present class Float; and Listing 3.10 presents a short test program.

Listing 3.4 _____

Implementation of class Numeric using early binding

```
// Implementation of class Numeric - Numeric.m

#import "Numeric.h"
#import <stdio.h>

@implementation Numeric

// Initialize methods
- initializeInt: (int) anInt
{
 intValue = anInt;
 type = int_type;
 return self;
}

- initializeFloat: (float) aFloat
{
 floatValue = aFloat;
 type = float_type;
 return self;
}

// Increment methods
- incrementByInt: (int) anInt
{
 intValue += anInt;
 return self;
}

- incrementByFloat: (float) aFloat
{
 floatValue += aFloat;
 return self;
}

// Access methods
- (int) getInt
{
 return intValue;
 }
 - (float) getFloat
 {
  return floatValue;
 }

- (numberType) getType
{
 return type;
}
@end
```

Listing 3.5 _____

A test program for class Numeric featuring early binding

```
// Test program for class Numeric
#import "Numeric.h"
#import <stdio.h>

main()
{
 int i;
 char choice;
 int value;
 float r;
 FILE *f;
 Numeric data[ 5 ]; // Static binding

 f = fopen( "choices.txt", "r" );
 for ( i = 0; i < 5; i++ )
 {
  choice = fgetc( f );
  printf( "\nWhat is the value: " );
  if ( choice == 'i' || choice == 'I' )
  {
   scanf( "%d", &value );
   [ data[ i ] initializeInt: value ];
  }
  else
  {
   scanf( "%f", &r );
   [ data[ i ] initializeFloat: r ];
  }
 }

 // Increment each value
 for ( i = 0; i < 5; i++ )
 {
  if ( [ data[ i ] getType ] == int_type )
  [ data[ i ] incrementByInt: 5 ];
  else
  [ data[ i ] incrementByFloat: 5.0 ];
 }

 // Print each value
 for ( i = 0; i < 5; i++ )
 {
  if ( [ data[ i ] getType ] == int_type )
  printf( "data[ %d ] = %d\n", i, [ data[ i ] getInt ] );
  else
  printf( "data[ %d ] = %f\n", i, [ data[ i ] getFloat ] );
 }
}
```

Listing 3.6 _____

Interface to class Integer using late binding

```
// Interface to class Integer - Integer.h

#import <Primitive.h>

@interface Integer: Object
{
 int value;
}

// Factory method
+ new: (int) anInt;

// Initialize method
- initialize: (int) anInt;

// Increment method
- incrementBy: (int) aValue;

// Print method

- print;

@end
```

Listing 3.7 _____

Implementation for class Integer using late binding

```
// Implementation of class Integer - Integer.m

#import "Integer.h"

@implementation Integer

// Factory method

+ new: (int) anInt
{
 id newInstance = [ super new ];
 [ newInstance initialize: anInt ];
 return newInstance;
}

// Initialize method
- initialize: (int) anInt
{
 value = anInt;
 return self;
}

// Increment method
- incrementBy: (int) aValue
{
```

(continues)

```
 value += aValue;
 return self;
}
// Print method
- print;
{
 printf( "%d\n", value );
}
@end
```

Listing 3.8 _____
Interface to class Float using late binding

```
// Interface to class Float - Float.h

#import <Primitive.h>

@interface Float: Object
{
 float value;
}
// Factory method
+ new: (float) aFloat;

// Initialize method
- initialize: (float) aFloat;

// Increment method
- incrementBy: (int) aValue;

// Print method
- print;

@end
```

Listing 3.9 _____
Implementation for class Float using late binding

```
// Implementation of class Float - Float.m

#import "Float.h"

@implementation Float

// Factory method
+ new: (float) aFloat
{
 id newInstance = [ super new ];
 [ newInstance initialize: aFloat ];
 return newInstance;
}
```

```
// Initialize method
- initialize: (float) aFloat
{
 value = aFloat;
 return self;
}
// Increment method
- incrementBy: (int) aValue
{
 value += aValue;
 return self;
}
// Print method
- print
{
 printf( "%f\n", value );
}

@end
```

Listing 3.10
A test program for late binding

```
// Test program to illustrate late binding
#import "Integer.h"
#import "Float.h"

main()
{
 int i;
 char choice;
 int value;
 float r;
 FILE *f;

 id data[ 5 ];  // Late binding
 f = fopen( "choices.txt", "r" );
 for ( i = 0; i < 5; i++ )
 {
  choice = fgetc( f );
  printf( "\nWhat is the value: " );
  if ( choice == 'i' || choice == 'I' )
  {
   scanf( "%d", &value );
   data[ i ] = [ Integer new: value ];
  }
```

(continues)

```
else
{
  scanf( "%f", &r );
  data[ i ] = [ Float new: r ];
}
}

// Increment each value
for ( i = 0; i < 5; i++ )
  [ data[ i ] incrementBy: 5 ];

// Print each value
for ( i = 0; i < 5; i++ )
  [ data[ i ] print ];
}
```

The test program in Listing 3.10 depicts the typical nature of a late-binding solution. The array id data[5] specifies that data contains an array of five arbitrary objects. Each of the five objects is created on the fly using the factory method new:, defined in classes Integer and Float.

After the user is prompted to load five Integer or Float objects into this data array, each object is incremented by sending the message [data[i] incrementBy: 5] to each object in succession. The operation incrementBy remains constant, whereas the type of object receiving the message varies. The behavior suffered by each object remains constant. The Objective-C run-time system, using a dispatch table, couples the message incrementBy to the appropriate method (either in class Integer or class Float) dynamically. Most importantly, the consumer is unburdened from having to test the type of the receiving object in order to determine the precise action to take. Late-binding polymorphism takes care of this. This capability is one of the cornerstones of object-oriented programming.

To show the real payoff to the late-binding architecture, we perform some simple maintenance on the system. Specifically, type fraction is added to each solution. The maintenance on the early binding solution requires that additions be made to class Numeric. Two new instance variables, numerator and denominator are added. In addition, some additional instance methods for incrementing and accessing are provided. The revised class Numeric is presented in Listings 3.11 and 3.12. The revised test program is presented in Listing 3.13.

The telltale characteristic of early-binding solutions is again evident in the test program of Listing 3.13. The software consumer must again take responsibility for allocating the flow of control for each of the three numeric types. Now an if else, else if, else construct is required to distribute the appropriate message for the type of receiving object. This construct is repeated several times in function main.

The maintenance required for the late-binding solution is quite trivial. A new class, Fraction, is defined that encapsulates the behavior of this new numeric type. All maintenance is localized to this new class definition. Listings 3.14 and 3.15 present the new class Fraction. The revised test program presented in Listing 3.16 is almost a carbon copy of the original test program; only the input section is changed. The sections of the test program that increment each of the objects and then print each of the objects is un-

Listing 3.11 _____
Interface to revised class Numeric featuring early binding

```
// Interface to class Numeric - Numeric.h
#import <Primitive.h>

typedef enum { int_type, float_type, fraction_type } numberType;

@interface Numeric : Object
{
 int intValue;
 float floatValue;
 int numerator;
 int denominator;
 numberType type;
}
// Initialize methods
- initializeInt: (int) anInt;
- initializeFloat: (float) aFloat;

- initializeFractionWithNumerator: (int) num denominator: (int) den;

// Increment methods
- incrementByInt: (int) anInt;

- incrementByFloat: (float) aFloat;

- incrementFractionByInt: (int) anInt;

// Access methods
- (int) getInt;

- (float) getFloat;

- (int) getNumerator;

- (int) getDenominator;

- (numberType) getType;

@end
```

_____

Listing 3.12 _____
Implementation of revised class Numeric featuring early binding

```
// Implementation of class Numeric - Numeric.m
#import "Numeric.h"
#import <stdio.h>

@implementation Numeric

// Initialize methods
```
(continues)

```
- initializeInt: (int) anInt
{
 intValue = anInt;
 type = int_type;
 return self;
}

- initializeFloat: (float) aFloat
{
 floatValue = aFloat;
 type = float_type;
 return self;
}

- initializeFractionWithNumerator: (int) num denominator: (int) den
{
 numerator = num;
 denominator = den;
 type = fraction_type;
 return self;
}

// Increment methods
- incrementByInt: (int) anInt
{
 intValue += anInt;
 return self;
}

- incrementByFloat: (float) aFloat
{
 floatValue += aFloat;
 return self;
}

- incrementFractionByInt: (int) anInt
{
 numerator += denominator * anInt;
 return self;
}

// Access methods
- (int) getInt
{
 return intValue;
 }

 - (float) getFloat
{
 return floatValue;
}

- (int) getNumerator
{
 return numerator;
}
```

```
- (int) getDenominator
{
      return denominator;

}
- (numberType) getType
{
 return type;
}

@end
```

Listing 3.13 _____
Revised test program featuring early binding

```
// Test program for class Numeric

#import "Numeric.h"
#import <stdio.h>

main()
{
 int i;
 char choice;
 int value;
 int num, den;
 float r;
 FILE *f;

 Numeric data[ 5 ]; // Static binding

 f = fopen( "choices.txt", "r" );

 for ( i = 0; i < 5; i++ )
 {
  choice = fgetc( f );
  if ( choice == 'i' || choice == 'I' )
  {
   printf( "\nWhat is the value: " );
   scanf( "%d", &value );
   [ data[ i ] initializeInt: value ];
  }
  else if ( choice == 'r' || choice == 'R' )
  {
   printf( "\nWhat is the numerator: " );
   scanf( "%d", &num );
   printf( "\nWhat is the denominator: " );
   scanf( "%d", &den );
   [ data[ i ] initializeFractionWithNumerator: num denominator: den ];
  }
```

(continues)

```
else
 {
  printf( "\nWhat is the value: " );
  scanf( "%f", &r );
  [ data[ i ] initializeFloat: r ];
 }
}

// Increment each value
for ( i = 0; i < 5; i++ )
{
 if ( [ data[ i ] getType ] == int_type )
  [ data[ i ] incrementByInt: 5 ];
 else if ( [ data[ i ] getType ] == float_type )
  [ data[ i ] incrementByFloat: 5.0 ];
 else
  [ data[ i ] incrementFractionByInt: 5 ];
}

// Print each value
for ( i = 0; i < 5; i++ )
{
 if ( [ data[ i ] getType ] == int_type )
  printf( "data[ %d ] = %d\n", i, [ data[ i ] getInt ] );
 else if ( [ data[ i ] getType ] == float_type )
  printf( "data[ %d ] = %f\n", i, [ data[ i ] getFloat ]);
 else
  printf( "data[ %d ] = %d/%d\n", i, [ data[ i ] getNumerator ], [ data[ i ] getDenominator ] );
}
}
```

changed. Late binding assures us that each object responds to the messages incrementBy and print in an appropriate way.

In terms of the number of lines of code, the early-binding and late-binding solutions are about the same, but we have demonstrated that the architectures of the two solutions are significantly different. The early-binding solution trades off potentially higher performance against increased complexity and cost of maintenance. The late-binding solution provides another benefit that has not yet been mentioned—reusability. The classes Integer, Float, and Fraction might be useful in other applications (with more protocol added to make them practical). The class Numeric is cumbersome and is therefore not an ideal candidate for reuse.

The focus thus far has been on early versus late binding. What about type checking? It is often assumed that static type checking goes hand-in-hand with early binding and that dynamic type checking goes hand-in-hand with late binding. This may be true for some languages like Ada, which features static type checking and early binding, or Smalltalk-80, which features dynamic type checking and late binding. But Objective-C is a hybrid language. It can pick and choose the best features of other languages.

Listing 3.14 _____
Interface to class Fraction using late binding

```
// Interface to class Fraction - Fraction.h

#import <objc/Object.h>

@interface Fraction: Object
{
 int numerator;
 int denominator;
}

// Factory method
+ new: (int) num  denominator: (int) den;

// Initialize method
- initialize: (int) num : (int) den;

// Increment method
- incrementBy: (int) aValue;

// Print method
- print;

@end
```

Listing 3.15 _____
Implementation of class Fraction using late binding

```
// Implementation of class Fraction - Fraction.m

#import "Fraction.h"

@implementation Fraction
// Factory method
+ new: (int) num  denominator: (int) den
{
 id newInstance = [ super new ];
 [ newInstance initialize: num : den ];
 return newInstance;
}
// Initialize method
- initialize: (int) num : (int) den
{
 numerator = num;
 denominator = den;
 return self;
}
```

(continues)

```
// Increment method
- incrementBy: (int) aValue
{
 numerator += denominator * aValue;
 return self;
}

// Print method
- print
{
 printf( "%d/%d\n", numerator, denominator );
 return self;
}

@end
```

Listing 3.16 _____
Revised test program featuring late binding

```
// Test program to illustrate late binding
#import "Integer.h"
#import "Float.h"
#import "Fraction.h"

main()
{
 int i;
 char choice;
 int value;
 int num, den;
 float r;
 FILE *f;
 id data[ 5 ];  // Late binding

 f = fopen( "choices.txt", "r" );
 for ( i = 0; i < 5; i++ )
 {
  choice = fgetc( f );

  if ( choice == 'i' || choice == 'I' )
  {
   printf( "\nWhat is the value: " );
   scanf( "%d", &value );
   data[ i ] = [ Integer new: value ];
  }
  else if ( choice == 'r' || choice == 'R' )
  {
   printf( "\nWhat is the numerator: " );
   scanf( "%d", &num );
   printf( "\nWhat is the denominator: " );
```

```
    scanf( "%d", &den );
    data[ i ] = [ Fraction new: num  denominator: den ];
  }
  else
  {
    printf( "\nWhat is the value: " );
    scanf( "%f", &r );
    data[ i ] = [ Float new: r ];
  }
}

// Increment each value
for ( i = 0; i < 5; i++ )
  [ data[ i ] incrementBy: 5 ];

// Print each value
for ( i = 0; i < 5; i++ )
  [ data[ i ] print ];
}
```

Objective-C supports static checking and early binding, static checking and late binding, and dynamic checking and late binding. Currently, the NeXT version of Objective-C does not support early binding; it supports only late binding with either static or dynamic type checking. The early-binding solutions given above also feature static checking. That is, if the consumer attempts to send an illegal message to a Numeric object, the compiler provides a warning. The late-binding solutions given above also feature dynamic checking. If an illegal message is sent to any of the objects, the error is reported at run time.

The combination of static checking with late binding may be achieved by declaring a pointer to an underlying object. For example, if the array data were declared as follows:

*Integer *data[5];*

then static checking with late binding would prevail. The compiler would check for the legality of messages sent to all the objects stored in the array data (with respect to the protocol of class Integer) while dynamically binding messages to methods.

Objective-C's ability to mix static and dynamic type checking with early or late binding affords the object-oriented software developer an important degree of freedom in determining the best trade-off between efficiency and flexibility. Generally, we prefer late-binding solutions because this architecture supports easier maintenance and provides more opportunity for code reuse.

3.5 THE MECHANICS OF MESSAGING

This section describes in general terms the actions that occur when a message is sent to an object. Dynamic binding is assumed. The details are slightly different in various Objective-C systems; the basis for this discussion is the implementation on the NeXT computer.

The messaging process begins when a message is sent to an object. Suppose, as shown below, aMessage is sent to anObject with aParameter.

[anObject aMessage: aParameter];

The compiler converts this to a call of a messaging function, such as

objc_msgSend(anObject, selector, aParameter)

The Stepstone system uses the messaging function _msg(). The messaging function objc_msgSend(anObject, selector, aParameter) performs the following tasks when called at run time:

1. It determines the exact method that the selector refers to by determining the class that the receiver (anObject) belongs to.
2. It invokes the method, passing in the instance variables of anObject along with aParameter.
3. It passes the return value of the method as its own return value.

The Objective-C compiler or translator includes the following for every class that is compiled:

1. A pointer to the superclass
2. A dispatch table

The dispatch table associates method selectors with the addresses of the methods to which they refer. Whenever a new object from a given class is created, it includes a pointer to the class to which it belongs, called the isa pointer.

When a message is sent to an object, the messaging function follows the object's isa pointer to the class structure. It then determines the method selector in the dispatch table. If it cannot find the selector, it follows the pointer to the superclass and attempts to find the selector in its dispatch table. It continues this search up the class hierarchy until it reaches the ultimate superclass, Object. When it finds the appropriate selector, the messaging function calls the method entered in the appropriate dispatch table and passes it the receiving object's instance variables. If it cannot find the selector, it emits a run-time error message and provides a backtrace for debugging purposes.

To speed this potentially slow process, Objective-C caches the selectors of methods currently in use. There's a separate cache for each class, and it can contain selectors for inherited methods as well as for methods given in the class. This cache is checked before searching the dispatch table for a class. If the method is found in the cache, the messaging overhead is only slightly slower than for an ordinary function call. The memory for the caches grows dynamically as more and more messages are sent.

Figure 3.1 depicts the messaging process starting with anObject which receives a message. To improve efficiency, Objective-C does not use the full name of a selector in the compiled code. The compiler writes each selector into the dispatch table and pairs the selector with a unique unsigned integer that serves as its proxy. Such a compiled selector is of type SEL.

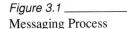
Figure 3.1
Messaging Process

Object class
- selector
- selector
- ...
- selector

Super class
- selector
- selector
- ...
- selector

Class
- selector
- selector
- ...
- selector

anObject
isa
instance
vars ...

The @selector() function may be used to access the SEL for a given selector. For example,

```
SEL someAction;
someAction = @selector( put:at: );
```

What might be done with the SEL, someAction? The methods perform:, perform:with:, and perform:with:with:, from class Object take a SEL argument as their first parameter. For example,

```
[ myArray perform: someAction with: 10  with:  5 ]
```

might be equivalent to

```
[ myArray put: 10  at: 5 ];
```

Can a SEL type be determined at run time (i.e., can we dynamically determine what message gets sent to an object)? The answer is yes. The function, sel_getUid("put:at:"), returns the SEL number of the selector put:at: when called at run time.

We have already seen that dynamic-binding polymorphism allows the same message to be applied to varying objects that are members of subclasses that respond to the message. Now we have seen that the message that is sent to an object itself can be determined at run time. This combination of being able to vary the receiver at run time, to vary the message at run time, or to do both provides the Objective-C developer with great flexibility and power.

The identifier _cmd refers to the SEL associated with a given method. The code

```
if ( _cmd == someAction )
    ...
```

might be useful.

Each implementation of Objective-C provides a set of C functions like sel_getUID( ). Many of these functions are used internally by the system and should not be directly invoked by the programmer. It is advisable to check the technical reference manual for your Objective-C system to see a list of these functions and their purpose. Only the most important of these functions are mentioned in this book.

All implementations of identically named methods must have the same return type and the same argument types since the messaging function has access to method implementations only through selectors, and thus treats all methods with the same selector alike.

Listing 3.17 illustrates a violation of this important rule: the classes Class1 and Class2 define a method action with different arguments and the same return type. The compiler emits the following warnings when the program is compiled:

```
test.m: In function main:
test.m:9: warning: multiple declarations for method 'action:'
Class1.h:10: using '-action:(int )aValue'
Class2.h:10: also found '-action:(float )aValue'
test.m:10: warning: multiple declarations for method 'action:'
Class1.h:10: using '-action:(int )aValue'
Class2.h:10: also found '-action:(float )aValue'
```

The compiler has detected that method action has two signatures. It uses the first signature encountered, namely the one that takes an int argument for aValue. The output of the program is

```
For class1, value = 5
For class2 value = 0.000000
```

3.6 THE OBJECT CLASS

The Object class is an abstract superclass that is the interface to the Objective-C run-time system. It is the root class of all inheritance hierarchies; it has no superclass. Since Object is an abstract superclass, instances of Object are rarely created. Rather, instances of subclasses of Object are created. All subclasses inherit the instance variables and the methods defined in Object.

Listing 3.17 _____

Violation of rule dealing with identically named methods

```objc
#import <objc/Object.h>

@interface Class1 : Object
{
 int value;
}

+ new;

- action: (int) aValue;

- print;

@end
------------------------
#import "Class1.h"
#import <stdio.h>
@implementation Class1

+ new
{
 return [ super new ];
}

- action: (int) aValue
{
 value = aValue;
 return self;
}

- print
{
 printf( "For class1, value = %d\n", value );
 return self;
}

@end
------------------------
#import <objc/Object.h>

@interface Class2 : Object
{
 float value;
}

+new;

- action: (float) aValue;
- print;

@end
------------------------
```

(continues)

```
#import "Class2.h"
#import <stdio.h>
@implementation Class2

+ new
{
 return [ super new ];
}

- action: (float) aValue
{
 value = aValue;
 return self;
}

- print
{
 printf( "For class2 value = %f\n", value );
 return self;
}

@end
```

The NeXT and Stepstone implementations of Objective-C provide different versions of class Object. In the remainder of this section we present an overview of the protocol in class Object and discuss the similarities and differences in the two versions.

Inheritance Properties of Class Object

The inheritance properties for methods defined in class Object are different from those defined in other classes. More specifically, the following inheritance properties apply to protocol in class Object.

- Instance methods are inherited by all objects. This includes classes since they are also objects (factory objects). Object is the only class from which inherited instance methods also apply to class objects.
- Factory methods are inherited by factory objects (classes). Instances do not respond to factory methods.
- Instance variables from superclasses are inherited by all instances of a class.

The following example illustrates the significant inheritance features for instance and factory methods.[1] Given a hierarchy of three classes with methods defined in each class as indicated below (factory methods are preceded by a +, and instance methods are preceded by a -),

---

[1] This example is based on the NeXT version of Objective-C. Class List is one of the common classes provided with NextStep.

Object (+ new, - hash)

    List (- count)
        SpecialList ( )

the following expressions yield the indicated results.

```
id aList = [ List new ];          // create a new instance of List
id bList = [ SpecialList new ];   // create a new instance of SpecialList

[ aList hash ];                   // hashes instance aList
[ bList hash ];                   // hashes instance bList
[ List hash ];                    // hashes factory object List
[ SpecialList hash ];             // hashes factory object SpecialList

[ aList new ];                    // error - factory method not valid for instance
[ aList count ];                  // answer number of objects in aList
[ bList count ];                  // answer number of objects in bList
[ SpecialList count ];            // error - only the instance methods in
                                  //       class Object apply to factory objects
```

Method Categories in Class Object

Generally, the methods defined in Object are considered to be applicable to all objects. In many cases the actual implementation of a method in class Object assumes a default that must be redefined in appropriate subclasses to have specific meaning. The protocol for class Object is further described by grouping its methods into categories, which are given in the documentation for both the NeXT and Stepstone versions of class Object. Table 3.1 lists the categories for the NeXT implementation, and Table 3.2 lists the categories for the Stepstone implementation.[2] Listings of the interface files for class Object are given in Appendix A for both the Stepstone and NeXT implementations.

Comparison of NeXT and Stepstone Implementations of Class Object

The following comparisons are made between the implementations of class Object by Stepstone and NeXT. The Stepstone implementation of class Object consists of 3 instance variables, 13 factory methods, and 55 instance methods. The NeXT implementation of class Object is smaller, with 1 instance variable, 10 factory methods, and 27 instance methods.

With some minor differences in type designations, there are 1 instance variable, 8 factory methods, and 21 instance methods that are common to both implementations. This leaves 2 factory methods and 6 instance methods unique to the NeXT implementation. There are 2 instance variables, 5 factory methods, and 34 instance methods that are unique to the Stepstone implementation. Table 3.3 begins with a list of the shared protocol and then lists the protocol that is unique to each implementation.

---

[2] The material in Tables 3.1 and 3.2 is abstracted from documentation provided with the NeXT and Stepstone versions of Objective-C.

Table 3.1 _____

Method categories for class Object: NeXT implementation

Factory Method Categories

Initializing the class

The Objective-C run-time system always initializes a class before any other messages are sent to it. Method initialize is in this category. It may be redefined for any subclass.

Creating and freeing instances

Factory method new creates instances, and factory method free is implemented to prevent the deletion of a class object. Method new may be augmented in subclasses.

Identifying classes

Methods class and superclass return self and the superclass factory object for a given class, respectively.

Testing class functionality

Method instancesRespondTo: (SEL) aSelector returns a Boolean true if instances of the class respond to aSelector.

Obtaining method handles

Method instanceMethodFor: (SEL) aSelector locates and returns the address of the instance method represented by aSelector.

Posing

Method poseAs: aClassObject allows the receiver class to pose as the class represented by aClassObject. The receiver must be a subclass of aClassObject. There are some additional restrictions on the receiver class.[1]

Archiving

Methods version and setVersion: (int) aVersion are used for version control of archived classes.

Instance Method Categories

Copying and freeing

Methods copy and free are used to either copy or free instances.

Identifying classes

Methods class and superclass return the class and the superclass factory objects for a given instance, respectively. Method name returns a type (const char *) that is a name string for the class of the receiving instance. Method findClass: (STR) aClassName returns the class object represented by string aClassName.

Identifying and comparing instances

Method self returns the receiving instance. Method isEqual: anObject compares the id's of the receiver and anObject and returns a Boolean true if they are the

	same. Method hash returns an unsigned int hash value for the receiver instance.
Testing inheritance relationships	Method isMemberOf: aClassObject answers if the receiver is an instance of class aClassObject. Method isKindOf: aClassObject answers if the receiver is an instance of class aClassObject or any of its superclasses. Methods isKindOfGivenName: (STR) aClassName and isMemberOfGivenName: (STR) aClassName perform similar functions using the name string for a class instead of the class object (id).
Testing class functionality	Method respondsTo: (SEL) aSelector returns a Boolean true if the receiver instance responds to aSelector.
Sending messages determined at run time	Methods perform: (SEL) aSelector, perform: (SEL) aSelector mined with: anObject, and perform: (SEL) aSelector with: object1 with: object2 allow the user to send a run-time-specified message (assigned to aSelector) with zero, one, or two parameters.
Obtaining method handles	Method methodFor: (SEL) aSelector locates and returns the address of the instance method represented by aSelector.
Enforcing intentions	Method notImplemented: (SEL) aSelector is a shortcut implementation used in the body of a method whose detailed implementation is to be completed later. This message is sent to self. Method shouldNotImplement: (SEL) aSelector is used in a superclass method to indicate (by error) that subclasses should not override the superclass version of aSelector. Method subclassResponsibility: (SEL) aSelector generates an error if method aSelector is not overridden in a subclass. Abstract superclasses often implement key methods as subclass responsibilities.
Error handling	Message doesNotRecognize: (SEL) aSelector is sent by the Objective-C run-time system whenever it does not recognize aSelector as a valid message for the receiving object. Method error: (STR) aString, ... creates an error message. Parameter aString has a variable number of arguments and has the style of a printf format string.
Archiving	Methods read: (NXTypedStream *) stream and write: (NXTypedStream *) stream read from or write to the typed stream, stream, the instance variables of the receiver. Implementation of these methods by

subclasses should first do a call to super. Method
awake is used to reinitialize an instance after it has
been unarchived using a read: message. Method
finishUnarchiving is used to replace an unarchived
object with a new object if necessary. The default for
this last method is to return nil.

NOTES

[1]The posing subclass cannot define any new instance variables and the poseAs: message must be
sent before any instances of aClass Object are created.

Table 3.2
Method categories for class object: Stepstone implementation

Factory Method Categories

Sent by the run-time system	The Objective-C run-time system always initializes a class before any other messages are sent to it. Method initialize is in this category.
Posing as another class	Method poseAs: (SHR) aFactoryId allows the receiving class to pose as the class represented by aFactoryId.
Instance creation	Methods new and new: (unsigned) arg create new instances. The second method creates an instance with arg indexed instance variables.
Freeing	Method free prevents statically allocated factory objects from being deallocated.
Automatic I/O	Method readFrom: (STR) aFileName is used to file-in and reconstruct an object from aFileName. The receiving factory object need have no relation to the object being filed-in.
Inheritance tree information	Methods self and class return the receiver. Method superClass returns the parent of the receiver. Method instancesRespondTo: (STR) aSelector answers if the instances of the receiver can respond to the message represented by aSelector. Method isSubclassOf: aClass answers if the receiver is a subclass of aClass.
Method implementation location	Method instanceMethodFor: (SEL) aSelector returns the address of the implementation for aSelector for instances of the receiver.
Inquiry[1]	Method ndxVarSize answers the size of individual variables for a receiver that has indexed instance variables. The default is to return zero.

Instance Method Categories

Location of classes at run time	Methods findClass: (STR) aClassName , idOfSTR: (STR) aClassName, and findClass: (STR) aClass requestor: (STR) requestor provide three options for returning the id of aClassName.
Object identification	Method name returns the class name of the instance as a C string. Method str returns a C string. The default in Object is to return the class name. This method is typically overridden in subclasses to return more useful information.
General object interrogation	Method size returns the number of items in the receiver.
Comparison	Method isEqual: anObject returns true if the receiver and anObject are equal. The default is that they must be the same object to be equal. This method is typically overridden in subclasses to define other equality rules. Method hash returns an unsigned value. Two objects have the same hash value if they satisfy the rules as given by isEqual:. Methods notEqual: anObject, compare: anObject, invertCompare: anObject, isSame: anObject, and notSame: anObject provide additional variations on comparison of the receiver with anObject.
Freeing	Method free frees the memory occupied by an instance and returns nil.
Automatic I/O	Method storeOn: (STR) aFileName stores a complete representation of the receiver object on aFileName. It can later be reconstructed using factory method readFrom:.
Support for deep methods	Method asGraph: (BOOL) unique returns an IdArray containing a list of all objects referenced by the receiver, including the receiver itself.
Printing objects	Method printOn: (IOD) anIOD is a key method that defines how an object is to be printed. The default is to print information about the class of the receiver. It typically is overridden in subclasses. Methods show, print, and printString: (STR) aBuf provide additional variations on displaying or printing a description of the object.
Inheritance tree information	Method self returns the receiver. It is useful for concatenation of messages to an object. Methods class

and superClass return the factory objects representing the class or superclass of the receiver. Method isMemberOf: aClass answers if the receiver is an instance of aClass. Method isKindOf: aClass answers if the receiver is an instance of aClass or any of its superclasses. Method respondsTo: (STR) aSelector answers if the receiver responds to aSelector.

Copying

Methods copy, deepCopy, and shallowCopy provide three options for making copies of an object. A deep copy duplicates all objects referenced by the receiver; a shallow copy does not. Method copy is often redefined in subclasses.

Method implementation location

The address of the implementation for a method is returned by the use of methodFor: (SEL) aSelector.

Performing

A run-time-modifiable message may be sent to an object by using methods perform: (STR) aSelector, perform: (STR) aSelector with: anObject, perform: (STR) aSelector with: obj1 with: obj2, and perform: (STR) aSelector with: obj1 with: obj2 with: obj3. The methods represent selectors with zero, one, two, or three parameters.

Methods to enforce intentions

Methods subclassResponsibility and subclassResponsibility: (SEL) aSelector provide the means for a superclass to pass responsibility for the implementation of methods to its subclasses. Methods shouldNotImplement and shouldNotImplement: (SEL) aSelector from: superclass are used to indicate that subclasses should not override the superclass implementation. Methods notImplemented and notImplemented: (SEL) aSelector are used to identify incomplete implementations.

Error handling

Method doesNotRecognize: (STR) aMessage is invoked by the system when no method can be found for a message sent to an object. Method error: (STR) aCStr, ... is used to create error traps with meaningful messages. The parameter has the style and format of the printf format string and parameter list.

AsciiFiler methods

Methods awake, sys$awake (an older version of awake), describe (returns code for type of an indexed instance variable), and capacity (returns the number of indexed instance variables in the receiver; default is zero) support the AsciiFiler class for archiving purposes.

Checking instance types[2]   Methods isStaticInstance, isDynamicInstance,
                                   isIndexable, and isMarked are used to check typing
                                   and status information about the receiver.

Other methods   There are five other methods in class Object. They are
                                   elements, initialize, initialize: (unsigned) arg, identity,
                                   and release.

NOTES

[1]This category is defined by the authors, not Stepstone.
[2]This category is defined by the authors, not Stepstone.

Table 3.3 _____
Comparison of NeXT and Stepstone implementations of class Object

Protocol Common to Both Implementations

NeXT   Stepstone

Instance Variables

Class isa;   struct_SHARED *isa;[1]

Factory Methods

initialize;   initialize;
new;   new;
free;   free;
class;   (SHR) class;
superClass;   (SHR) superClass;[2]
poseAs: aClassObject;   poseAs: aFactoryId;
(BOOL) instancesRespondTo: (BOOL) instancesRespondTo:
    (SEL) aSelector;[3]   (STR) aSelector;[4]
(IMP) instanceMethodFor: (IMP) instanceMethodFor:
    (SEL) aSelector;   (SEL) aSelector;

Instance Methods

awake;   awake;
class;   (SHR) class;
copy;   copy;
doesNotRecognize: (SEL) aSelector;   doesNotRecognize: (STR) aMessage;
error: (STR) aString, ...;   error: (STR) aCStr, ...;
findClass: (STR) aClassName;   findClass: (STR) aClassName;
free;   free;
(unsigned int) hash;   (unsigned) hash;
(BOOL) isEqual: anObject;   (BOOL) isEqual: anObject;
(BOOL) isKindOf: aClassObject: (BOOL) isKindOf: aClass;
(BOOL) isMemberOf: aClassObject;   (BOOL) isMemberOf: aClass;

(IMP) methodFor: (SEL) aSelector;   (IMP) methodFor: (SEL) aSelector;[5]
(const char*) name;   (STR) name;
notImplemented: (SEL) aSelector;   notImplemented: (SEL) aSelector;
perform: (SEL) aSelector;   perform: (STR) aSelector;
perform: (SEL) aSelector with: anObject;   perform: (STR) aSelector with: anObject;
perform: (SEL) aSelector with: object1   perform: (STR) aSelector with: obj1
    with: object2;   with: obj2;
(BOOL) respondsTo: (SEL) aSelector;   respondsTo: (STR) aSelector;
self;   self;
subclassResponsibility: (SEL) aSelector;   subclassResponsibility: (SEL) aSelector;
superClass;   (SHR) superClass;

Protocol Unique to the NeXT Implementation

Instance Variables

Factory Methods

version;   // archiving version control
setVersion;   // archiving version control

Instance Methods

(BOOL) isKindOfGivenName: (STR) aClassName;   // inheritance testing
(BOOL) isMemberOfGivenName: (STR) aClassName;   // inheritance testing
shouldNotImplement: (SEL) aSelector;   // enforcing intentions
write: (NXTypedStream *) stream;   // archiving
read: (NXTypedStream *) stream;   // archiving
finishUnarchiving;   // archiving

Protocol Unique to the Stepstone Implementation

Instance Variables

unsigned short attr;   // instance attribute fields
unsigned short objID;   // address independent id for instances

Factory Methods

new: (unsigned) arg;   // create instance with indexed
                                                //   instance variables

(SHR) self;   // inheritance tree information
readFrom: (STR) aFileName;   // automatic I/O for filing in objects
(BOOL) isSubclassOf: aClass;   // inheritance tree information
(unsigned) ndxVarSize;   // returns size of an individual indexed
                                                //   instance variable

Instance Methods

(STR) elements;   //
(STR) describe;   // return AsciiFiler type,
                                                //   for indexed instance variable

(unsigned) capacity;	// number of indexed instance variables
(BOOL) isStaticInstance;	// answer if static type
(BOOL) isDynamicInstance;	// answer if dynamic type (id)
(BOOL) isIndexable;	// answer if indexable
(BOOL) isMarked;	// answer if marked
initialize;	//
initialize: (unsigned) arg;	//
(unsigned short) identity;	//
release;	//
idOfSTR: (STR) aClassName;	// returns id of aClassName
findClass: (STR) aClass requestor: (STR) requestor;	// returns id of aClass
(STR) str;	// returns a C string (name of class)
(unsigned) size;	// returns number of items in object
(BOOL) notEqual: anObject;	// negation of isEqual:
(int) compare: anObject;	// equivalent to C function strcmp
(int) invertCompare: anObject;	// returns negation of compare:
(BOOL) isSame: anObject;	// test if receiver & anObject are the same
(BOOL) notSame: anObject;	// returns negation of isSame:
(BOOL) storeOn: (STR) aFileName;	// archive entire object graph of receiver
asGraph: (BOOL) unique;	// IdArray of all reference objects
	// of receiver
show;	// display an object
print;	// print an object on stdout
printString: (STR) aBuf;	// call sprintf and return the receiver
printOn: (IOD) anIOD;	// print an object on anIOD[6]
shallowCopy;	// no copy made of referenced objects
deepCopy;	// copies made of all referenced objects
perform: (STR) aSelector with: obj1 with: obj2 with: obj3;	// run-time selection of a method with // 3 parameters
subclassResponsibility;	// enforce intentions
shouldNotImplement;	// enforce intentions
shouldNotImplement: (SEL) aSelector from: superclass;	// enforce intentions
notImplemented;	// enforce intentions
sys$awake;	// old version of awake

NOTES

[1]Both Class and struct_SHARED* are pointers to the structure for a class.

[2]Type SHR is a pointer to the shared part of an object.

[3]Type BOOL is type char.

[4]Both types STR and SEL are char*.

[5]Type IMP is defined as a pointer to a function returning an id, e.g., typedef id (* IMP)( );

[6]Defined as typedef FILE * IOD;.

3.7 SOME PROTOCOL FROM CLASS OBJECT

This section examines some of the protocol of class Object that relates to memory management, posing, and inheritance.

Support for Memory Management

Current versions of Objective-C do not perform automatic garbage collection. Releasing unneeded objects is the responsibility of the programmer. The fundamental operations associated with memory management are: creation, deletion, duplication, and resizing.

Object Creation. Class Object defines a factory method, new, that may be used to create objects from any subclass. For example, myWidget = [Widget new] creates a new Widget object, myWidget. The factory method new uses the interface file for class Widget to determine the appropriate memory allocation size. The instance variables for myWidget are initialized to zero. Method new returns the id of the newly created instance.

Most subclasses redefine factory method new. Their implementation usually does a call to method new from class Object (e.g., id newInstance = [super new]).

Object Deletion. Class Object defines an instance method, free. This method may be used to deallocate storage for any object in the Objective-C system. As in the case of method new, many subclasses redefine method free.

It is sound programming practice for the owner of an object to be responsible for freeing it when it is no longer needed. The programmer should not assume that because an object is created within a function (using new), the run-time system will deallocate storage for the object when leaving the scope of the function. All that will be deallocated is the variable that holds the id of the object. The actual space for the object must be deallocated by the programmer, using free.

Listing 3.18 shows a simple example that illustrates this point. Class Integer contains the method add. This method creates a new object that is the sum of the receiver and the object used as a parameter in the add message.

Listing 3.18 contains a commented line in the main driver program near the bottom of the listing. This line, [int3 free], applies the method free to the object int3. When this line is commented out (as in Listing 3.18), 200,000 new objects are created during the execution of the loop, one for each add operation. If the program is run on a virtual memory system such as the NeXT, the paging environment uses caching to keep the flow of new objects pouring from the method add. On the other hand, if the program is run using Stepstone's MS-DOS version on a PC, the program grinds to a halt with a heap overflow error when no more heap space is left to continue the generation of new objects. When the commented line is put into the program, the PC version runs fine. This illustrates the point that the owner of an object, for example function main in Listing 3.18, is responsible for deallocating storage for an object when it is no longer needed. Before each new addition operation, the newly allocated object int3 is no longer needed and therefore must be freed.

As an interesting postscript, when the version shown in Listing 3.18 (with the free message commented out) is run on the NeXT computer, its execution time is about 15 percent faster than the version that uses the free message. This can be explained by the fact that virtual memory paging is more efficient than the memory deallocation function resulting from the use of method free. This result is machine-dependent, and no general

Listing 3.18 _____
Using method free

```
// Interface to class Integer

#import <objc/Object.h>

@interface Integer : Object
{
 int value;
}
// Factory methods
+ new : (int) aValue;

// Access methods
- value: (int) aValue;

- (int) value;

// Arithmetic methods
-  add: anInt;

@end
------------------------

// Implementation of class Integer

#import "Integer.h"
#import <string.h>
#import <stdio.h>
@implementation Integer;

// Factory methods
+ new : (int) aValue
{
 id newInt = [ super new ];
 [ newInt value: aValue ];
 return newInt;
}
// Access methods
- value: (int) aValue
{
 value = aValue;
 return self;
}

- (int) value
{
 return value;
}
```

(continues)

```
// Arithmetic methods
- add : anInt
{
 return [ Integer new: value + [ anInt value ] ];
}

@end
------------------------

#import "Integer.h"
#import <stdio.h>
#import <stdlib.h>

main()
{
 Integer  *int1 = [ Integer new: 17 ];
 Integer *int2 = [ Integer new: 500 ];
 Integer *int3;
 int i;

 for ( i = 1; i <= 200000; i++ )
 {
  int3 = [ int1 add: int2 ];
  // [ int3 free ];
 }
}
```

conclusions can be drawn. It is better programming to deallocate storage after each addition operation than to rely on virtual memory caching to do the dirty work of creating 200,000 objects when only one is necessary.

Object Copying. In this section we examine the subtle differences between method copy from class Object, the assignment operator, and the notion of deep copy. The interface to method copy in the NeXT version of Objective-C is

```
- copy;
/*
 * TYPE: Creating; Returns a copy of the receiver
 *
 * Returns a new instance that's an exact copy of the receiver.
 */
```

The comment "Returns a new instance that's an exact copy of the receiver" is misleading. Although technically true, it masks the fact that the object produced by the copy is prone to serious aliasing effects; it is not a deep copy. Let us explain.

In Smalltalk and the Stepstone version of Objective-C, a distinction is made between a shallow copy and a deep copy. No protocol for a deep copy exists in class Object in the current NeXT version of Objective-C. A shallow copy produces only a reference to the source. This is best seen in ordinary C from the following code segment:

```
int data1[ 5 ] = { 1, 2, 3, 4, 5 };
int *data2;

data2 = data1;
```

The last assignment statement demonstrates a shallow copy. The variable data2 is not independent of data1. If a change is made to data1 (e.g., data1[2] = 25), then the same change will be induced in data2.

Continuing with ordinary C, a deep copy would be achieved as follows:

```
int data1[ 5 ] = { 1, 2, 3, 4, 5 };
int *data2 = ( int* ) malloc( 5 * sizeof( int ) );

memcpy( data2, data1, 5 * sizeof( int ) );
```

Now the variable data2 is autonomous in relation to data1.

To understand better the limitations of method copy, given in the protocol of Object, consider the example in Listing 3.19, in which two simplified classes, Integer and String, are introduced. Objects of class Integer contain an object of class String.

Listing 3.19 _____
An examination of method copy from class Object

```
// Interface to class Integer

#import <objc/Object.h>
#import "String.h"

@interface Integer : Object
{
 int value;
 String *string; // Name of object
}
// Factory methods
+ new;

+ new : (int) aValue;

+ new: (int) aValue  withName: (char*) aName;

// Accessing methods
- createString;

- (int) value;

- value: (int) aValue;

- name: (char*) aName;

- (char*) name;

// Printing method
- print;

@end
```

(continues)

```
// Implementation of class Integer

#import "Integer.h"
#import <string.h>
#import <stdio.h>

@implementation Integer;

// Factory methods

+ new
{
 id newInt = [ super new ];

 [ newInt value: 0 ];
 [ newInt name: "None" ];
 return newInt;
}

+ new : (int) aValue
{
 id newInt = [ super new ];

 [ newInt value: aValue ];
 [ newInt name: "None" ];
 return newInt;
}

+ new: (int) aValue  withName: (char*) aName
{
 id newInt = [ super new ];

 [ newInt value: aValue ];
 [ newInt createString ];
 [ newInt name: aName ];
 return newInt;
}

// Access methods
- createString
{
 string = [ String new ];
 return self;
}

- (int) value
{
 return value;
}

- value: (int) aValue
{
 value = aValue;
 return self;
}
```

```
- name: (char*) aName
{
 [ string name: aName ];
 return self;
}

- (char*) name
{
 return [ string name ];
}

// Printing method
- print
{
 printf( "The value of %s is %d\n", [ string name ], value );
 return self;
}

@end
```

```
// Interface to class String

#import <objc/Object.h>

@interface String : Object
{
 char value[ 80 ];
}

// Factory method
+ new;

// Access methods
- (char*) name;

- name: (char*) aName;

@end
```

```
// Implementation of class String
#import "String.h"
#import <string.h>

@implementation String

// Factory method
+ new
{
 return [ super new ];
}

// Access methods
- (char*) name
{
 return value;
}
```

(continues)

```
- name: (char*) aName
{
strcpy( value, aName );
return self;
}

@end
------------------------

#import "Integer.h"
#import <stdio.h>
main()
{

// Create an Integer object int1 with name "one"
Integer *int1 = [ Integer new: 17 withName: "one" ];
Integer *int2;

printf( "Printing object int1:  " );
[ int1 print ];
// Copy object int1 to int2
int2 = [ int1 copy ];
// Output object int2
printf( "Printing object int2 after invoking int2 = [ int1 copy ]:  " );
[ int2 print ];

// Reassign object int1 to have the name "two" and value 5
[ int1 name: "two" ];
[ int1 value: 5 ];
printf( "Printing object int1:  " );
[ int1 print ];
printf( "Printing object int2:  " );
// Display object int2
[ int2 print ];
}

/* Program output
Printing object int1:  The value of one is 17
Printing object int2 after invoking int2 = [ int1 copy ]:  The value of one is 17
Printing object int1:  The value of two is 5
Printing object int2:  The value of two is 17
*/
```

Objects int1 and int2 have two instance variables, int value and String string. It is clear from the output in Listing 3.19 that the statement int2 = [int1 copy] effectively copies the value field from object int1 to int2 but not the string field. That is because method copy does not create an autonomous object, string, in object int2.

What would happen if the assignment statement int2 = int1 were used instead of the method copy? The last line of output would then be Printing object int2: The value of two is 5. The assignment statement produces a shallow copy in the sense described earlier in the ordinary C code segment.

Listing 3.20 _____
Method deepCopy in class Integer

```
- deepCopy
{
// This performs a deep copy
 return [ Integer new: value  withName: [ string name ] ];
}
```

The method copy, from class Object, produces neither a shallow copy nor a deep copy but something in between. How can this problem be corrected? The code in Listing 3.20 shows how to solve this problem. The method deepCopy is introduced into the protocol of class Integer. This method could have been called copy, in which case it would redefine or supersede the method copy given in class Object.

The copy method in Listing 3.20 creates a new object of class Integer whose value is the same as that of the receiver and whose name is the same as the receiver's. If the statement int2 = [int1 deepCopy] were used in the main program, the last line of output would be Printing object int2: The value of one is 17.

Posing

A subclass can take the place of its superclass at run time; this is called posing. Posing provides a mechanism for adding methods to an existing class definition even when one has no access to the implementation details for the class. Any messages sent to the superclass get diverted to the posing subclass. The following rules apply to the posing subclass:

1. The posing subclass must be an immediate subclass of the class that it is to pose as.
2. The posing subclass may define or redefine only methods.
3. The posing subclass cannot introduce any new instance variables.
4. The redefinition must be done before any instances of the posed-as class are created. The run time system does not check for the existence of instances.

Using categories is a better way of adding methods to an existing class (see earlier section, "Adding Methods to a Class: Categories"). Listing 3.21 shows how methods can be added to a class, Parent, using posing or using categories.

Support for Inheritance

Several methods in class Object allow an object to identify its position in the class hierarchy. These include class, name, superClass, isMemberOf, isMemberOfGivenName, isKindOf, and isKindOfGivenName. Some typical message calls for each of these methods, with accompanying explanations, follows:

```
// Returns the id of the receiver's class
id myObject = [ Parent class ];
```

Listing 3.21 _____
Adding methods to a class using posing and using categories

```
// Interface to class Parent

#import <objc/Object.h>

@interface Parent : Object
{
 int value;
}

// Factory method
+ new: (int) aValue;

// Initialize method
- initialize: (int) aValue;

// Access methods
- (int) value;

- value: (int) aValue;

@end
------------------------

// Implementation for class Parent

#import "Parent.h"

@implementation Parent

// Factory method
+ new: (int) aValue
{
 id newInstance = [ super new ];
 [ newInstance initialize: aValue ];
 return newInstance;
}

// Initialize method
- initialize: (int) aValue
{
 value = aValue;
 return self;
}

// Access methods
- (int) value
{
 return value;
}

- value: (int) aValue
{
 value = aValue;
 return self;
}
```

```
@end
------------------------
// Interface to class Parent1 - Parent1.h

#import <objc/Object.h>
#import "Parent.h"
@interface Parent( MoreMethods )

// Arithmetic
- doubleValue;

// Printing
- print;

@end
------------------------
// Implementation of class Parent1 - Parent1.m

#import "Parent1.h"
#import <stdio.h>

@implementation Parent( MoreMethods )

// Arithmetic
- doubleValue
{
 value *= 2;
 return self;
}
// Printing
- print
{
 printf( "%d\n", value );
 return self;
}

@end
------------------------
// Test program for categories

#import "Parent1.h"
#import <stdio.h>

main()
{
 Parent *myObject = [ Parent new: 25 ];

 [ myObject value: 35 ];
 [ myObject doubleValue ];
 printf( "\nPrinting myobject:  " );
 [ myObject print ];
 return 0;
}
```

(continues)

```
/* Program output
Printing myobject:  70
*/
------------------------

// Interface to class Parent2 - Parent2.h

#import <objc/Object.h>
#import "Parent.h"

@interface Parent2 : Parent
{
}

// Arithmetic method
- doubleValue;

// Printing method
- print;

@end
------------------------

// Implementation for class Parent2 - Parent2.m

#import "Parent2.h"
#import <stdio.h>

@implementation Parent2

// Arithmetic method
- doubleValue
{
 value *= 2;
 return self;
}

// Printing method
- print
{
 printf( "%d\n", value );
 return self;
}

@end
------------------------

// Test program for posing

#import "Parent2.h"
#import <stdio.h>

main()
{
 Parent *myObject;

 [ Parent2 poseAs: [ Parent class ] ];
```

```
myObject = [ Parent new: 25 ];
[ myObject value: 35 ];
[ myObject doubleValue ];
printf( "\nPrinting myobject:  " );
[ myObject print ];
return 0;
}

/* Program output
Printing myobject:  70
*/
```

```
// Returns the name of the receiver's class as a string
const char *myObjectClassName = [ Parent name ];

// Returns the id of the receiver's superclass
 id superClass = [ Parent2 superClass ];

//Tests whether the receiver is an instance of of a particular class
int boolean = [ myObject isMemberOf: [ Parent class ] ];

//Tests whether the receiver is an instance of of a particular class
int boolean = [ myObject isMemberOfGivenName: "Parent" ];

//Tests whether the receiver inherits from a particular class
int boolean = [ myObject isKindOf: [ Parent class ] ];

//Tests whether the receiver is an instance of of a particular class
int boolean = [ myObject isKindOfGivenName: "Parent" ];
```

3.8 SUPPORT FOR STREAMS AND PERSISTENCE IN NeXT OBJECTIVE-C

The NeXT version of Objective-C handles persistence differently than the Stepstone version. This section describes the NeXT approach to persistence, which uses streams.

Streams

A stream is an abstraction that represents a data channel connecting an application program with a source or a destination of data. A typed stream is used for archiving data objects. A stream may be connected to memory, a file, or an output port as either a source or a destination.

The Objective-C functions that write to or read from a stream may be grouped according to whether they

1. write or read a single character at a time,

2. write or read a specified number of bytes of data, or

3. convert data using a format string.

These functions take a pointer to a stream as an argument.

Writing and Reading Characters. The macros NXPutc( ) and NXGetc( ) are modeled after putc( ) and getc( ) in ordinary C. NXPutc( ) appends a character to a stream. For example,

```
NXPutc( aStream, 'A' );
```

NXGetc( ) retrieves the next character from the stream. For example,

```
char aChar = NXGetc( aStream );
```

The macro, NXUngetc( ) puts the last character read back into the stream. For example,

```
NXUngetc( aStream );
aChar = NXGetc( aStream );
```

Writing and Reading Bytes of Data. The functions NXWrite( ) and NXRead( ) write or read multiple bytes of data. For example,

```
NXWrite( aStream, &myObject, sizeof( myObject ) );
NXRead( aStream, &myObject, sizeof( myObject ) );
```

write or read myObject to aStream.

Writing and Reading Formatted Data. Four functions may be used to format strings of data in reading from or writing to a stream. They are NXPrintf( ), NXScanf( ), NXV-Printf( ), and NXVScanf( ). The last two functions are the same as the first two except that instead of being invoked with a variable number of arguments, they are called with a va_list, which is defined in the header file stdarg.h.

   Some examples of the usage of NXPrintf( ) and NXScanf( ) follow:

```
int mortgagePayment = 400;
char month = "January";
```

```
NXPrintf( aStream, "My mortgage payment for the month of %s is %d\n",
       month, mortgagePayment );
```

```
int x;
float r;
```

```
NXScanf( aStream, "%d%dr", &x, &r );
```

With the stream of data -12 24.6, this statement assigns -12 to *x* and 24.6 to *r*.

Flushing and Filling. File and port streams are buffered. This means that data is actually written to a buffer and not directly to a file or port. When the buffer is filled, it is flushed, and all the data is sent to the file or port. Before a stream is disconnected from its destination, the contents of the buffer are flushed. The function NXFlush( ) may be used to flush the buffer before it is filled. For example,

```
NXFlush( aStream );
```

When reading from a file or port, data is loaded into a buffer and then read from the buffer. The buffer is automatically filled after all the data has been read from it. To explicitly fill the buffer, invoke NXFill( ). For example,

```
NXFill( aStream );
```

Setting the Position within a Stream. The function, NXSeek( ) is used to establish a position within a stream. For example,

```
NXSeek( aStream, 12, NX_FROMSTART );
```

moves 12 bytes forward from the beginning of the stream. The function NXTell( ) returns an integer location indicating the current position in the stream.

Connecting Streams to a Source or Destination

Connecting to Memory. The function NXOpenMemory( ) is used to open a temporary buffer for writing or reading data. For example,

```
NXStream *aStream;
stream = NXOpenMemory( NULL, 0, NX_WRITEONLY );
```

The first two arguments are NULL and 0 to allow the amount of memory to be automatically adjusted as more data is written. If NX_READONLY is specified, a memory stream is set up for reading data beginning at the location specified by the first argument.

When a memory stream is completed, it should be closed using NXCloseMemory( ). For example,

```
NXCloseMemory( aStream, NX_FREEBUFFER );
```

Connecting to Files. There are two functions available for connecting a stream to a file: NXMapFile( ) and NXOpenFile( ). The first function, NXMapFile, maps a file into memory and then opens a memory stream. The second function, NXOpenFile, connects a stream to a file. Some examples follow:

```
NXStream *aStream;
aStream = NXMapFile( "myFile.txt", NX_READONLY );
```

A memory stream is opened and initialized with the contents of the file "myFile.txt". Before ending, invoke

```
NXSaveToFile( aStream, "myFile.txt" );
NXCloseMemory( aStream, NX_FREEBUFFER );

NXStream *aStream;
aStream = NXOpenFile( fd, NX_WRITEONLY );
...
NXClose( aStream );
```

The file descriptor, fd, was obtained using the C function open( ) with one of three flags:

O_WRONLY, O_RDONLY, or O_RDWR. The sense of this flag must match that used in the call to NXOpenFile. The function NXOpenFile can be used to connect to stdin, stdout, and stderr by obtaining their file descriptors with the C library function fileno( ). For example,

```
int fd;
NXStream *aStream;

fd = fileno( stdin );
aStream = NXOpenFile( fd, NX_READONLY );
...
NXClose( aStream );
```

Archiving Objects to a Typed Stream

Typed streams save information about a data structure along with the actual data being stored. In the case of objects, the object's class hierarchy is archived as well. A typed stream assures that objects are written only once, even when several members of a data structure reference the same object.

To archive an object, the functions NXWriteRootObject( ) or NXWriteObject( ) may be used. Each of these functions takes a pointer to a typed stream and an object id as an argument. They send the object a write: message, using the typed stream as a parameter. The function, NXWriteRootObject( ) expects to be able to archive every object referred to by id instance variables, whereas NXWriteObject( ) expects to be able to archive every object referred to by id instance variables, as well as objects referred to by those objects, and so forth. Using NXWriteRootObject( ), some id instance variables may point to nil when they're unarchived.

All Application Kit classes and common classes supplied with the NeXT Objective-C system implement a write: method that archives their instance variables. The application developer must supply a write: method for any class that contains instance variables and for which archiving is desired. The Write: messages are not sent directly to objects. They are invoked by the functions NXWriteRootObject( ) or NXWriteObject( ).

When writing a customized write: method, the programmer should begin with a message to super. For example,

```
- write: ( typedStream* ) typedStream
{
  [ super write: typedStream ];
  /* Code for writing instance variables declared in class */
}
```

This ensures that the object's class hierarchy and its inherited instance variables are archived. The details of the write: method use appropriate functions to archive the instance variables defined for the class. The example presented in Listing 3.22 demonstrates how this can be done.

To archive the id instance variables of a class, the function NXWriteObject( ) can be used. To unarchive an object, the function NXReadObject( ) can be used. This function initializes the object's instance variables by sending it a read: message, which reads values for the instance variables from the typed stream. The method read: is defined in all Application Kit and common classes delivered with the NeXT Objective-C system. It is the programmer's responsibility to supply a read: method for every class that will be unarchived.

Every read: method should begin with a message to super. For example,

```
- read: (typedStream* ) typedStream
{
  [ super read: typedStream ];
  /* Code for reading instance variables defined for class */
}
```

The details of method read: use appropriate functions to unarchive the instance variables defined in the class. The example presented in Listing 3.22 demonstrates how this can be done.

The function NXOpenTypedStreamForFile( ) returns a pointer to a typed stream opened on a user defined file. The function NXOpenTypedStream( ) takes an already opened NXStream structure as an argument and returns a pointer to a typed stream.

Listing 3.22 demonstrates the archiving and unarchiving of objects using many of the functions described above. Particular attention should be paid to the methods write: and read: in class Parent. Note that these methods store the value of the Integer object as well as the object itself. This allows the object to be rebuilt when it is unarchived.

Listing 3.22 _____
Archiving and unarchiving objects

```
// Interface to class Integer

#import <objc/Object.h>
@interface Integer : Object
{
 int value;
}

// Factory methods
+ new : (int) aValue;

- value: (int) aValue;

- (int) value;

// Arithmetic methods
-  add: anInt;

// Printing method
- print;

@end
------------------------
```
                                                                    (continues)

```
// Implementation of class Integer

#import "Integer.h"
#import <string.h>
#import <stdio.h>

@implementation Integer;

// Factory methods
+ new : (int) aValue
{
 id newInt = [ super new ];

 [ newInt value: aValue ];
 return newInt;
}

- value: (int) aValue
{
 value = aValue;
 return self;
}

- (int) value
{
 return value;
}

// Arithmetic methods
- add : anInt
{
 return [ Integer new: value + [ anInt value ] ];
}

// Printing method
- print
{
 printf( "%d\n", value );
 return self;
}

@end
-----------------------

// Interface to class Parent

#import "Integer.h"
#import <objc/Object.h>
#import <appkit/appkit.h>

@interface Parent : Object
{
 int a;
 float b;
 char c;
```

```
 char d[ 40 ];
 Integer *e;
}
```

// Factory method
```
+ new: (int) value1 : (float) value2 : (char) value3 : (char*) value4 :
    (int) value5;
```

// Initialize method
```
- initialize: (int) value1 : (float) value2 : (char) value3 : (char*) value4 :
    (int) value5;
```
// Archiving methods
```
- write: (NXTypedStream*) typedStream;

- read: (NXTypedStream*) typedStream;
```

// Print method
```
- print;
```

```
@end
```

// Implementation of class Parent

```
#import "Parent.h"
```

```
@implementation Parent
```

// Factory method
```
+ new: (int) value1 : (float) value2 : (char) value3 : (char*) value4 :    (int) value5
{
 id newInstance = [ super new ];
 [ newInstance initialize: value1 : value2 : value3 : value4 : value5 ];
 return newInstance;
}
```
// Initialize method
```
- initialize: (int) value1 : (float) value2 : (char) value3 : (char*) value4 :        (int) value5
{
 a = value1;
 b = value2;
 c = value3;
 strcpy( d, value4 );
 e = [ Integer new: value5 ];
 return self;
}
```
// Archiving methods
```
- write: (NXTypedStream*) typedStream
{
 int eValue = [ e value ];

 [ super write: typedStream ];
 NXWriteTypes( typedStream, "ifc@i", &a, &b, &c, &e, &eValue );
```

(continues)

```
NXWriteArray( typedStream, "c", 40, d );
return self;
}

- read: (NXTypedStream*) typedStream
{
int eValue;
[ super read: typedStream ];
NXReadTypes( typedStream, "ifc@i", &a, &b, &c, &e, &eValue );
NXReadArray( typedStream, "c", 40, d );
[ e value: eValue ];
return self;
}

// Printing method
- print
{
printf( "a = %d\n", a );
printf( "b = %f\n", b );
printf( "c = %c\n", c );
printf( "d = %s\n", d );
printf( "e = " );
[ e print ];
return self;
}

@end
------------------------

// Test program for archiving and unarchiving

#import "Parent.h"

main()
{
NXTypedStream *writeStream;
NXTypedStream *readStream;
Parent *myParent = [ Parent new: 3 : 4.0 : '5' : "678" : 9 ];
Parent *anotherParent;

printf( "\nThe object myParent before archiving:  " );
[ myParent print ];

//Archive the object myParent
writeStream = NXOpenTypedStreamForFile( "myArchive", NX_WRITEONLY );
NXWriteObject( writeStream, myParent );
NXCloseTypedStream( writeStream );

// Unarchive the object myParent
readStream = NXOpenTypedStreamForFile( "myArchive", NX_READONLY );
anotherParent = NXReadObject( readStream );
```

```
printf( "\nThe object anotherParent after unarchiving: " );
[ anotherParent print ];
return 0;
}
/* Output of test program
The object myParent before archiving:  a = 3
b = 4.000000
c = 5
d = 678
e = 9

The object anotherParent after unarchiving:  a = 3
b = 4.000000
c = 5
d = 678
e = 9
*/
```

3.9 SUPPORT FOR PERSISTENCE USING STEPSTONE OBJECTIVE-C

Persistence is supported through classes Object and AsciiFiler in the Stepstone version of Objective-C. The two key methods that support persistence are storeOn: and readFrom:, both given in class Object. Since all Objective-C classes inherit from class Object, persistence is supported in all classes through these two key methods.

The technique used for implementing storeOn: and readFrom: involves storing the complete graph of an object (all objects contained in the object and all objects contained in those objects, etc.) in ASCII text format, based on the underlying C type of each field in the object. This information is based on static descriptions of instance variable types given at compile/link time. The output file encodes references to classes by name. It is assumed that the stored and retrieved data structures are the same and that all AsciiFiler-built files are reconstructed whenever these data structures change.

The underlying C types that are supported by class AsciiFiler follow:

- signed and unsigned char
- signed and unsigned short int
- signed and unsigned int
- signed and unsigned long int
- single- and double-precision floating-point numbers (float, double)
- enumeration types
- pointer types (assumed to hold a null-terminated array of char)
- object types (id type)
- aggregate types (arrays, structures, and unions; bitfields not supported)

At compile-time, information about instance variables is encoded by using the following mapping:

C Type	Code
char	'c'
unsigned char	'C'
short	's'
unsigned short	'S'
int	'i'
unsigned int	'I'
long	'l'
unsigned long	'L'
float	'f'
double	'd'
void	'v'
id	'@'
char*	'*'
struct_SHARED*	'#'
pointer-to-other	'$'
unknown type	'?'
begin array	'['
end array	']'
begin struct	'{'
end struct	'}'
begin union	'('
end union	')'

All scalar types are saved in a format that includes their type descriptor followed by an ASCII representation of their value.

Factory id types are saved as '#' followed by the name of the class.

Pointers to type char are saved as C strings. Pointers to other types are saved simply as '$' followed by the constant 0. When read back in, any such pointer instance variables are set to 0.

Array members are saved in increasing subscript order according to their individual types. Struct members are saved in the order of their declaration according to types.

When an object receives the message storeOn:, first all reachable objects are read in, and then each of these objects receives the message awake. The awake method can be implemented to do any initializing, or it can read in other objects.

Writing Objects

The instance methods available for writing objects to a file are the following:

```
- (BOOL) store: anObject on: (STR) aFileName;
// This method opens aFileName for writing, writes the object graph, then closes the file.
//  The C function used to open the file is, iod = fopen( afileName, "w" ).
```

- (BOOL) fileOut: anObject on: (IOD) anIOD;
// Writes anObject and all referenced objects to the file with IOD (FILE*) anIOD.

Reading Objects

The instance methods available for reading objects from a file are the following:

- readFrom: (STR) aFileName;
// Opens aFileName for reading using the C function, iod = fopen(aFileName, "r").
// The message fileIn: is sent and then the file is closed.

fileIn: (IOD) anIOD;
// This method reads the file and builds a new instance and transfers all of the stored data
// to this new instance.

An Example

Listing 3.23 demonstrates how an object can be written to file and recovered from a file.

Listing 3.23 _____
Writing and reading objects

```
#import <Primitive.h>
#import <Filer.h>
#import <StringCl.h>
#import <IdArray.h>

main()
{
 AsciiFiler *myFiler = [ AsciiFiler new ];
 id inputData = [ IdArray new: 4 ];
 id outputData;
 String *str1, *str2, *str3, *str4, *str5;

 str1 = [ String str: "abc" ];
 str2 = [ String str: "def" ];
 str3 = [ String str: "ghi" ];
 str4 = [ String str: "jkl" ];

 [ inputData at: 0  put: str1 ];
 [ inputData at: 1  put: str2 ];
 [ inputData at: 2  put: str3 ];
 [ inputData at: 3  put: str4 ];
 [ myFiler store: inputData  on: "mydata" ];

 [ outputData = [ Object readFrom: "mydata" ];
 str5 = [ outputData at: 1 ];
 printf( "The value of str5 = %s\n", [ str5 str ] );
}
```

In Listing 3.23, a Filer object, myFiler, is created using the factory method new. An object, inputData, is declared and initialized as an IdArray with four elements. An object, outputData, is declared but not initialized. String objects str1, str2, str3, str4 are declared and initialized in the body of code. The object inputData is loaded with the string objects. Using the key method store: on:, the graph of the inputData object is stored on the file mydata. Using the key method readFrom:, operating on the class variable Object since a new object is being formed, the previously saved object is recovered. This is verified in the final line of output.

The data file mydata appears as follows:

```
#AsciiFiler i3
4 #IdArray i4 $0 @2 @3 @4 @5
4 #String i3 i3 *3"abc
4 #String i3 i3 *3"def
4 #String i3 i3 *3"ghi
4 #String i3 i3 *3"jkl
```

3.10 DEFEATING DATA HIDING AND OTHER WAYS TO WEAKEN AN OBJECT-ORIENTED SOLUTION

Public Instance Variables

The topics covered in this section may be skipped. We recommend against using any of the capabilities presented in this section because they violate one or more of the basic principles of object-oriented programming. We include these topics for completeness only.

An Objective-C programmer who wishes to increase the efficiency of an application, at the expense of compromising data hiding, can do so by declaring a public section in a class definition. This is illustrated below.

```
@interface MyClass : Object
{
    ... // Private instance variables
    @public
    // Public instance variables
    int data;
}
```

A statically typed object can now directly access the public instance variable data as follows:

```
MyClass *myObject;
myObject -> data = 17;
```

The Address of a Method

It is possible to obtain a pointer to the function that implements a method, as illustrated below.

```
id ( *functionAddress ) ( );
functionAddress = [ myObject methodFor: @selector( doubleValue ) ];
...
( *functionAddress )( myObject, @selector( doubleValue: );
```

Using the last line of code allows dynamic binding to be circumvented.

Getting the Data Structure of an Object

The directive @defs( ) produces the declaration list for an instance of a class. This directive provides another way to remove the objectivity from an Objective-C solution; its use is illustrated below.

```
struct ParentDef
{
   @defs( Parent )
} *public;

id aParent = [ Parent new ];
public = ( struct ParentDef* ) aParent;

public -> value = 5;
```

As indicated at the beginning of this section, **we recommend against using any of these techniques for sidestepping object-oriented programming.**

3.11 THE MAJOR DIFFERENCE BETWEEN STEPSTONE AND NeXT VERSIONS OF OBJECTIVE-C: STATIC OBJECTS

This section examines the major difference between the two variants of Objective-C, Stepstone and NeXT. Additional differences exist in the underlying classes that support programming in the Stepstone and NeXT versions of this language, particularly in class Object. The differences in class Object are explored in Chapter 4; other differences may be gleaned from usage throughout this book. The best reference for predefined class libraries is the *Library Reference Guide* provided with each Objective-C system.

There is no "standard" Objective-C language. It is fair to say, however, that the Stepstone and NeXT versions are very similar. The most significant difference between Stepstone and NeXT Objective-C is that using static objects is legal in the Stepstone version but not in the NeXT version. The reader may wish to review Section 3.4 and Listing 3.3 to see an example of the use of static objects.

A statically allocated object is declared (in the Stepstone version only) as follows:

```
ClassName objectName;
```

This usage resembles an ordinary C type declaration. The identifier objectName represents an instance of class ClassName. Storage for this object is allocated at compile/link time with no initialization of any of the fields of objectName except the isa field. No factory (class) method(s) is automatically invoked to initialize the fields of this object; one or more instance methods must be used for this purpose.

When a message such as [objectName aMessage] is sent, static type checking and static binding are used by the compiler, as with an ordinary C type. This may potentially improve the efficiency of such a "function call" at the expense of programming flexibility. The degree of improvement in code execution time would depend primarily on the hardware being used and the context in which the statically declared object is declared.

## CHAPTER 4

Foundation Classes: Using Stepstone's ICpak 101 Library

Stepstone's version 4.0 of Objective-C includes a set of sixteen foundation classes in a hierarchy under root class Object. The hierarchy of these ICpak 101 classes is shown in Figure 4.1. These classes offer the Objective-C software developer a coherent, Smalltalk-like set of reusable software components that may be used as an initial framework for building applications. The application developer can add to any of these classes, using categories or the technique of posing (described in the previous chapter), create subclasses of any particular class, or build customized classes that inherit directly from Object. Before making such decisions, the developer should become familiar with the behaviors provided in this set of foundation classes.

This chapter presents limited examples that show how selected classes in ICpak 101 may be used. The examples are tutorial in nature and illustrate part of the available protocol in a class. Section 4.1 gives a general description of the ICpak 101 classes and the purpose of each. Sections 4.2 through 4.5 give examples of the use of ICpak 101 classes; additional examples are given in Chapter 5. Summaries of the ICpak 101 classes are given in Appendix B.

4.1 FOUNDATION CLASSES

The Array Classes

There are three array classes in ICpak 101. Class Array is an abstract superclass representing all array classes. Subclasses of Array represent arrays with various types of elements. Two subclasses of Array are included in ICpak 101; class IdArray contains elements of type id, and class IntArray contains elements of type int.

Instances of class Array should not be created since it is an abstract class. In fact many of its key methods are implemented as subclassResponsibility, indicating that any useful functionality is subclass-dependent. All array instances consist of indexable

Figure 4.1 _____
ICpak 101 hierarchy of foundation classes

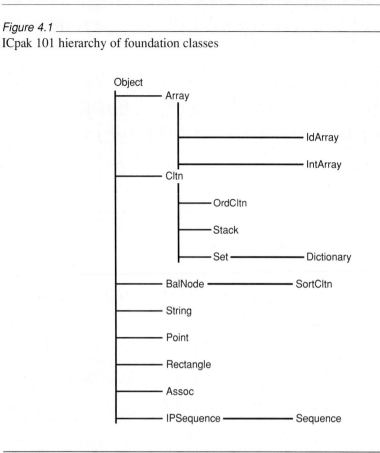

instance variables that are the elements in the array (accessible through the instance variable elements, which is of type void *). The instance variable capacity is a count of the current number of elements in an array instance.

The protocol listed in class Array includes methods for creation, copying, initialization, interrogation, resizing, printing, comparison, and sorting. Several of these methods are dependent on the type of element in the array and are implemented as subclass-Responsibility in Array. Noticeably missing are methods for accessing elements at a given index in the array. The return type of an accessing method is different for each array subclass. This has the effect that different message identifiers must be used for each subclass (thus no common message may be included in abstract class Array).[1] For example,

_____

[1] The return type and the types of any parameters for a given message cannot be different, even in different classes. This defining method (id) at: (unsigned) index in class IdArray prohibits the definition of method (int) at: (int) index in class IntArray.

[anIdArray at: index];   // returns type id
[anIntArray intAt: index];   // returns type int.

Class IdArray is a subclass of Array that contains elements of type id. In other words it contains objects. The objects may be instances of any class, which allows a generic mix of different kinds of objects. In addition to redefining those methods inherited as subclassResponsibility from Array, IdArray defines new methods for random access, adding, removing, sequencing, performing, locating, freeing, and conversion. Methods in the performing category allow a message to be sent sequentially to each element in the array.

Array subclass IntArray represents arrays of int elements. It provides new methods for random access and sorting.

The Collection Classes

Collections are groups of items. In a general sense collections differ in terms of the types of items in the group, ordering of the items, rules for duplicate items, and whether the items are indexable. In this sense arrays are also collections.

In ICpak 101 arrays are hierarchically separated from collections, as already indicated. Collections are dependent on arrays since the contents of collections are always stored as instances of IdArray. Thus collections are groups of objects (items with type id). There are five classes in ICpak 101 representing collections. Some of the properties of each are described below.

Class Cltn is an abstract superclass representing all the collection subclasses. It is a subclass of Object. It defines instance variables contents (a pointer to an instance of IdArray) which is the group of objects, and capacity, which is the number of objects in the collection. The default capacity for a newly created instance of a collection subclass is ten objects. Class Cltn defines methods for instance creation, initialization, adding, removing, sequencing, performing (sending a message to each element in the collection), printing, freeing, conversion (among collection subclasses), copying, interrogation, and comparing. Key methods for adding, removing, and interrogation are implemented as subclassResponsibility. Instances of class Sequence are used to loop over the contents of collections.

Class OrdCltn represents collections whose elements are ordered. This class adds a new instance variable, firstEmptySlot, which is the unsigned index of the first empty slot in the contents of the ordered collection. No nil entries are allowed in an instance of OrdCltn. Protocol is included for adding, removing, locating, or accessing items at any index position in the ordered collection. Thus, instances of this class may be implemented to represent ordinary stack, queue, deque, or linked-list data structures.

Class Stack is used to implement a stack data structure. This class could have been subclassed under OrdCltn; however, as a subclass of Cltn, it inherits less excess baggage (methods that do not apply to stacks). Methods for normal stack operations are given the names push: anObject, topElement, and pop. Methods for manipulating elements other than the top element are also included in this class.

Class Set represents mathematical sets. It does not allow duplicate elements. Objects are placed in a set based on their hash value (obtained by sending the message hash to the object). Sets are not dynamic in the sense that modified properties of an object are not reflected in the set. For example, if objectA is added to a set and then modified so it hashes to a different value, the modified objectA will not appear to be in the set. Other collections are dynamic in nature. A new instance variable, tally, is defined in class Set to keep track of the number of members in the set. Methods in the class provide for normal set operations such as adding, removing, interrogation, union, intersection, and difference.

Class Dictionary is a subclass of Set. Its elements are sets of associations (instances of class Assoc). Associations are linked pairs of objects (a key and a value). Class Dictionary adds new methods for manipulating the associations that are its elements.

The Binary Tree Classes

ICpak 101 has two classes that support the generation of binary tree data structures. Class BalNode is an abstract superclass that defines a binary node. Its instance variables include key, left, and right, which represent the fundamental components of a binary node. Methods in class BalNode provide ways to create, copy, and free nodes as well as to perform an in-order traversal of a tree structure whose root is an instance of BalNode.

Class SortCltn is a subclass of BalNode that represents a sorted AVL binary tree. The order of the binary tree is determined by a user-defined method on instance creation. Sorted collections respond to most of the same methods that other collections do. Class SortCltn adds new instance variables tally (the number of nodes in the tree), cmpSel (a pointer to a function that gives ordering details), addDupAction (providing options for adding, replacing, rejecting, or merging duplicates), and nameLength (maximum number of letters used in printing—default is 3). Methods are provided in the categories instance creation, initialization, instance-variable access, adding, collection adding, replacing, merging, removing, collection removing, sequencing, performing, conversion (to collection classes), interrogation, printing, and freeing.

The String Class

Class String is an example of encapsulating a C type, char *, into a class. It provides a way to build in extra error protection and to treat the C type as an object for consistency in the development of object-oriented solutions. Instances of String are null-terminated strings.

Class String defines three instance variables: length (the current length of the null-terminated string), size (the current buffer size used for storing the string), and string (the pointer to the storage buffer containing the string). Methods are provided for conversion between String instances and C strings. Other methods are provided for instance creation, initialization, other conversions, concatenations, comparison, printing, copying, random access (using an index), interrogation, and resizing.

The Geometry Support Classes

Classes Point and Rectangle are primitive classes that provide fundamental capability for building two-dimensional support for screen graphics. Points are represented by instance variables xLoc and yLoc (of type int). Rectangles are defined by instance variables origin (a Point that is the top-left corner of the rectangle) and corner (a Point that is the lower-right corner of the rectangle). A rich set of methods is provided for manipulating both points and rectangles.[2]

The Association Class

Instances of class Assoc are closely linked with the collection class Dictionary. They are stored as pairs of key and value objects. Instance variables defined in Assoc are key (typically the object used for searching) and value (the object associated with the key). Methods are provided for instance creation, accessing instance variables, comparison, interrogation, and printing.

The Sequence Classes

Two classes, IPSequence and its subclass, Sequence, are used for sequencing over collections. After a sequence is created for a collection, a loop is used wherein the next message is sent to the sequence object (to return the next element in the collection) until it reaches the end (at which time it returns nil). Accessing methods skip over empty slots in a collection.

Class IPSequence is retained for backward compatibility with earlier versions of ICpak 101, and it is faster than class Sequence. However, class Sequence is considered to be more reliable and is recommended by Stepstone for most applications. Class IPSequence defines two instance variables: contents, which points to an IdArray that holds the elements in a collection (no copy is made of the IdArray), and offset, which is the current place in the sequence. Methods are provided for instance creation, initialization, positioning, accessing, interrogation, freeing, and printing.

Class Sequence inherits and uses most of the protocol from its parent class, IPSequence. Methods for creating and freeing an instance of Sequence are different because a copy is made of the IdArray of the collection over which sequencing is being performed. Methods for sorting the IdArray are included since they will have no effect on the original in the collection.

4.2 USING THE ARRAY CLASSES

In this section we discuss some of the guidelines and rules for using the array classes. Class Array is an abstract superclass providing protocol common to its subclasses, IdArray and IntArray. We first look at instance creation and then examine some of the operations performed on arrays.

Although it is possible to create instances of class Array by using factory methods new and new: nElements, the resulting instances are not usable. These methods are defined in class Array so that they may be defined once and used by all subclasses. The normal way to create and initialize an array instance is with the factory method with: nArgs, ..., which is implemented as subclassResponsibility in class Array. Specific imple-

---

[2] The capabilities of the ICpak 101 implementations of Point and Rectangle are similar to those of the same classes in Smalltalk-80.

mentations details for method with: nArgs, ... are overridden in each subclass. For example, the following expressions have the indicated results.

```
id anArray = [ Array new: 20 ];   // creates an unusable instance of Array
                             // with a capacity for 20 elements.³

id objectArray = [ IdArray new: 20 ];  // creates an empty instance of IdArray
                                  // that has capacity for 20 objects.

id intArray = [ IntArray with: 5, -5, -4, -3 -2, -1 ];   // creates an instance of IntArray
                                            // containing the five ints (-5, -4, -3, -2 -1)

id twoDArray = [ IdArray with: 3, intArray, intArray, intArray ];  // creates a new
                             // instance of IdArray that contains 3 copies
                             // of the object, intArray.
```

Another key factory method implemented as subclassResponsibility in class Array is ndxVarSize, which returns the size of a single instance variable (element in the array).

Key instance methods implemented as subclassResponsibility in class Array include describe, printContentsOn: (IOD) anIOD, isEqual: anObject, hash, and sort. These methods must be redefined in any subclass of Array to reflect dependence on the type of elements in the array.[4]

If the size of an array needs to be changed, it is done with method capacity: nSlots in one of the Array subclasses. This method must have knowledge of the element type in the array. Other new methods provided in subclasses IdArray and IntArray include methods for accessing the indexed locations in the array (index values range from 0 to capacity -1). For example

```
[ intArray intAt: 2 put: 4 ];    // replaces -4 with 4 in intArray
[ intArray intAt: 4 ];           // returns -1 (the last element in intArray)

[ objectArray at: 1 put: obj1 ];    // puts obj1 in 2nd element of objectArray
[ objectArray at: 2 ];              // returns nil since this index is empty
[ objectArray add: obj2 ];          // puts obj2 in first element of objectArray⁵
```

There are several variations on the add: method, and there are methods for remove: as well in class IdArray. These methods are not available in class IntArray. Methods are defined in IdArray for sending a specified message to each object in the array. For example,

---

[3] The instance is unusable because there are no accessing methods in Array to allow any elements to be placed in the array. Accessing the methods defined in subclasses are not usable by instances of the parent class.

[4] When adding a new subclass to an abstract class, it is important that all key methods (those implemented as subclassResponsibility in the abstract class) be redefined to fit the properties of instances of the new class. Failure to do so will make other methods inherited from the abstract class fail to work properly.

[5] The add: anObject method puts anObject in the first empty slot (containing nil) in the array. An error occurs if the array is full.

```
[ objectArray elementsPerform: @selector( print ) ]; // sends the message print
                          // to each object in objectArray
```

Variations on this method allow messages with one, two, or three parameters to be sent to each object in the IdArray instance. Clearly these methods are not implemented in class IntArray since it is meaningless (produces an error) to send a message to an int.

4.3 USING THE COLLECTION CLASSES

Class Cltn is an abstract superclass representing groups of objects. Instances may be created of class Cltn, but like instances of Array, they are unusable. For example,

```
id aCltn = [Cltn new: 15 ];   // creates a new instance of Cltn with
                              // capacity initialized to 15 and
                              // contents initialized to an empty IdArray of
                              // 15 elements.6
```

Class Cltn is a good example of how a rich set of methods can be factored to depend on a very few key methods. There are thirty-three instance methods in the class, of which four are key methods (implemented as subclassResponsibility). New subclasses of Cltn need implement only those four key methods to make all the inherited protocol from Cltn valid. The four key methods are add: anObject, remove: anObject, find: anObject, and size. Implementation of these methods for various subclasses follows different rules for when and where to add, remove, or locate an object in the contents array. The size of a subclass instance is also managed differently. The size of a Cltn subclass instance is the actual number of objects it contains, which is usually different from capacity.

Some methods in class Cltn are implemented by sending an appropriate message to its contents instance variable, an instance of IdArray. For example, method elements-Perform: (SEL) aSelector is implemented by sending the message elementsPerform: a-Selector to contents. This behavior is inherited and usable by any subclass of Cltn that uses an IdArray to store its contents. All subclasses of Cltn in ICpak 101 use the inherited instance variable contents to store their elements.

Instances of subclasses of Cltn are created with the factory method with: nArgs, ... defined in class Cltn. Subclass dependency is enforced by the fact that the implementation for with: nArgs, ... depends on key method add: anObject. For example, the following expressions yield the indicated results.

```
id anOrdCltn = [ OrdCltn with: 3, obj1, obj2, obj2 ];
                    // create a new instance of
                    // OrdCltn containing objects obj1
                    // obj2 and obj2 again.7
```

---

[6] There is no way to add objects to the empty instance aCltn.

[7] Multiple copies of objects are allowed in OrdCltn and Stack but not in Set or Dictionary.

```
id aStack = [ Stack with: 2, obj1, obj2 ]; // create a Stack containing obj1
                // and obj2 with obj2 on top.
id aSet = [ Set with: 3, obj1, obj2, obj2 ]; // create a new Set with capacity of
                // 3 and insert obj1 and obj2.8
id aDictionary = [Dictionary with: 4, key0, value0, key1, value1];
                // create a Dictionary instance with
                // two associations (key0, value0)
                // and (key1, value1).9
```

Significant new protocol in class OrdCltn allows its instances to be used to represent collections with order and with a variety of accessing methods. More specifically, new objects may be inserted at the front, at the rear, at a given index, or before or after a given object. Methods for finding and/or removing objects in the collection are also very flexible.

New protocol in class Set provides methods for testing membership and for performing the operations of union, intersection, and difference between two sets. Class Dictionary adds new methods for dealing directly with associations (instances of Assoc), since the elements of a dictionary are associations.

4.4 USING THE BINARY TREE CLASSES

There are two classes, BalNode and SortCltn, that provide support for the development of AVL binary tree structures. BalNode is an abstract class that defines a binary node. SortCltn is really a collection class; however, it is not grouped with the other collection classes because it does not use an IdArray to store its contents. Rather its contents are stored in a linked collection of BalNode instances. This has the disadvantage that much of the protocol for collections must be redefined in SortCltn.

New instances of SortCltn may be created in a number of ways. Instance variable cmpSel is a selector that is used to compare the keys of objects being inserted into the tree. The default selector for cmpSel is compare: anObject. Recall that compare: anObject is defined in class Object, but it is implemented as subclassResponsibility. It is the software developer's responsibility to ensure that an appropriate comparison method exists in the class for any object to be stored in a SortCltn instance. The following expressions and cautions are given for using the binary tree classes.

```
id myTree = [ SortCltn new ];    // creates a new, empty tree with cmpSel
                // set to the default of compare: anObject.
id yourTree = [ SortCltn orderedBy: @selector( contrast: ) ];
                // creates a new, empty tree with cmpSel
                // set to contrast: anObject.
```

---

[8] The second copy of obj2 is not inserted, and the size of aSet is only 2.

[9] Associations are instances of class Assoc. Notice that method with: nArgs, ... is redefined in class Dictionary to accomodate only associations as elements.

```
id ourTree = [ SortCltn orderedBy: @selector( contrast: ) onDups: REJECT ];
                    // creates a new, empty tree with cmpSel
                    // set to contrast: anObject and with
                    // rejection of duplicate entries.
```

Instances of any class may be the objects inserted into one of the above-defined instances of SortCltn so long as the class defines the required method for comparison. For example,

```
[ myTree add: aWidget ];     // requires that compare: be defined in class Widget
[ yourTree add: aWidget ];   // requires that contrast: be defined in class Widget.
```

   Selectability of the comparison method allows trees with different structure and properties to be built from the same objects. Other methods defined in classes BalNode and SortCltn provide the usual list of operations on binary nodes and AVL trees. The SortCltn instance can be traversed and a selected message sent to the object at each node. There are methods for converting instances of SortCltn to instances of other collection classes containing the same elements.

4.5 USING THE GEOMETRY SUPPORT CLASSES

Classes Point and Rectangle provide protocol for representing two-dimensional points and rectangles. Their major emphasis is on representing coordinate locations and windows on the computer screen. As such, instances of Point are restricted to be coordinate pairs of integers. Further, since the top left of the screen is considered to be at coordinate location $(x, y) = (0, 0)$, some of the comparison methods appear to be upside down; for example, point (10, 20) is considered to be above point (10, 24).
   Instances of Point and Rectangle are created in the following ways.

```
aPoint = [ Point x: anX y: aY ];     // create a point at ( anX, aY )
rect1 = [ Rectangle origin: oPoint corner: cPoint ];
                    // create a rectangle defined by upper left
                    // corner oPoint and lower right corner
                    // cPoint
rect2 = [ Rectangle origin: oPoint extent: ePoint ];
                    // upper left corner is oPoint
                    // lower right corner is oPoint + ePoint
rect3 = [ Rectangle origin: oX : oY corner: cX : cY ];
                    // upper left corner = (oX, oY)
                    // lower right corner = ( cX, cY)
rect4 = [ Rectangle origin: oX : oY extent: eX : eY ];
                    // upper left corner = (oX, oY)
                    // lower right corner = (oX + eX, oY + eY)
```

These instance-creation expressions illustrate the missing keyword option in Objective-C. Further they indicate that arithmetic operations are possible on instances of Point. The following methods are provided.

```
[ point1 plus: point2 ];       // sum is aPoint = (x1 + x2, y1 + y2)
[ point1 minus: point2 ];      // difference is aPoint = (x1 - x2, y1 - y2)
[ point1 times: anInt ];       // returns aPoint = (anInt * x1, anInt * y1)
```

Other methods exist for moving, accessing x and y, equality testing, and printing of points.

Methods in class Rectangle provide ways to access or change any geometric feature of an instance. Other methods return Point instances corresponding to selected points on the rectangle; for example, bottomLeft returns a point with the coordinates of the bottom left of the rectangle. There are methods that move the rectangle without changing its size. Other interesting methods include the following:

```
[ aRect insetBy: xInt : yInt ];   // returns a rectangle whose sides are inset by xInt
                                  // and whose top and bottom are inset by yInt.
[ rect1 intersection: rect2 ];    // returns a rectangle that is the intersection of\
                                  // rect1 with rect2
[ rect1 union: rect2 ];       // returns the smallest rectangle that contains
                              // both rect1 and rect2.
[ rect1 intersects: rect2 ];    // returns true if rect1 intersects rect2
```

Classes Point and Rectangle provide fundamental support for the graphic user-interface classes.

4.6 SUMMARY

Classes such as those representing arrays, collections, strings, and sequences are important classes with a high degree of reusability. Their instances represent common data structures in computer problem solving.

This chapter has presented an overview of the functionality of the foundation classes in Stepstone's ICpak 101 and discussed several issues in terms of using those classes. Further insight is obtained in Chapter 5 from other examples that use the foundation classes.

More Examples
Using Foundation Classes

Good order is the foundation of all good things.

Edmund Burke, *1729–1797*

Chapter 4 presented an overview of Stepstone's ICpak 101 foundation classes. Figure 4.1 presented a hierarchy of these reusable software components. This chapter further explores the use of these components. The first few sections provide shorter examples illustrating the use of the most important array, collection, and sequence classes. The last section revisits the *Swamp Runner* program presented in Chapter 2 and presents the first complete implementation of this simulation. Needless to say, the use of key ICpak 101 classes plays a central role in the solution.

Before one can become proficient at writing, one must master the art of reading. In using languages such as Smalltalk or Objective-C, it is desirable to understand the protocol provided in the classes that form the development environment accompanying the language. This is particularly true in Smalltalk, where over 300 classes are supplied with the system.

As indicated earlier, Objective-C systems include rich support for general-purpose programming as well as support for developing user interfaces (e.g., the NeXT Application Kit or ICpak 201). To take proper advantage of this support, the beginning Objective-C developer must learn to read and understand the protocol in the basic foundation classes. Unlike the vast set of standard C functions that represent reusable software components for the C programmer, the classes in the foundation libraries provide concepts and abstractions for representing and manipulating basic information structures that can form the building blocks of a problem solution. Therefore, just learning the mechanics of using a particular class is not enough. The challenge that the Objective-C or OOP developer must face is learning to effectively design and then implement a solution in terms of these basic building blocks. The design and implementation of the *Swamp Runner* problem introduced in Chapter 2 and continued in this chapter demonstrates how some of the basic building blocks in the foundation classes may be used at a conceptual level to design the software architecture and at the implementation level to produce a working solution.

The foundation classes provide the basis for incremental problem solving. By adding to existing classes through categories or posing (see Chapter 3), or by composing classes that include objects from other classes, or by creating subclasses of existing foundation classes, the designer and programmer encounter many potentially powerful options for reusing existing software resources.

The first task in this chapter is to better understand some key ICpak 101 foundation classes by exploring their use in simple examples.

5.1 USE OF IdArray CLASS

Suppose that we wish to construct a two-dimensional array of String objects and allow the user to specify the number of rows and the number of columns in this array structure. Furthermore, we wish to allow the user the ability to insert or access a string at a given row and column. The code in Listing 5.1 uses the ICpak 101 classes IdArray and String to satisfy these requirements.

Listing 5.1 _____

Illustrative example that features IdArray

```
/*
This application builds a two-dimensional array of
strings using the ICpak101 foundation classes IdArray and
 String.
*/

#import <IdArray.h>
#import <StringCls.h>
#import <stdio.h>
#import <string.h>

main()
{
 IdArray *row;
 IdArray *data;
 unsigned numRows, numCols;
 int rowNum, colNum;
 char aString[ 51 ];

 printf( "Enter the number of rows: " );
 scanf( "%d", &numRows );
 printf( "Enter the number of columns: " );
 scanf( "%d", &numCols );

 // Allocate storage for data
 data = [ IdArray new: numRows ];
 for ( rowNum = 0; rowNum < numRows; rowNum++ )
 {
 // Allocate storage for row
 row = [ IdArray new: numCols ];
 [ data at: rowNum  put: row ];
 }
```

```
// Allow the user to insert strings at a given row and column
printf( "\nEnter row for insertion (-1 to quit): " );
scanf( "%d", &rowNum );
while ( rowNum != -1 )
{
 printf( "\nEnter column for insertion: " );
 scanf( "%d", &colNum );
 printf( "Enter string: " );
 scanf( "%s", aString );
 [ [ data at: rowNum ] at: colNum put: [ String str: aString ] ];
 printf( "\nEnter row for insertion (-1 to quit): " );
 scanf( "%d", &rowNum );
}

// Allow the user to access strings at a given row and columns
printf( "\nEnter the row for access (-1 to quit): " );
scanf( "%d", &rowNum );
while ( rowNum != -1 )
{
 printf( "\nEnter the column for access: " );
 scanf( "%d", &colNum );
 strcpy( aString, [ [ [ data at: rowNum ] at: colNum ] str ] );
 printf( "\nThe string at row %d  column %d = %s\n",
     rowNum, colNum, aString );
 printf( "\nEnter the row for access (-1 to quit): " );
 scanf( "%d", &rowNum );
}
 return 0;
}
```

The ICpak 101 class IdArray, which is the centerpiece of Listing 5.1, supports a one-dimensional array of arbitrary objects. In order to construct a two-dimensional array of arbitrary objects, the principal goal of this short application, two IdArrays are declared:

```
IdArray *row;
IdArray *data;
```

The array data holds numRows objects, each an IdArray object ultimately containing numCols String objects. The allocation of this two-dimensional IdArray of arbitrary objects is given as follows:

```
data = [ IdArray new: numRows ];
for ( rowNum = 0; rowNum < numRows; rowNum++ )
{
// Allocate storage for row
row = [ IdArray new: numCols ];
[ data at: rowNum  put: row ];
}
```

To insert a String object into a particular row and column, we use the following code:

```
[ [ data at: rowNum ] at: colNum put: [ String str: aString ] ];
```

The message expression [data at: rowNum] returns a row object. This row object, through message concatenation, receives the message [at: colNum put: [String str: aString]]. The protocol of at: and at:put: is part of class IdArray, which was presented in Chapter 4. The factory method str: is part of the protocol for class String, also presented in Chapter 4.

Finally, we use the following code to access a String object at a particular row and column:

```
[ [ [ data at: rowNum ] at: colNum ] str ] ];
```

5.2 USE OF CLASSES OrdCltn AND Sequence

Suppose we wish to build an ordered collection of Point objects that includes all points whose x- and y-coordinates are non-negative and are equal to or less than 5. The ordering of points is by row; that is, all the points with $y = 0$ are inserted first, and then the points with $y = 1$ are inserted. This continues until all the points with $y = 5$ are inserted into the ordered collection. Within each row, the points are ordered by column, starting from 0 and proceeding to 5.

After building this collection, we wish to remove all points for which the sum of the x- and y-coordinates is divisible by 3 (e.g., Point x: 2 y: 4 or Point x: 5 y: 1). Following this, we wish to output the collection of points. Listing 5.2 provides a solution to this problem.

Listing 5.2 _____
Illustrative example that features OrdCltn and Sequence

```
// Example illustrating classes OrdCltn and Sequence

#import <OrdCltn.h>
#import <Point.h>
#import <Sequence.h>

main()
{
 id collection = [ OrdCltn new ];
 id iterate;
 id aPoint;
 int row, col;

// Create collection of Points
 for ( row = 0; row <= 5; row++ )
  for ( col = 0; col <= 5; col++ )
    [ collection add: [ Point x: col y: row ] ];

// Remove the points whose x y coordinate sum is divisible by 3
 iterate = [ Sequence over: collection ];
```

```
aPoint = [ iterate next ];
while ( aPoint ) // elements left in the collection
{
 if ( ( [ aPoint x ] + [ aPoint y ] %)  3 == 0 )
   [ collection remove: aPoint ];
 aPoint = [ iterate next ];
}
// Output collection
[ iterate free ];
iterate = [ Sequence over: collection ];
aPoint = [ iterate next ];
while ( aPoint )
{
 [ aPoint print ];
 aPoint = [ iterate next ];
}
 return 0;
}
/* Program output
(1,0)(2,0)(4,0)(5,0)(0,1)(1,1)(3,1)(4,1)(0,2)(2,2)(3,2)(5,2)(1,3)(2,3)(4,3)(5,3)(0,4)(1,4)
(3,4)(4,4)(0,5)(2,5)(3,5)(5,5)
*/
```

In Listing 5.2, after creating an instance (object collection) from class OrdCltn, the method add: is used to fill the collection. To iterate over the collection, an object, iterate, an instance of class Sequence, is created. Using the method next, all of the elements of the collection are tested to determine which ones receive the message remove: .

5.3 USE OF CLASS Set

Suppose we wish to solve the same problem as in the previous section without being concerned about the order in which the points are inserted and printed. The Set class is used to hold the points, only two lines of code in Listing 5.2 have to be changed. Change

#import <OrdCltn.h> to #import <Set.h>

and change

collection = [OrdCltn new] to collection = [Set new]

The output of Listing 5.2 using class Set follows:

(1,1)(1,0)(2,0)(0,1)(4,0)(5,0)(3,1)(4,1)(0,2)(2,2)(3,2)(5,2)(1,3)(2,3)(4,3)(5,3)(0,4)
(1,4)(3,4)(4,4)(0,5)(2,5)(3,5)(5,5)

The output using class Set is in a different order than the input and is based on an internal hash method that method add: uses to position each new entry in the collection.

Sets are useful when it is desirable to avoid duplicates in a collection of objects. In the next application, we generate a sequence of 1000 points whose *x*- and *y*-coordinates are randomly chosen between 1 and 20. We insert each of these points into an ordered collection and into a set. We compare the sizes of each collection after the insertions. From the size of the set, we output the percentage of the 400 coordinates actually covered by the random insertion of 1000 points. Finally, the points not covered, if any, are printed. A solution to this problem is presented in Listing 5.3.

Listing 5.3 _____

Illustrative example that features class Set

```
// Example to exercise Set and OrdCltn classes

#import <Set.h>
#import <OrdCltn.h>
#import <Sequence.h>
#import <Point.h>
#import "Random.h"
#import <stdio.h>

main()
{
 Set *mySet = [ Set new ];
 OrdCltn *myCollection = [ OrdCltn new ];
 Random *random = [ Random new ];
 Point *aPoint;
 int row, col;
 int i;

 // Generate 1000 points and add them to mySet and myCollection
 for ( i = 1; i <= 1000; i++ )
 {
 col = [ random nextBetweenLow: 1  high: 20 ];
 row = [ random nextBetweenLow: 1  high: 20 ];
 aPoint = [ Point x: col y: row ];
 [ mySet add: aPoint ];
 [ myCollection add: aPoint ];
 }

 // Determine percentage of coverage
 printf( "Fraction of points covered = %0.2f\n", [ mySet size ] / 400.0 );

 // Determine the number of points in myCollection
 printf( "The number of points in myCollection = %d\n", [ myCollection size ] );

 // Determine the points in mySet not covered
 printf( "\nPoints not covered in mySet\n" );
 for ( row = 1; row <= 20; row++ )
 for ( col = 1; col <= 20; col++ )
 {
   aPoint = [ Point x: col y: row ];
   if ( ![ mySet contains: aPoint ] )
     [ aPoint print ];
 }
```

```
}
/* Program output
Fraction of points covered = 0.92
The number of points in myCollection = 1000

Points not covered in mySet
(7,2)(10,2)(12,2)(20,3)(17,4)(13,5)(18,5)(3,6)(4,6)(5,6)(14,6)(1,7)(2,7)(15,7)(16,7)
(13,8)(8,9)(12,9)(16,9)(17,9)(18,9)(12,10)(4,13)(20,13)(18,15)(7,17)(11,17)(5,18)
(1,19)(4,20)(16,20)(17,20)(19,20)
*/
```

The solution in Listing 5.3 begins by creating four objects, mySet, myCollection, random, and aPoint. Because each of the objects is declared as a pointer to a class, the compiler employs static checking. Nevertheless, dynamic binding associates messages with appropriate methods at run time.

The first task in the program is the generation of 1000 random points with x- and y-coordinates from 1 to 20. The message nextBetweenLow:high: is sent to object random to accomplish this task. The protocol for class Random is shown in Listing 5.4. This protocol has been tested using both Stepstone's Objective-C running on a Sun workstation and the NeXT computer (both using a variant of Berkeley 4.3 UNIX). The details may have to be modified on other systems.

The next task in the program is to determine the percentage of coverage. This is done by sending the message size to object mySet. To verify that duplicates are allowed in ordered collections (the only role that the object myCollection plays in this example), the size of myCollection is output. As expected, the result is 1000.

Finally, the actual points not covered in the rectangular grid are output. This is accomplished by using the the method contains: on object mySet as all 400 points are tested. The program output, given in Listing 5.3, indicates that 92 percent of the 400 points in the grid are covered by generating 1000 points. The actual points not covered are shown in the output. They appear to be randomly scattered about the grid.

Listing 5.4 _____
Protocol for class Random

```
// Interface to class Random

#import "Primitive.h"

@interface Random:Object
{
}

// Factory method
+ new;

// Access methods
- (int) nextBetweenLow: (int) lowerBound  high: (int) upperBound;

- (double) randReal;

@end
------------------------
```
                                                                        (continues)

```
// Implementation of class Random
#import "Random.h"
#import "sys/types.h"
#import "/usr/sys/h/timeb.h"

extern void ftime( struct timeb *tp );
extern void srandom( int seed );
extern long random( void );

@implementation Random

// Factory method
+ new
{
 id newRandom = [ super new ];
 struct timeb t;
 int seed;

 ftime( &t );
 seed = ( unsigned short ) t.millitm;
 srand( seed );
 return newRandom;
}

// Factory methods
- (int) nextBetweenLow: (int) lowerBound  high: (int) upperBound
{
 double r, t;
 int c;

 r = ( double ) upperBound - ( double ) lowerBound + 1.0;
 t = r * [ self randReal ];
 return lowerBound + ( int ) t;
}

- (double) randReal
{
 return  ( ( double ) rand() / 2147483648.0 );
}

@end
```

5.4 THE SWAMP RUNNER SIMULATION

The specifications and a language-independent design for the *Swamp Runner* simulation
are presented in Chapter 2. In this section the object-oriented design of this system is
used to produce a working implementation using Stepstone's Objective-C. Several
aspects of the language-independent design are modified to take account of some special
features of Objective-C.

Several important foundation classes, including Point, Sequence, IdArray, OrdCltn,
and Set, are used in the implementation. In addition to these classes, several customized
classes are developed, including the superclass SwampTraveler and its subclasses Genius,

Wit, Halfwit, and Dimwit. In addition to these, the superclass SwampCell and its subclasses TravelerCell,[1] QuickSand, and PathCell are constructed as part of the solution. Finally, the classes Swamp and SwampSimulation complete the programmer-generated classes that form the design and implementation of this system.

This simulation is important for the following reasons:

1. It demonstrates the use of several important foundation classes in the context of a larger application.
2. It demonstrates how programmer-defined classes can be effectively mixed with existing foundation classes.
3. It demonstrates how an object-oriented design gives way to an object-oriented program.
4. It represents the first substantial Objective-C and object-oriented software solution presented thus far.

The Hierarchy of Classes

Based on the design presented in Chapter 2 (with small modifications), the hierarchy of classes, not including the foundation classes, used to solve the *Swamp Runner* problem is presented in Figure 5.1. Because of the extensive discussion of the specifications and design of this system presented in Chapter 2, such discussion is minimized in this chapter. The class hierarchy shown in figure 5.1 includes the use of composition (container-ship) and derivation (inheritance).

Figure 5.1 _____

Hierarchy of classes for *Swamp Runner* simulation

Object

Swamp(numRows, numCols, thePath, minPathLength, random, offsets, marked)
SwampSimulation(aSwamp, swampTraveler)

SwampTraveler(coordinate, numSteps, numAttempts, targetSwamp)
  Dimwit( )
  Halfwit(cellsVisited, pathVisited)
    Wit(firstMove, lastPathCoordinate)
      Genius( )

SwampCell(image, coordinate)
  QuickSand( )
  PathCell( )
  TravelerCell( )

_____

[1] Class TravelerCell is added to the original hierarchy of classes for the purpose of more consistently displaying the image of one of the SwampTraveler objects.

With respect to composition, the SwampSimulation object includes a Swamp object and a SwampTraveler object. A Swamp object includes an OrdCltn object (thePath), a Set object (marked), and a Random object (random). A SwampTraveler object includes a Point object (coordinate) and a Swamp object (targetSwamp). A Halfwit object includes two Set objects (cellsVisited and pathVisited). With respect to derivation, it should be apparent that a Genius is a kind of Wit, which is a kind of Halfwit, which is a kind of Dimwit.

The Main Simulation Driver Program

The main driver program for the simulation is given in Listing 5.5.

An instance of SwampSimulation, simulation, is created by sending the message new to SwampSimulation. After initializing this object, the message run: is sent to the object simulation with the parameters [Genius class], [Wit class], [Halfwit class], and [Dimwit class].

SwampSimulation Class

The protocol for class SwampSimulation is presented in Listing 5.6.

An instance of SwampSimulation contains an instance of Swamp (theSwamp) and SwampTraveler (aSwampTraveler). The method intializeSwamp causes a new Swamp object to be created. In the next section the details of initializing a Swamp object are described.

The method run: is interesting. It takes aTravelerClass as a parameter. At compile time, there is no way that the system can bind a particular class variable such as Dimwit, Halfwit, Wit, or Genius to the method createOn:, which is used to produce the object aSwampTraveler. Here is another example where late binding provides the necessary flexibility to accomplish this design.

The run: method is typical of the methods used at the highest level of system design. The message travel, specified in class SwampTraveler, is sent repeatedly to aSwamp-Traveler until the integer variable completedPath is nonzero.

Swamp Class

The Swamp class encapsulates the physical features of the swamp that a swamp traveler must traverse. The protocol for this class is presented in Listing 5.7.

A Swamp object contains the object swampCells, a two-dimensional array of SwampCells. A SwampCell is a superclass, with PathCell, TravelerCell, and QuickSand as its subclasses. The two-dimensional array of SwampCells is built, as described in Section 5.1, using the foundation class IdArray.

A Swamp object also contains the objects thePath (an instance of OrdCltn), random (an instance of Random), offsets (an instance of OrdCltn), and marked (an instance of Set). It is fair to say that the foundation classes play a key role in the design and implementation of this simulation.

Listing 5.5 _____
Main simulation driver program

```
// Main driver program for Swamp Runner simulation
#import "SwampSimulation.h"
#import "Genius.h"
#import "Wit.h"
#import "Halfwit.h"
#import "Dimwit.h"

main()
{
 id simulation = [ SwampSimulation new ];

 [ simulation initializeSwamp ];
 [ simulation run: [ Genius class ] ]; // in Stepstone version use [simulation run: Genius ];
 [ simulation run: [ Wit class ] ];
 [ simulation run: [ Halfwit class ] ];
 [ simulation run: [ Dimwit class ] ];
 return 0;
}
```

Listing 5.6 _____
SwampSimulation class

```
#import <Primitive.h>
@interface SwampSimulation : Object
{
 id theSwamp;
 id aSwampTraveler;
}
// Initialize methods
- initializeSwamp;

// Run method
- run: aTravelerClass;

// Statistics method
- stats;

@end
-------------------------

// Implementation of class SwampSimulation

#import "Swamp.h"
#import "SwampSimulation.h"
#import "SwampTraveler.h"
#import "Dimwit.h"
#import "Halfwit.h"
#import "Wit.h"
#import "Genius.h"
```

(continues)

```objc
@implementation SwampSimulation

// Initialize methods
- initializeSwamp
{
 theSwamp = [ [ Swamp new ] initialize ];
 return self;
}

// Run method
- run: aTravelerClass
{
 int completedPath;

 aSwampTraveler = [ aTravelerClass createOn: theSwamp ];
 completedPath = [ aSwampTraveler travel ];
 while ( ( [ aSwampTraveler numberAttempts ] < 1000 ) &&
    !completedPath )
  completedPath = [ aSwampTraveler travel ];
 [ theSwamp display ];
 [ self stats ];
 [ theSwamp refresh ];
 [ aSwampTraveler free ];

 return self;
}

// Statistics method
- stats
{
 char dummy;
 printf( "\n Performance of %s\n", [ aSwampTraveler className ] );
 printf( "\nLength of path traversed:    %d\n",
  [ [ theSwamp path ] size ] );
 printf( "Number of attempts:    %d\n",
  [ aSwampTraveler numberAttempts ] );
 if ( [ aSwampTraveler numberAttempts ] == 1000 )
  printf( "Total number of steps:
       Path not completed\n" );
 else
  printf( "Total number of steps:    %d\n",
   [ aSwampTraveler numberSteps ] );
 printf( "\n                         Hit return to continue ..." );
 scanf( "%c", &dummy );
 return self;
}

@end
```

Listing 5.7 _____
Swamp class

// Interface to class Swamp

#import <Primitive.h>

@interface Swamp : Object
{
 id swampCells;
 // 2D IdArray of SwampCells

 int numRows;
 int numCols;

 id thePath;
 // OrdCltn
 int minPathLength;

 id random;
 // Random

 id offsets;
 // OrdCltn

 id marked;
 // Set of Points
}
// Display method
- display;

// Initialize method
- initialize;

- initializeMarked;

- refresh;

- promptForRowsandCols;

- setPath;

- setSwampCells;

// Access methods
- (int) numCols;

- numCols: (int) anInteger;

- (int) numRows;

- numRows: (int) anInteger;

- swampCells;

- path;   *(continues)*

- offsets;

- random;

- setOffsets;

```
// Methods for building path
- getFirstCoordinate;

- getNextCoordinateFrom: currentCoordinate;

- (int) isOutOfBounds: aCoord;

- (int) isOnBorder: aCoord;

@end
------------------------

// Implementation of class Swamp

#import <stdio.h>
#import <OrdCltn.h>
#import <Set.h>
#import <IdArray.h>
#import <Point.h>
#import <Sequence.h>
#import "Swamp.h"
#import "PathCell.h"
#import "QuickSand.h"
#import "TravelerCell.h"
#import "Random.h"
#import "curses.h"

static int MaxRows = 30; // Class variable
static int MaxCols = 80; // Class variable
static int firstDisplay = 1;

@implementation Swamp

// Display method
- display
{
 int rowNum, colNum;
 if ( firstDisplay )
 {
  initscr();
  clear();
  firstDisplay = 0;
 }
 for ( rowNum = 0; rowNum < numRows; rowNum++ )
 for ( colNum = 0; colNum < numCols; colNum++ )
   [ [ [ swampCells at: rowNum ] at: colNum ] display ];
refresh();
return self;
}
```

```
// Initialize method
- initialize
{
 random = [ Random new ];
 [ self setOffsets ];
 [ self initializeMarked ];
 [ self promptForRowsandCols ];
 [ self setSwampCells ];
 [ self setPath ];
 [ self display ];
 return self;
}

- initializeMarked
{
 marked = [ Set new ];
 return self;
}
- refresh
{
 int rowNum, colNum;

 for ( rowNum = 0; rowNum < numRows; rowNum++ )
  for ( colNum = 0; colNum < numCols; colNum++ )
    if ( [ [ [ swampCells at: rowNum ] at: colNum ] class ] ==
      [ TravelerCell class ] )
    {
      [ [ swampCells at: rowNum ] at: colNum put: [ QuickSand create ] ];
      [ [ [ swampCells at: rowNum ] at: colNum ] coordinate:
            [ Point x: colNum y: rowNum ] ];
    }
 [ self display ];
 return self;
}

- promptForRowsandCols
{
 printf( "Enter the number of rows in the swamp: " );
   scanf( "%d", &numRows );
 if ( numRows > MaxRows )
 {
  printf( "The number of rows is set to %d\n", MaxRows );
  numRows = MaxRows;
 }
 if ( numRows < 5 )
 {
  printf( "The number of rows is set to 5\n" );
  numRows = 5;
 }
 printf( "Enter the number of columns in the swamp: " );
 scanf( "%d", &numCols );
```

(continues)

```
if ( numCols > MaxCols )
{
 printf( "The number of columns is set to %d\n", MaxCols );
 numCols = MaxCols;
}
if ( numCols < 5 )
{
 printf( "The number of columns is set to 5\n" );
 numCols = 5;
}
 return self;
}
- setPath
{
 id currentCoordinate;
 id iterate;
 id nextCoord;

 beginning: thePath = [ OrdCltn new ];
 minPathLength = ( numRows > numCols ) ? numCols : numRows;
 currentCoordinate = [ self getFirstCoordinate ];
 [ thePath add: currentCoordinate ];
 do
 {
  currentCoordinate = [ self getNextCoordinateFrom:
    currentCoordinate ];
  if ( currentCoordinate )
    [ thePath add: currentCoordinate ];
 }
 while ( ( currentCoordinate != nil )&&
  ![ self isOnBorder: currentCoordinate ] );

 if ( currentCoordinate == nil )
  goto beginning;
 // Add thePath to swampCells
 iterate = [ Sequence over: thePath ];
 nextCoord = [ iterate next ];
 while ( nextCoord )
 {
 [ [ [ swampCells at: [ nextCoord y ] ]
       at: [ nextCoord x ] ] free ];
 [ [ swampCells at: [ nextCoord y ] ]
       at: [ nextCoord x ]
       put: [ PathCell create ] ];
 [ [ [ swampCells at: [ nextCoord y ] ]
     at: [ nextCoord x ] ]
     coordinate: [ Point x: [ nextCoord x ]
                         y: [ nextCoord y ] ] ];
     nextCoord = [ iterate next ];
 }
 [ iterate free ];
 return self;
}
```

```
- setSwampCells
{
// Create an initial numRows x numCols of Quicksand cells
int rowNum, colNum;
id swampRow;

swampCells = [ IdArray new: numRows ];
for ( rowNum = 0; rowNum < numRows; rowNum++ )
{
 id swampRow = [ IdArray new: numCols ];

 for ( colNum = 0; colNum < numCols; colNum++ )
   [ swampRow  at: colNum
     put: [ QuickSand create ] ];
 [ swampCells at: rowNum
   put: swampRow ];
}
for ( rowNum = 0; rowNum < numRows; rowNum++ )
 for ( colNum = 0; colNum < numCols; colNum++ )
   [ [ [ swampCells at: rowNum ] at: colNum ]
   coordinate: [ Point x: colNum y: rowNum ] ];
return self;
}

// Access methods
- (int) numCols
{
 return numCols;
}

- numCols: (int) anInteger
{
 numCols = anInteger;
 return self;
}

- (int) numRows
{
 return numRows;
}

- numRows: (int) anInteger
{
 numRows = anInteger;
 return self;
}

- swampCells
{
 return swampCells;
}

- path
{
```

(continues)

```
return thePath;
}

- offsets
{
return offsets;
}

- random
{
return random;
}

- setOffsets
{
int deltaX, deltaY;
offsets = [ OrdCltn new ];
for ( deltaX = -1; deltaX <= 1; deltaX++ )
 for ( deltaY = -1; deltaY <= 1; deltaY++ )
   if ( ![ [ Point x: deltaX  y: deltaY ] isEqual:  [ Point x: 0 y: 0 ] ] )
    [ offsets add: [ Point x: deltaX  y: deltaY ] ];
return self;
}

// Methods for building path
- getFirstCoordinate
{
// Start all paths on y = 0
return [ Point x: [ random nextBetweenLow: 0 high: numCols - 1 ]
              y: 0 ];
}

- getNextCoordinateFrom: currentCoordinate
{
int index;
id validCoords;
id nextCoord;
id nextOffset;
id iterate;

iterate = [ Sequence over: offsets ];
nextOffset = [ iterate next ];
validCoords = [ OrdCltn new ];
// Get all valid neighbors
while ( nextOffset )
{
 nextCoord = [ currentCoordinate plus: nextOffset ];
 if ( [ thePath size ] >= minPathLength - 1 )
 {
   if ( ( ![ marked contains: nextCoord ] ) &&
     ( ![ self isOutOfBounds: nextCoord ] ) )
     [ validCoords add: nextCoord ];
 }
```

```
    else
      if ( ( ![ self isOutOfBounds: nextCoord ] ) &&
        ( ![ self isOnBorder: nextCoord ] ) &&
        ( ![ marked contains: nextCoord ] ) )
        [ validCoords add: nextCoord ];

  // Mark all the neighbors of currentCoordinate
  [ marked add: nextCoord ];
  nextOffset = [ iterate next ];
  }
  [ iterate free ];
  if ( [ validCoords size ] > 0 )
  {
   index = [ random nextBetweenLow: 0
          high: [ validCoords size ] - 1 ];
   return [ validCoords at: index ];
  }
  else
  {
   [ marked freeContents ];
   return nil;
  }
}

- (int) isOutOfBounds: aCoord
{
 if ( [ aCoord x ] < 0 ||
  [ aCoord x ] >= numCols ||
  [ aCoord y ] < 0 ||
  [ aCoord y ] >= numRows )
  return 1;
 else
  return 0;
}

- (int) isOnBorder: aCoord
{
 if ( ( [ aCoord x ] == 0 ) || ( [ aCoord x ] == numCols - 1 ) ||
  ( [ aCoord y ] == 0 ) || ( [ aCoord y ] == numRows - 1 ) )
    return 1;
 else
  return 0;
}

@end
```

Method initialize creates the objects random, offsets, marked, swampCells, and the-Path. The method setSwampCells creates and loads up the two IdArrays (two-dimensional array of SwampCell objects) with QuickSand objects. The code is similar to that used in the example presented in Listing 5.1.

The method setPath inserts a sequence of PathCell objects into random coordinate positions in the SwampCells object. This is perhaps the most complex method in the software system, so it is described in detail.

An object, thePath, is created as an instance of OrdCltn. The instance variable min-PathLength is set as the smaller of the numRows or numCols. The point current-Coordinate is assigned to a random coordinate on the top border of the swamp (using the method getFirstCoordinate). This point is added to thePath, using the method add:. In a do-while loop, the method getNextCoordinateFrom: currentCoordinate is used to obtain the next cell location, which is then added to thePath.

The method getNextCoordinateFrom: works as follows. An object, validCoord, of class OrdCltn is created. It is loaded with all adjacent coordinates of currentCoordinate that satisfy the following conditions. If the size of thePath is equal to or greater than minPathLength -1, then

1. the adjacent coordinate is not in the set of marked coordinates (not adjacent to the existing path created prior to currentCoordinate), and

2. the adjacent coordinate is not out of the boundaries of the swamp.

If the size of thePath is less than minPathLength -1, then the same two conditions hold, and

3. the adjacent coordinate is not on the border of the swamp.

As each adjacent neighbor of currentCoordinate is generated, it is added to the set of marked coordinates. This ensures that future coordinates will not be adjacent to the currentCoordinate.

The reader should verify that this algorithm for generating the next coordinate can box itself in. This is because of the requirement that the total path size be equal to or greater than the minPathLength. If this event occurs, the method getNextCoordinateFrom: returns nil. The method setPath uses a goto statement (every book on C must have a token goto statement!) to create a new path, thePath, and start from scratch.

After a valid path has been generated in the ordered collection thePath, an iteration over this collection is performed, using object iterate from class Sequence, to insert PathCell objects into the object SwampCells at the appropriate coordinate positions.

SwampCell Class

Class SwampCell is a superclass that establishes protocol for the subclasses TravelerCell, PathCell, and QuickSand. As indicated in the preceding section, a Swamp object contains a two-dimensional array of SwampCell objects. In fact no SwampCell objects inhabit a Swamp; instead, subclass objects of SwampCell occupy the two-dimensional array within a Swamp object. Late-binding polymorphism allows the same messages (defined in the superclass SwampCell) to be sent to objects of classes TravelerCell, PathCell or QuickSand. The appropriate action occurs at run time.

Listing 5.8 presents the protocol for class SwampCell.

Listing 5.8 _____

SwampCell class

```
// Interface to class SwampCell

#import <Primitive.h>

@interface SwampCell : Object
{
 char image;
 id coordinate;
}

// Factory methods
+ create;

// Initialize method
- initialize;

// Display method
- display;

// Accessing methods
- coordinate;

- coordinate: aCoordinate;

- (char) image;

- setImage: (char) aChar;

// Private methods
- gotoCol: (int) yCoord  row: (int) xCoord;

@end
------------------------

// Implementation of class SwampCell

#import "SwampCell.h"
#import <Point.h>
#import <curses.h>

@implementation SwampCell

// Factory methods
+ create
{
 id newInstance = [ super new ];

 [ newInstance initialize ];
 return newInstance;
}

// Initialize method
- initialize
{
 return [ self subclassResponsibility ];
}
```

(continues)

```
// Display method
- display
{
 int xCoord = [ coordinate x ];
 int yCoord = [ coordinate y ];
 char imageString[ 2 ];

 imageString[ 0 ] = image;
 imageString[ 1 ] = '\0';
 [ self gotoCol: 10 + yCoord  row: 10 + xCoord ];
 printw( imageString );
 return self;
}

// Accessing methods
- coordinate
{
 return coordinate;
}

- coordinate: aCoordinate
{
 coordinate = aCoordinate;
 return self;
}

- (char) image
{
 return image;
}

- setImage: (char) aChar
{
 image = aChar;
 return self;
}

// Private methods
- gotoCol: (int) yCoord  row: (int) xCoord
{
 move( yCoord, xCoord );
 return self;
}

@end
```

Note the following points. Each SwampCell or subclass object contains the instance variables image and coordinate (instance of class Point). The display method uses function printw from the UNIX C library curses to output the string imageString at a particular *x*- and *y*-coordinate on the output device. Method initialize is implemented as subclassResponsibility. That is, each of the subclasses must perform its own initialization. The other methods in SwampCell are relatively simple access methods.

QuickSand Class

The QuickSand class is one of three subclasses of the SwampCell class. Its protocol is given in Listing 5.9.

The only method defined in class QuickSand is initialize. This method sets the image of a QuickSand cell to be the character Q. All the other protocol of QuickSand is inherited from the parent class SwampCell.

PathCell Class

The protocol for class PathCell, another subclass of SwampCell, is presented in Listing 5.10.

The only method defined in class PathCell, as in class QuickSand, is initialize. This method sets the image of a PathCell to be the character P. All the other protocol of PathCell is inherited from the parent class SwampCell.

TravelerCell Class

The protocol for class TravelerCell, the third subclass of SwampCell, is given in Listing 5.11.

Listing 5.9
QuickSand class

```
// Interface to class QuickSand

#import <Primitive.h>
#import "SwampCell.h"

@interface QuickSand : SwampCell
{
}

- initialize;

@end
------------------------
// Implementation of class QuickSand'

#import "QuickSand.h"

@implementation QuickSand

- initialize
{
 [ self setImage: 'Q' ];
 return self;
}

@end
```

Listing 5.10 _____
PathCell class

```
// Interface to class PathCell

#import <Primitive.h>
#import "SwampCell.h"

@interface PathCell : SwampCell
{
}

- initialize;

@end
------------------------

// Implementation of class PathCell

#import "PathCell.h"

@implementation PathCell

- initialize
{
[ self setImage: 'P' ];
 return self;
}

@end
```

Like the other two subclasses of SwampCell, method initialize in TravelerCell sets the image to a character—in this case, *X*.

SwampTraveler Class

The second superclass in the *Swamp Runner* simulation is class SwampTraveler. It is the top of a hierarchy of four subclasses, each a child of the other. The subclasses are the following:

SwampTraveler(coordinate, numSteps, numAttempts, targetSwamp)
 Dimwit( )
  Halfwit(cellsVisited, pathVisited)
   Wit(firstMove, lastPathCoordinate)
     Genius( )

The protocol in the superclass SwampTraveler is shared by subclasses Dimwit, Halfwit, Wit, and Genius, which represent swamp travelers with increasing degrees of intelligence.
 The protocol for class SwampTraveler is given in Listing 5.12.
 Every SwampTraveler object contains targetSwamp, an instance of Swamp. As discussed in Chapter 2, this enables such an object to access information about and modify the swamp that it traverses. At every coordinate that a SwampTraveler object hits as it

Listing 5.11 _____
TravelerCell class

```
// Interface to class TravelerCell

#import <Primitive.h>
#import "SwampCell.h"

@interface TravelerCell : SwampCell
{
}

- initialize;

@end
------------------------

// Implementation of class TravelerCell
#import "TravelerCell.h"

@implementation TravelerCell

- initialize
{
[ self setImage: 'X' ];
return self;
}

@end
```

Listing 5.12 _____
SwampTraveler class

```
// Interface to class SwampTraveler

#import <Primitive.h>

@interface SwampTraveler : Object
{
 id coordinate;
 int numSteps;
 int numAttempts;
 id targetSwamp;
}
// Factory methods
+ createOn: aTarget;

// Initialize methods
- initialize;

// Access methods
- target;
```
                                                              (continues)

- target: aTarget;

- (int) numberAttempts;

- (int) numberSteps;

// Travelling methods
- (int) atEndOfPath;

- chooseNeighbor;

- makeNextMove;

- moveTo: aCoordinate;

- (int) travel;

- (int) isOutOfBounds: aCoord;

@end

// Implementation of class SwampTraveler

```
#import "SwampTraveler.h"
#import "Swamp.h"
#import "SwampCell.h"
#import "QuickSand.h"
#import "TravelerCell.h"
#import "Halfwit.h"
#import "PathCell.h"
#import "Random.h"
#import <stdio.h>
#import <OrdCltn.h>
#import <Point.h>
#import <IdArray.h>

@implementation SwampTraveler

// Factory methods
+ createOn: aTarget
{
 id newInstance = [ super new ];

 [ newInstance target: aTarget ];
 [ newInstance initialize ];
 return newInstance;
}

// Initialize methods
- initialize
{
 numSteps = 0;
 numAttempts = 1;
 coordinate = [ [ targetSwamp path ] firstElement];
 return self;
}
```

```
// Access methods
- target
{
 return targetSwamp;
}

- target: aTarget
{
 targetSwamp = aTarget;
 return self;
}

- (int) numberAttempts
{
 return numAttempts;
}

- (int) numberSteps
{
 return numSteps;
}
// Traveling methods
- (int) atEndOfPath
{
 return [ coordinate isEqual:
  [ [ targetSwamp path ] lastElement ] ];
}

- chooseNeighbor
{
 return [ self subclassResponsibility ];
}

- makeNextMove
{
 [ self moveTo: [ self chooseNeighbor ] ];
 return self;
}

- moveTo: aCoordinate
{
 return [ self subclassResponsibility ];
}

- (int) travel
{
 [ self makeNextMove ];
 return [ self atEndOfPath ];
}
// Private methods
- (int) isOutOfBounds: aCoord
{
 if ( [ aCoord x ] < 0 ||
```

(continues)

```
[ aCoord x ] >= [ targetSwamp numCols ] ||
[ aCoord y ] < 0 ||
[ aCoord y ] >= [ targetSwamp numRows ] )
return 1;
else
return 0;
}

@end
```

crosses the swamp, it produces and inserts a TravelerCell in the two-dimensional Swamp-Cells object contained within the swamp.

The factory method createOn: is used to build a new SwampTraveler object. The instance variable targetSwamp is bound to the parameter aTarget, which is the swamp that must be crossed. In addition, the initial value of the instance variable coordinate is assigned the result of sending the message firstElement to the path of targetSwamp.

The two key methods chooseNeighbor and makeNextMove are implemented as subclassResponsibility. The details of these two methods in the four subclasses are dependent on the level of intelligence of the particular SwampTraveler subclass.

The method atEndOfPath uses the protocol of methods isEqual (from ICpak 101 class Point) and lastElement (from ICpak 101 class OrdCltn) to determine whether the value of instance variable coordinate equals the last coordinate in the targetSwamp path.

The other methods of class SwampTraveler should be clear without additional comments.

Dimwit Class

The protocol for class Dimwit, a subclass of SwampTraveler, is presented in Listing 5.13.

The only two methods in subclass Dimwit are the two key methods chooseNeighbor and moveTo:. The method chooseNeighbor uses the ICpak 101 classes Sequence and OrdCltn to obtain a random neighbor of the current coordinate that is not out of the boundaries of the swamp. The ordered collection offsets, from class targetSwamp, is used to locate all of the neighbors of coordinate. The method moveTo: assigns a TravelerCell to the coordinate aCoordinate if the cell is not a TravelerCell or PathCell. The coordinate is reset to the beginning of the path (using firstElement) if the cell is a QuickSand or TravelerCell.

Halfwit Class

The protocol for class Halfwit, a subclass of Dimwit, is presented in Listing 5.14.

Objects of class Halfwit contain the additional instance variables cellsVisited and pathVisited, both instances of the ICpak 101 class Set. The instance variable cellsVisited keeps track of the QuickSand cells hit on the current and previous attempts at traversing the swamp. The instance variable pathVisited allows a Halfwit object to remember and not revisit the path cells visited on the current turn only. This instance variable is erased at the end of each attempt and initialized before the beginning of every new attempt.

Listing 5.13 _____
Dimwit class

```
// Interface to class Dimwit
#import <Primitive.h
#import "SwampTraveler.h"

@interface Dimwit : SwampTraveler
{
}

// Methods for traveling
- chooseNeighbor;

- moveTo: aCoordinate;

@end
------------------------

// Implementation of class Dimwit

#import "Dimwit.h"
#import "Swamp.h"
#import "SwampCell.h"
#import "QuickSand.h"
#import "TravelerCell.h"
#import "Halfwit.h"
#import "PathCell.h"
#import "Random.h"
#import <stdio.h>
#import <OrdCltn.h>
#import <Point.h>
#import <IdArray.h>

@implementation Dimwit

// Methods for traveling
- chooseNeighbor
{
 id newCoords;
 int index;
 id iterate;
 id nextOffset;
 id nextCoord;

 newCoords = [ OrdCltn new ];
 iterate = [ Sequence over: [ targetSwamp offsets ] ];
 nextOffset = [ iterate next ];
 while ( nextOffset )
 {
  if ( ![ self isOutOfBounds: [ nextOffset plus: coordinate ] ] )
    [ newCoords add: [ nextOffset plus: coordinate ] ];
  nextOffset = [ iterate next ];
 }
```

(continues)

```
[ iterate free ];
index = [ [ targetSwamp random ]
    nextBetweenLow: 0  high: [ newCoords size ] - 1 ];
return [ newCoords at: index ];
}

- moveTo: aCoordinate
{
 id aSwampCell;
 id swampcells = [ targetSwamp swampCells ];
 // Get cell associated with aCoordinate
 aSwampCell = [ [ swampcells at: [ aCoordinate y ] ]  at: [ aCoordinate x ] ];

 // If aSwampCell is not a PathCell or TravelerCell,
 // mark it as a TravelerCell
 if ( ( [ aSwampCell class ] != [ PathCell class ] ) &&
  ( [ aSwampCell class ] != [ TravelerCell class ] ) )
 {
 [ [ swampcells at: [ aCoordinate y ] ]
    at: [ aCoordinate x ]
    put: [ TravelerCell create] ];
 [ [ [ swampcells at: [ aCoordinate y ] ]
    at: [ aCoordinate x ] ]  coordinate: aCoordinate ];
 }
 coordinate = aCoordinate;
 numSteps++;

 // Test to see whether move is into quicksand
 if ( ( [ aSwampCell class ] == [ QuickSand class ] ) ||
  ( [ aSwampCell class ] == [ TravelerCell class ]  ) )
 {
 numAttempts++;
 coordinate = [ [ targetSwamp path ] firstElement ];
 }
 return self;
}

@end
```

---

*Listing 5.14*_____
Halfwit class

```
// Interface for class Halfwit

#import <Primitive.h>
#import "Dimwit.h"

@interface Halfwit : Dimwit
{
 id cellsVisited; // Set of Quicksand cells
 id pathVisited;  // Set of pathCells, erased for each turn
}
```

```
// Method for initialize
- initialize;

// Method for traveling
- chooseNeighbor;

- moveTo: aCoordinate;

@end
------------------------

// Implementation of class Halfwit

#import "Halfwit.h"
#import "Swamp.h"
#import "SwampCell.h"
#import "QuickSand.h"
#import "TravelerCell.h"
#import "Halfwit.h"
#import "PathCell.h"
#import "Random.h"
#import <stdio.h>
#import <OrdCltn.h>
#import <Point.h>
#import <IdArray.h>

@implementation Halfwit

// Method for initialize
- initialize
{
 cellsVisited = [ Set new ];
 pathVisited = [ Set new ];
 [ super initialize ];
 return self;
}

// Method for traveling
- chooseNeighbor
{
 id newCoords;
 int index;
 id iterate;
 id nextOffset;
 id nextCoord;
 id aCoord;

 newCoords = [ OrdCltn new ];
 iterate = [ Sequence over: [ targetSwamp offsets ] ];
 nextOffset = [ iterate next ];
 while ( nextOffset )
 {
  aCoord = [ nextOffset plus: coordinate ];
  if ( ![ self isOutOfBounds: aCoord ] &&
     ![ cellsVisited contains: aCoord ]  &&
```

(continues)

```
        ![ pathVisited contains: aCoord ] )
        [ newCoords add: aCoord ];
    nextOffset = [ iterate next ];
    }
    [ iterate free ];
    index = [ [ targetSwamp random ]
        nextBetweenLow: 0  high: [ newCoords size ] - 1 ];
    return [ newCoords at: index ];
}

- moveTo: aCoordinate
{
    id aSwampCell;
    id swampcells = [ targetSwamp swampCells ];

    // Get cell associated with aCoordinate
    aSwampCell = [ [ swampcells at: [ aCoordinate y ] ]
                        at: [ aCoordinate x ] ];
    if ( [ aSwampCell class ] == [ PathCell class ] )
    [ pathVisited add: aCoordinate ];

    // If aSwampCell is not a PathCell or TravelerCell,
    // mark it as a TravelerCell
    if ( ( [ aSwampCell class ] != [ PathCell class ] ) &&
    ( [ aSwampCell class ] != [ TravelerCell class ] ) )
    {
    [ [ swampcells at: [ aCoordinate y ] ]
            at: [ aCoordinate x ]
            put: [ TravelerCell create] ];
    [ [ [ swampcells at: [ aCoordinate y ] ]
                at: [ aCoordinate x ] ]  coordinate: aCoordinate ];
    }
    coordinate = aCoordinate;
    numSteps++;

    // Test to see whether move is into quicksand
    if ( ( [ aSwampCell class ] == [ QuickSand class ] ) ||
    ( [ aSwampCell class ] == [ TravelerCell class ]  ) )
    {
    numAttempts++;
    coordinate = [ [ targetSwamp path ] firstElement ];
    [ cellsVisited add: aCoordinate ];
    [ pathVisited freeContents ];
    pathVisited = [ Set new ];
    }
    return self;
}

@end
```

The method initialize for class Halfwit creates new instances of the Set objects cells-Visited and pathVisited before invoking the initialize method in the parent class Dimwit. Since the protocol of class Dimwit does not contain method initialize, the method initialize in Dimwit's parent, SwampTraveler, is used.

The key method chooseNeighbor, redefined in class Halfwit, obtains a random neighbor (from coordinate) that satisfies the following three conditions:

1. It is not a QuickSand cell previously visited.
2. It is not a pathCell visited on the current attempt.
3. It is not out of the boundaries of the swamp.

Again, the ICPak 101 foundation classes OrdCltn and Set are most useful in implementing the details of this method.

The method moveTo: is almost the same as the method moveTo: in the parent class Dimwit. The only difference is the manipulation of instance variables cellsVisited and pathVisited. Note that when a QuickSand cell is hit and a new attempt is to occur (coordinate set back to the initial path cell), the method freeContents is sent to Set pathVisited, followed by the factory method new applied to the class variable Set.

Wit Class

The protocol for class Wit, a subclass of Halfwit, is presented in Listing 5.15.

Class Wit introduces two additional instance variables, firstMove (an int) and lastPathCoordinate (an instance of Point). The instance variable firstMove allows the method chooseNeighbor to start the traversal at the last successful path cell attained on the previous attempt instead of having to start from the initial path cell on each new attempt. The test for firstMove in method chooseNeighbor allows for this branching logic.

When firstMove has the value 1, coordinate is assigned to lastPathCoordinate, and numSteps is incremented by the number of elements in the instance variable pathVisited. This instance variable is not erased after each attempt, as it is with the parent class Halfwit. The ability for a Wit object to remember the cumulative path successfully attained on previous attempts lowers the number of steps and the number of attempts required to successfully traverse the swamp. When firstMove is 0, the logic proceeds in the same manner as in the chooseNeighbor method in the parent class Halfwit.

The method moveTo: in class Wit is similar to the method in the parent class, except the pathVisited is not cleared after each attempt.

Genius Class

The protocol for class Genius, a subclass of Wit, is presented in Listing 5.16.

The protocol for class Genius introduces no additional instance variables. The additional method quickSandCell: returns 1 if the parameter aCoordinate is a QuickSand cell; otherwise it returns 0.

Listing 5.15 _____
Wit class

// Interface for class Wit

```
#import <Primitive.h>
#import "Halfwit.h"

@interface Wit : Halfwit
{
 int firstMove; // Set to 1 at beginning of attempt
 id lastPathCoordinate;
}

// Method for traveling
- chooseNeighbor;

- moveTo: aCoordinate;

@end
------------------------

// Implementation of class Wit

#import "Wit.h"
#import "Swamp.h"
#import "SwampCell.h"
#import "QuickSand.h"
#import "TravelerCell.h"
#import "Halfwit.h"
#import "PathCell.h"
#import "Random.h"
#import <stdio.h>
#import <OrdCltn.h>
#import <Point.h>
#import <IdArray.h>

@implementation Wit
// Method for initialize
- initialize
{
 firstMove = 1;
 [ super initialize ];
 lastPathCoordinate = coordinate;
 [ pathVisited add: coordinate ];
 return self;
}

// Method for traveling
- chooseNeighbor
{
 id newCoords;
 int index;
 id iterate;
 id nextOffset;
```

```
id nextCoord;
id aCoord;

// Use added intelligence to go to end of known path
if ( firstMove == 1 )
{
 coordinate = lastPathCoordinate;
 numSteps += [ pathVisited size ];
 firstMove = 0;
}

newCoords = [ OrdCltn new ];
iterate = [ Sequence over: [ targetSwamp offsets ] ];
nextOffset = [ iterate next ];
while ( nextOffset )
{
 aCoord = [ nextOffset plus: coordinate ];
 if ( ![ self isOutOfBounds: aCoord ] &&
     ![ cellsVisited contains: aCoord ]  &&
     ![ pathVisited contains: aCoord ] )
   [ newCoords add: aCoord ];
 nextOffset = [ iterate next ];
}
[ iterate free ];
index = [ [ targetSwamp random ]
 nextBetweenLow: 0  high: [ newCoords size ] - 1 ];
return [ newCoords at: index ];
}

- moveTo: aCoordinate
{
id aSwampCell;
id swampcells = [ targetSwamp swampCells ];

// Get cell associated with aCoordinate
aSwampCell = [ [ swampcells at: [ aCoordinate y ] ]
      at: [ aCoordinate x ] ];
if ( [ aSwampCell class ] == [ PathCell class ] )
{
 [ pathVisited add: aCoordinate ];
 lastPathCoordinate = aCoordinate;
}
// If aSwampCell is not a PathCell or TravelerCell,
// mark it as a TravelerCell
if ( ( [ aSwampCell class ] != [ PathCell class ] ) &&
 ( [ aSwampCell class ] != [ TravelerCell class ] ) )
{
 [ [ swampcells at: [ aCoordinate y ] ]
    at: [ aCoordinate x ]
    put: [ TravelerCell create] ];
 [ [ [ swampcells at: [ aCoordinate y ] ]
    at: [ aCoordinate x ] ]  coordinate: aCoordinate ];
}
```

(continues)

```
coordinate = aCoordinate;
numSteps++;
// Test to see whether move is into quicksand
if ( ( [ aSwampCell class ] == [ QuickSand class ] ) ||
  ( [ aSwampCell class ] == [ TravelerCell class ] ) )
{
 numAttempts++;
 coordinate = [ [ targetSwamp path ] firstElement ];
 [ cellsVisited add: aCoordinate ];
 firstMove = 1;
}
 return self;
}

@end
```

Listing 5.16 _____
Genius class

```
// Interface for class Genius

#import <Primitive.h>
#import "Wit.h"

@interface Genius : Wit
{
}
```

```
// Method for traveling
- chooseNeighbor;

- (int) quickSandCell: aCoordinate;
```

```
@end
------------------------
```

```
// Implementation of class Genius

#import "Genius.h"
#import "Swamp.h"
#import "SwampCell.h"
#import "QuickSand.h"
#import "TravelerCell.h"
#import "Halfwit.h"
#import "PathCell.h"
#import "Random.h"
#import <stdio.h>
#import <OrdCltn.h>
#import <Point.h>
#import <IdArray.h>
```

```
@implementation Genius
// Method for traveling
- chooseNeighbor
{
 id newCoords;
 int index;
 id iterate;
 id nextOffset;
 id nextCoord;
 id aCoord;

 // Use added intelligence to go to end of known path
 if ( firstMove == 1 )
 {
  coordinate = lastPathCoordinate;
  numSteps += [ pathVisited size ];
  firstMove = 0;
 }
 newCoords = [ OrdCltn new ];
 iterate = [ Sequence over: [ targetSwamp offsets ] ];
 nextOffset = [ iterate next ];
 while ( nextOffset )
 {
  aCoord = [ nextOffset plus: coordinate ];
  if ( ![ self isOutOfBounds: aCoord ] &&
     ![ cellsVisited contains: aCoord ]  &&
     ![ pathVisited contains: aCoord ] &&
     ![ self quickSandCell: aCoord ] )
    [ newCoords add: aCoord ];
  nextOffset = [ iterate next ];
 }
 [ iterate free ];
 index = [ [ targetSwamp random ]
     nextBetweenLow: 0  high: [ newCoords size ] - 1 ];
 return [ newCoords at: index ];
}

- (int) quickSandCell: aCoordinate
{
 id swampcells = [ targetSwamp swampCells ];
 id aSwampCell = [ [ swampcells at: [ aCoordinate y ] ]
                            at: [ aCoordinate x ] ];

 return ( ( [ aSwampCell class ] == [ QuickSand class ] ) ||
     ( [ aSwampCell class ] == [ TravelerCell class ] ) );
}

@end
```

The key method chooseNeighbor, again redefined in the subclass Genius, only returns a neighboring coordinate if the following conditions are satisfied:

1. The neighboring cell is not within the Set of QuickSand cells visited (which will be empty for this class).
2. The neighboring cell is not within the Set of path cells.
3. The neighboring cell is not a QuickSand cell.

Absent from subclass Genius is the method moveTo:. The method moveTo: from the parent class Wit suffices to move Genius objects.

Some Comments About Portability. The simulation presented above was implemented first on a Sun workstation using Stepstone's ICpak 101 foundation classes. The code was then ported to the NeXT computer, which currently does not support these foundation classes. Prototypes for the key methods of Set, OrdCltn, IdArray, Point, and Sequence were written using the same interfaces for the methods as those given in ICpak 101. After testing each prototype method, the application was linked and run on the NeXT computer. As expected, it ran perfectly the first time. Therefore, the conceptual framework provided by the Stepstone ICpak 101 classes provided a great deal of leverage in porting this application to a totally different environment. Only the key methods of each of the critical ICpak 101 classes had to be implemented.

Conclusions

It should be apparent from inspecting the code listings in this section that the ICpak 101 foundation classes Set (with methods new, add: contains:, freeContents), OrdCltn (with methods new, size, firstElement, lastElement, add:), IdArray (with methods new, at:, at: put:), Point (with methods x: y:, isEqual:, x, y, plus), and Sequence (with methods over: next) play a critical role in designing and implementing the software solution.

One of the touted benefits of object-oriented programming is the ease with which maintenance can be performed. The reader may wish to experiment with this notion by adding one or more additional subclasses to SwampTraveler. It is our conjecture that such maintenance would be relatively easy to accomplish using the existing protocol and hierarchical class structure. In some sense such an experiment would provide a real test of the quality of the current object-oriented design of the *Swamp Runner* simulation.

Examples of Object-Oriented Design Using Objective-C

Example is always more efficacious than precept.

Samuel Johnson, *1709–1784*

Two simple examples of object-oriented design using Objective-C are presented in this chapter.

6.1 SOLITAIRE SIMULATION: AN IDENTIFICATION OF IMPORTANT OBJECTS AND CLASSES

Specifications

We wish to simulate the game of solitaire—the Las Vegas gambling variety. The layout of the game is shown in Figure 6.1. The goal of Las Vegas solitaire is to get as many cards onto the foundation piles as possible by playing the available cards, which come from the talon, tableau, or hand. The specific rules of play are the following:

1. Cut and shuffle a deck of fifty-two cards until they are mixed.

2. Deal cards to the tableau as follows: Deal one card face-up in column 1, then six cards face-down in the same row toward the right. Deal one card face-up in column 2, then five cards face-down in the same row toward the right. Continue this pattern until a face-up card is dealt to column 7. The top card in each tableau pile is face-up; the remaining cards are face-down. After the tableau cards are dealt, the remaining cards form the hand. Play resumes by taking one card at a time from the deck and placing it face-up on the talon. Each card is available for placement on the tableau or foundation.

3. Each foundation pile contains cards of one suit (either clubs, hearts, diamonds, or spades). Each pile begins with an ace followed by two, three, four, . . . , ten, jack, queen, and king of the given suit. These cards are face-up. A card once placed on the foundation may not thereafter be removed.

Figure 6.1 _____

Solitaire layout

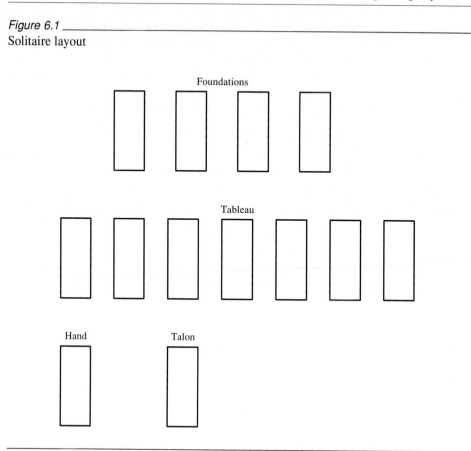

4. The face-up card in each tableau pile is the highest-ranking card in the pile (rankings go from king-high to ace-low). Other face-up cards can be placed below the top card if they are of next lower rank and opposite color. For example, if the top card in a tableau pile is the ten of clubs, then either a nine of diamonds or a nine of hearts can be placed, face-up, below the ten of clubs.

5. All face-up cards on a tableau pile can be moved as a unit onto a card of next higher rank and opposite color in another tableau pile. When such a transfer occurs, the top face-down card of the pile that is transferred from is turned face-up and becomes available. The top card of the talon is always available.

6. If a tableau pile is completely transferred to another tableau pile and a space is created, this space can only be filled with a king.

7. On every play, an attempt is made to place the bottom tableau card from a tableau pile onto a foundation pile (foundation cards provide the payoff). An attempt is made to place the top talon card onto the foundation. An attempt is made to move the face-up cards from one tableau pile to another, thus uncovering the top-card of a pile. An attempt is made to place the top talon card onto a tableau pile. These attempts are made repeatedly until none of the above events are possible. Then, as a last resort,

the hand is played. If the hand card cannot be put on the foundation or bottom of some tableau pile, it is placed on top of the talon pile (a stack of cards). The game ends when all of the hand cards have been played, and there are no available cards that can be moved to the foundation, to a tableau pile, or transferred from one tableau pile to another.

Analysis

The first step in the analysis of the *Solitaire* simulation is to identify the set of primary objects in the solution space. The simulation consists of a deck, a hand, a talon, a tableau, and a foundation. These physical entities map directly into objects in the software system. Each of these objects requires a class protocol description. Therefore, the primary object classes are Deck, Hand, Talon, Tableau, and Foundation. Secondary objects are identified when the instance variables of the primary objects are developed in more detail.

Tableau Class. A tableau object (there is only one in this simulation) contains seven stacks of cards, each with a top face-up card and each with a bottom face-up card. From this observation the secondary objects Card and Stack are identified.

The instance variables for this class are given as follows:

```
Tableau : Object
{
Stack* pile[ 7 ];
Card* top[ 7 ];
Card* bottom[ 7 ];
}
```

Foundation Class. A foundation object (there is only one in this simulation) contains four stacks of cards, each with face-up cards.

The instance variables for this class are given as follows:

```
Foundation : Object
{
Stack* pile[ 4 ];
}
```

Talon Class. A talon may be implemented as a stack of Cards.

Stack Class. A stack is a generic component that supports a last-in, first-out queue discipline. The fundamental stack operations of push, for insertion, and pop, for deletion, are independent of the base type of element stored in the stack. Objective-C, with its generic object type, id, provides strong support for building a Stack class. The instance variables of such a class are given as follows:

```
Stack : Object
{
Node* firstNode;
}
```

```
Node : Object
{
 id contents;
 Node* next;
}
```

The supporting class Node provides the mechanism for a Stack object containing an arbitrary object, contents.

Card Class. The supporting class Card contains the following instance variables:

```
Card : Object
{
 suitType suit;      // club, diamond, heart, spade
 stateType state;   // up, down
 char value;         // 2, 3, ..., T, J, Q, K  A
}
```

Deck Class. A deck is a special type of pile containing exactly fifty-two cards. Therefore, the class Pile is first defined. Class Deck is defined as a subclass of Pile.

```
class Pile : Object
{
 Card* * cards;   // An array of cards - space must be allocated dynamically
 unsigned size;   // Capacity of dynamically dimensioned array of cards
 unsigned index; // Position of next card to be inserted or removed (0 .. size - 1)
}
```

```
class Deck : Pile
{
}
```

Class Hierarchy. The class hierarchy for the *Solitaire* simulation is given in Figure 6.2.

Figure 6.2 _____

Hierarchy of classes for *Solitaire* simulation

```
Object( ... )

  Tableau( pile, top, bottom )

  Foundation( pile )

  Card( suit, state, value )

  Pile( cards, size, index )

   Deck( )

  Stack( firstNode )

  Node( contents, next )

  Talon -> implemented as a Stack
```

Significant Messages in the Simulation. The significant messages that drive the simulation are used in the main driver program. This driver program is written before any of the details of each class are created.

Listing 6.1 presents the main driver program of the *Solitaire* simulation. The significant messages used in this driver program are shown in bold-faced type.

Listing 6.1 _____
Main driver function of *Solitaire* simulation

```
// Main driver program - solitaire.m
// If one or more command line arguments are used
// program produces an integer score to standard output
// Should be run using script file run

//  run script file
/*
#Script file to run Solitaire program
#usage:  time run #times > output
set i = 0
while ( $i < $1 )
 solitaire NoOutput
 @ i++
end
*/

// This script file produces a set of scores for complete Solitaire games without showing
// any of the events that contribute to each game score.

#import "Stack.h"
#import "Deck.h"
#import "Tableau.h"
#import "Foundation.h"
#import <stdio.h>

int output; // If 1, all events are output to the standard output device

main( int argc, char* argv[] )
{
 Deck *myDeck = [ Deck new ];
 Tableau *myTableau = [ Tableau new ];
 Foundation *myFoundation = [ Foundation new ];
 Stack *myTalon = [ Stack new ];
 Card *card;
 int i;
 output = ( argc == 1 );

 [ myDeck cut ];
 // Thoroughly cut and shuffle deck of cards
 for ( i = 1; i <=5; i++ )
 {
 [ myDeck shuffle ];
 [ myDeck cut ];
 if ( output )
```

(continues)

```
    printf( "Deck shuffled and cut\n" );
}
[ myDeck resetIndex ];
if ( output )
 printf( "\n\n" );

[ myTableau initializeWithDeck: myDeck ];
card = [ myDeck remove ];
[ card setState: up ];
[ myTalon push: card ];
if ( output )
{
 printf( "\nThe initial conditions after dealing cards. " );
 printf( "There are %d cards in the hand and 1 card on the talon\n",
      [ myDeck remainingNumber ] );
 [ myTableau viewWith: myFoundation  andWith: myTalon ];
}
[ myTableau processWithTalon: myTalon
       withFoundation: myFoundation
         withDeck: myDeck ];
if ( !output )
 printf( "%d\n", [ myFoundation score ] );

if ( output )
{
 printf( "\nThe final game position\n" );
 [ myTableau viewWith: myFoundation  andWith: myTalon ];
 printf( "\n\nThe final score of the game = %d\n\n", [ myFoundation score ] );
}
}
```

After creating objects myDeck, myFoundation, myTableau, and myTalon, shuffling and cutting myDeck, and initializing myTableau with the important message initializeWith-Deck:, the main action of the simulation is accomplished with the important message from class Tableau, processWithTalon:withFoundation:withDeck:.

The highest-level architecture of the simulation is established in the main driver program, using the significant messages discussed above. The remaining details of this software system may be implemented in a variety of ways and are not presented in this book. Our emphasis here has been on the identification of the important objects and classes of the system.

Simulation Output

It is interesting to run the *Solitaire* simulation many times and compute scoring statistics. In particular, it is interesting to compute the average score obtained over many runs. For a simulation run of over 1000 games, the average winnings are close to zero, suggesting a fair gambling game. This is especially significant considering that a player would have to put $52,000 at risk ($52.00 per game x 1000 games). A Las Vegas gambling hall makes money because, in short runs (only a few consecutive games), the player will typically achieve no perfect games. It appears from our statistics that the probability of achieving a perfect game (score of $260.00) is approximately 2.4 percent. It would take, on average, approximately 40 games of solitaire before achieving a perfect game. The 28 perfect games achieved over 1000 games add a great deal of cumulative earnings to the total score. Only by depriving the player of an opportunity to allow the law of averages to yield a perfect score can the house beat the player.

6.2 GENERALIZED NUMERIC CLASSES

In Objective-C there are two predefined types of numbers, namely, int and float, each with several varieties (e.g., long, short, double). Along with these predefined numeric types, there are predefined operators such as +, -, *, and / that may be used to perform arithmetic operations on these types.

A programmer may wish to promote numbers from predefined scalar types to objects. In this case numeric classes must be defined that encapsulate the state and operations associated with a particular numeric class. In this section, the numeric classes Integer, Fraction, Float, and Complex are designed as subclasses of an abstract superclass, Number.

Specifications

For the numeric classes Integer, Fraction, Float, and Complex, the following arithmetic operations must be supported: add, subtract, multiply, and divide. These are the primary methods of each numeric class.

The principal challenge is in performing an arithmetic operation on two numeric objects that belong to different classes. In this case one of the numeric objects must be coerced to the class of the other. Late-binding polymorphism plays a central role in meeting this challenge.

Design

The abstract superclass Number provides an interface for all the basic operations that must be performed on any numeric subclass. Objects of class Number are never created, but some of the protocol in this superclass is used in each numeric subclass through inheritance.

In addition to the arithmetic operations add, subtract, multiply, and divide, definitions of the printing method print, the conversion methods coerce: and asFloat, and the coercion method retry:coerce: appear in the Number superclass. Only the method retry:coerce: is actually implemented in this superclass. This method provides the key to successfully performing arithmetic operations on objects of different classes.

Each numeric class defines a generality number that all objects of the class assume. Whenever two numeric objects of different classes are combined through an arithmetic operation, the numeric object with the lower generality number is coerced to an equivalent numeric object of the higher-generality class by using the method retry:coerce:.

Figure 6.3 _____
Hierarchy of numeric classes

```
Object( ... )

  Number( )

   Integer( val )

   Float( val )

   Fraction( top, bottom )

   Complex( real, imag )
```

Since Objective-C does not support the overloading of operators, as does C++, the arithmetic methods add:, subtract:, multiply:, and divide: must be used.

The hierarchy of numeric classes with their attributes is shown in Figure 6.3.

Selected Implementation Details

Listing 6.2 presents the interface for the abstract superclass Number.

The methods add:, subtract:, multiply:, divide:, and other methods are implemented as subclassResponsibility, since they are each key methods. They must be redefined in each of the subclasses. The details for method add: are shown below.

```
- add: operand
{
 return [ self subclassResponsibility: _cmd ];
}
```

Support for arithmetic among objects of different classes is provided by the methods generality, coerce: and retry: coerce: . Each subclass is responsible for its own level of generality and its method for coercion. The logic for retrying an operation with coercion of one Number subclass to another is the same for all subclasses and is implemented as follows in the abstract superclass Number.

```
// Retry coerce method
- retry: (SEL) anOperation  coerce: aNumber
{
 if ( [ self generality ] < [ aNumber generality ] )
  return [ ( [ aNumber coerce: self ] ) perform: anOperation
             with: aNumber ];
 else
  return [ self perform: anOperation
         with: ( [ self coerce: aNumber ] ) ];
}
```

Listing 6.2 _____
Interface for class Number

```
// Interface to class Number
// Abstract super class
#import <objc/Object.h>

@interface Number : Object
{
}
// Generality method
- (int) generality;

// Arithmetic methods
- add: operand;

- subtract: operand;

- multiply: operand;

- divide: operand;

// Printing method
- print;

// Conversion methods
- coerce: aNumber;

- asFloat;

// Retry coerce method
- retry: (SEL) anOperation  coerce: aNumber;

@end
```

If the generality of the receiver of an arithmetic message is lower than the generality of its parameter (e.g., [myInt add: myFloat]), the receiver is coerced to have the same generality as the parameter. The arithmetic operation is then retried and will invoke the method in the class of higher generality (note that both the receiver and the parameter are of the same generality). The same principle applies in reverse if the generality of the receiver is higher than that of the parameter. Retrying an operation with one parameter is supported by the method perform:with: inherited from class Object.

We define the generality of Integer objects as 10, Fraction objects as 20, Float objects as 30, and Complex objects as 40. This is consistent with the requirement that a number of lower generality can always be coerced to an equivalent number of higher generality.

To illustrate how subclasses redefine the arithmetic methods to take advantage of generality, the details of method add: from class Integer are presented below.

```
- add: operand
{
id newInteger;

if ( [ operand class ] == [ Integer class ] )
{
 newInteger = [ Integer new: val + [ operand getValue ] ];
 return newInteger;
}
else
 return [ self retry: @selector( add: ) coerce: operand ];
}
```

In the method add:, if the generality of the receiver equals the generality of the operand, a new Integer object is created with state equal to the sum of the int values of each operand. If the generality of the receiver does not equal the generality of the operand, the method retry:coerce:, described above, is sent to the receiver. Here, a selector is used as a parameter of this message. The other arithmetic methods are implemented in a similar manner in each of the subclasses.

## CHAPTER 7

Software Development Environments: User Interfaces and Visual Programming

An important feature of the object-oriented approach to problem solving is the availability of a software development environment that makes it possible and convenient to take advantage of reusable software components. Predefined classes with high reusability and supporting software tools to examine details of classes are key features of such an environment. The environment may further enhance software productivity through the application of visual programming methods for otherwise tedious and often-used operations, such as the development of user interfaces.

In this chapter we discuss the desirable features of an object-oriented software development environment and discuss in particular the NeXT environment for the development of object-oriented software applications. The chapter ends with several examples illustrating the development of Objective-C applications on the NeXT computer. These examples illustrate key features of the Application Kit™ classes and the Interface Builder™ that are provided as part of the NextStep® software development environment.

7.1 HARDWARE AND SOFTWARE ENVIRONMENTS

A software development environment can be divided into hardware components and software components. Together these components provide the tools available for software development. In this section we discuss those features of hardware and software environments that have come to be associated with object-oriented problem solving.

Object-Oriented Programming Environments

One of the primary motivations for using object-oriented programming is its support for the development of reusable software components through inheritance and the creation of abstract classes with high reusability. If one indeed produces an increasing number of reusable classes, we make the following observations:

- Strong support exists for incremental problem solving based on the use of existing classes and messages.
- A need exists for tools that allow the programmer to examine the structure and interfaces for existing classes.
- A need exists for tools that make it easy to incorporate the programmer's new classes into the existing hierarchy of classes.
- A need exists for tools that expedite the repetitive, time-consuming operations that are part of most software projects. These operations include those that are part of a user interface plus interactions with files and printers.

These needs lead to requirements for an object-oriented programming software environment. Some of these needs also imply the existence of characteristics in the hardware environment such as the following:

- A high-resolution display
- A pointing device for user interaction with displayed windows
- Increased memory capacity for interacting with multiple windows
- A high-resolution printer
- Supporting coprocessors to increase efficiency and speed

One only need track the progress of computer systems over the past few years to see that these hardware and software environments are becoming more commonly available.

Visual Programming

We begin with definitions for the following terms:

— *Visual*
of, relating to, or employing visual aids
— *Programming*
to work out a sequence of operations to be performed

A variety of definitions for visual programming is given in the literature. Software that provides windows and interaction with a pointing device such as a mouse is sometimes said to support visual programming. A more strict definition for visual programming is *the use of icons and connections among icons to visually construct working software*. The more strict approach to visual programming is supported by several software development environments, including Prograph® and the Interface Builder.

Prograph uses the concepts of data flow and object-oriented programming to allow the user to graphically construct software systems. It comes with several predefined classes and is based on its own language. Prograph runs on the Apple Macintosh® and provides access to the toolbox.

The Interface Builder supports visual programming through the provision of icons for selected user interface objects. These icons may be arranged in windows and connected graphically to invoke specified actions. Components of the interface may also be connected to actions provided in classes generated by the software developer. Classes may be defined with appropriate outlets and actions from within the Interface Builder. A template for the class is automatically generated, saving the software developer much time in completing the implementation.

The Interface Builder runs on the NeXT computer, has over forty predefined classes representing user-interface objects, and is based on the Objective-C language. A number of examples using the Interface Builder are given in Section 7.4.

Supporting Software Development Tools

One of the most important supporting software development tools for object-oriented problem solving is a tool for examining the protocol of existing classes. It should also provide the capability for adding new classes at appropriate locations within the existing hierarchy. Such a tool is often called a *browser*. A well-designed browser will assist in the organization of classes and their messages and provide operations for examining dependencies among classes or messages.

The Interface Builder provides a browser for adding new classes to the existing hierarchy. It also provides an *inspector* for any selected class, which allows one to list the outlets (instance variables) and actions (target messages). It is also possible to add new outlets and actions to a class from the inspector. Details of the actions must be added externally using a text editor. A full-featured browser is available for use with the Objective-C system from Stepstone also.

Other tools for supporting software development include a source-level debugger, editors, and make utilities.

7.2 BUILDING APPLICATIONS WITH THE NeXT ENVIRONMENT

The NeXT computer uses an application called the Workspace Manager™ as a graphic interface to the file system. It takes the place of the UNIX® shell; however, a UNIX shell may be opened within a window in the Workspace Manager. The Workspace Manager provides a convenient graphic interface for performing all operations on the NeXT, including the execution of applications.

Applications on the NeXT may be window-based or they may run within a UNIX shell. Window-based applications make use of the Application Kit classes provided with the system to create windows, menus and, user-interactive display objects.

NextStep: Hardware, Applications, Windows, and Window Server

NextStep is an operating environment that provides several layers of support for the development of software systems on the NeXT computer. These layers bridge the gap from user applications to the hardware. NextStep, consisting of four software components (the Window Server™, the Workspace Manager, the Application Kit, and the Interface

Builder), in conjunction with the Mach[1] operating system and the NeXT hardware, provides the following support layers for the development of software systems.[2]

- *Top layer: Applications*
  These are the classes and software components generated by a software developer. Each application must have an instance of class Application if it is to use the windowing environment of the Workspace Manager. The Workspace Manager is automatically launched when the system is booted.

- *Second layer: Interface Builder*
  The Interface Builder is itself an application that is a tool for the development of user interfaces for any other application. It bridges the gap between applications and the underlying kit classes that support user-interface operations. Although applications can directly access the kit classes, using the Interface Builder is a great time-saver. Many complicated and tedious operations are implemented visually from the Interface Builder.

- *Third layer: Kit classes*
  There are three categories of kit classes: Application Kit, Music Kit, and Sound Kit. Together they provide over seventy predefined classes. These classes are accessible either directly or from the Interface Builder.

- *Fourth layer: Window Server and supporting C libraries*
  Between the Objective-C classes or the user-defined classes and the operating system are the Window Server and supporting C libraries. The Window Server is a low-level background process that is launched with the Workspace Manager when the system is booted. The Window Server is used by the Application Kit to manage windows and to send user events, such as mouse and keyboard actions, back to an application. Included in the Window Server is a Display PostScript® interpreter that's used for all drawing of text and graphics on the screen or printed page. The Window Server manages all windows on the screen and is the interface between those windows and applications that use them. It receives and carries out instructions from an application for drawing windows and their contents.

- *Fifth layer: Mach operating system*
  The Mach operating system is a multitasking system that provides complete compatibility with UNIX 4.3 BSD (Berkeley Software Distribution). Enhancements added by Mach include

  1. a faster and more consistent system of interprocess communication,

  2. larger virtual memory space,

  3. memory-mapped files,

  4. and multiple threads of execution within a single address space.

---

[1] The Mach operating system was developed by Carnegie-Mellon University.

[2] The NextStep software development environment has been licensed by IBM for use on their R-6000 workstations as well.

- *Bottom layer: Hardware*
  The NeXT computer comes with several powerful hardware processors including

1. the microprocessor,
2. a digital signal processor, and
3. a floating-point processor.

It also comes with an erasable optical disk as well as a magnetic disk.

Essential Components of an Application

Working software programs on the NeXT are called *applications*. An application must have several essential components if it is to take advantage of the windowing environment offered by the Workspace Manager.

- *Application object*
  Every application has an object that is an instance of the Application Kit class Application. It is through this object that the Window Server can interact with the application.
- *Listener object*
  This object is an instance of class Listener. Its purpose is to receive communications from other applications or external events. An instance of Listener is automatically created when the application object is created.
- *Speaker object*
  This object is an instance of class Speaker. Its purpose is to communicate with external applications and the Window Server. An instance of Speaker is automatically created when the application object is created.
- *Window object*
  An application may have one or more windows that are instances of class Window or its subclasses. The application object keeps a list of its windows in an instance variable called windowList.

Predefined Classes and Software Development Tools

The NextStep environment comes with four categories of predefined classes in Objective-C. They are

1. common classes (those that support any application),
2. Application Kit classes (supportive of the development of graphic user interfaces),
3. Music Kit classes (for developing software that deals with music), and
4. Sound Kit classes (providing an interface to the supporting sound hardware).

In addition to predefined classes, the NeXT environment provides the application called Interface Builder, which supports the graphic construction of user interfaces and

software systems. It is used to access existing classes as well as for adding new classes to
the hierarchy.

7.3 ACCESS TO THE NeXT ENVIRONMENT USING OBJECTIVE-C

The NeXT environment is accessed through Objective-C programming by using the predefined classes in the Application Kit, Music Kit, Sound Kit, and common classes. In
addition, an application may use the Interface Builder to create a window-based interface,
or this may be done by direct use of the predefined classes.

In this section we begin with an overview of the common classes as well as selected
classes in the Application Kit. We then discuss some of the details of program development by direct application of these predefined classes. We end with a discussion of the
key features of the Interface Builder.

Overview of the Common Classes and Application Kit Classes

There are five predefined classes that are grouped into a category called *common classes*.
The common classes and their hierarchical relationships are given in Figure 7.1. The
common classes may be imported and used in any application. A brief description of each
class follows.

- Object
  This is the abstract superclass of all classes in the Objective-C system. It contains protocol that is representative of all classes of objects. It provides the
  interface between all other classes and the Objective-C run-time system. It contains the instance variable, isa, which is a pointer to an object's class structure.
  Class Object contains about thirty methods that are applicable to all objects.

- List
  Class List represents dynamic and generic collections of objects. The collections
  may be fixed in size or variable. A list may function as a set or an ordered
  collection.

- Storage
  This class represents a dynamic array with arbitrary classes of objects as its
  elements.

Figure 7.1 _____
The common classes on the NeXT computer

```
Object
   List
   Storage
   HashTable
      StreamTable
```

Figure 7.2 _____

Organization of classes in the Application Kit

```
Object
    MySpecialClass
    Other Object subclasses ---
    Responder
        Application
            MyApplicationClass
        Window
            Panel
                Other Panel subclasses ---
                Menu
        View
            Text
            Other View subclasses ---
            Control
                Control subclasses ---
    Cell
        Cell subclasses ---
```

_____

- HashTable

  This class represents a hash table object. It maps keys into values. The keys and values are restricted to be 32-bit quantities such as types id, int, char* or void*.

- StreamTable

  This class represents sets of independent data structures that are mapped onto a stream. Its primary use is for incremental saving of files.

Figure 7.2 gives an abbreviated hierarchy of the Application Kit classes. The two classes, MySpecialClass and MyApplicationClass are inserted to show the most likely locations for adding user classes to the hierarchy. A descriptive summary of selected classes in the Application Kit follows.

There are approximately forty classes in the Application Kit, arranged in the hierarchy shown in Figure 7.2. Of the forty classes, the following are of primary interest in the development of window-based applications.

- Responder

  Inherits from Object. It is an abstract superclass of all objects that can respond to events from the NextStep environment (events are usually initiated by mouse-clicks, or keyboard input, or from the Window Server or another application. As an abstract class, Responder will have no instances created; instances of its subclasses are created.

- Application

  Inherits from Responder–Object. An instance of this class is the major object for developing a new application. It responds to events sent by the Window Server and dispatches events to an appropriate window. It maintains a list of all its windows in the instance variable windowList. An active application object is assigned to the global variable NXApp. An application object is automatically assigned a Listener object and a Speaker object for communicating with the Window Server and other applications.

- Window

  Inherits from Responder–Object. For each Window object, the Window Server creates a window that is identified by a window number. The Window object is identified by an id; it manipulates the window through methods that interface with the Window Server.

  Every window has its own view hierarchy with at least two views: a frameView and a contentView. The frameView draws the frame, title bar, and border of a window. It has a nil superview and is private (the user cannot change its hierarchy). The user can, however, specify the size of frameView by setting instance variable frame, an NXRect.

  Window objects are drawn in screen coordinates and cannot be rotated. Changing frame does not affect the actual display of a window. Only instructions sent to the Window Server will resize a window. This results in an event being sent to a window via its application that allows the window to update its views.

- The contentView is a public view that can be redefined by the user. It fills the entire border of the frame and may have subviews added. It is an instance variable in Window.

- Message display sent to a window object causes the message display to be sent to all its views, where the actual display work is done.

- Message printPSCode: prints a window and all its views.

- Other instance variables of interest in Window include

  1. delegate, the object that receives notification messages from the window object;
  2. firstResponder, the object that should handle the next event received by the window object; and
  3. fieldEditor, a placeholder for a Text object for interacting with Control objects that may be part of the window.

- Panel

  Inherits from Window–Responder–Object. Panel objects display information and accept inputs from a user. They are often used for selection of fonts and for providing information or help. Panels are different from other windows in that they are typically hidden until displayed as the result of some program action. A special kind of Panel called an attention panel is one that requires a user response before the program can continue execution.

- Menu

  Inherits from Panel–Window–Responder–Object. Menus are panels with user options attached to target messages and objects. Selection of an option in the menu list sends the target message to the target object. Menu objects consist of MenuCell objects that are selectable.

- View

  Inherits from Responder–Object. This class provides protocol for drawing on the screen and refines inherited Responder protocol for handling events specific to Views.

  All graphic objects in the NeXT user interface are instances of View. A View is attached to a Window where it can be displayed and is part of a View hierarchy for that window. Each View knows its window, superview, and subviews.

  Each View has a frame that is a rectangle specified by origin, width, and height. The frame is relative to the origin of the superview. A view cannot draw outside its own frame. The frame of a view may be rotated or scaled.

- The message display sent to a view sends the message, drawSelf::. Every subclass of View must implement a method for drawSelf::.

- The major message for printing a view and its subviews is printPSCode:.

- Archiving (to files) is accomplished with major messages read: and write: for View objects as well as other kinds of objects.

- View subclasses fall into three major groups:

  1. Views that display data and allow the user to manipulate or change it (e.g., Text);

  2. Views that capture instructions from the user and pass them on to other objects, called targets (e.g., all the Control subclasses); and

  3. Views that are used in conjunction with other views to enhance or regulate the display (e.g., Box and ScrollView).

- Control

  Inherits from View–Responder–Object. Control is an abstract superclass for all objects that follow the control-action paradigm. Subclass objects of Control interpret user responses and send actions to other objects (targets). Control objects are associated with Cell objects. The Cell object is used to store internal characteristics of the Control object, such as how it looks, how it should respond to user actions, and so forth. A Control object may have one or more Cell objects associated with it.

- Cell

  Inherits from Object. It is an abstract superclass representing various kinds of cells. Cell objects have the ability to display text or icons and accept user inputs as numbers, text, or by selection. They have less overhead than View objects. Some View classes (e.g., Matrix) allow multiple Cell objects to be grouped together without requiring a separate View for each.

- Text

  Inherits from View–Responder–Object. This class represents objects that can display and edit text. It is one of the more complicated classes in the Application Kit. As a subclass of View, it has all the protocol for displaying on the screen and for printing.

Program Development from a UNIX Shell

Objective-C programs may be developed from a UNIX shell window. This window is an application operating under the Workspace Manager. From the shell, normal UNIX commands may be invoked for the compilation, linking, and execution of software systems. It also supports the normal UNIX editors such as vi. A separate application for text editing is also available and is very useful for developing source code.

The normal compile-edit cycle of a nonwindowing system is available on the NeXT. As an option, this approach may also be used for debugging, even for systems that used the Interface Builder for initial development.

Interface objects may be generated directly by using protocol in the Application Kit classes and building the necessary windows, menus, and other interface objects. Connections of these objects to appropriate messages and outlets can also be made directly, without the Interface Builder.

Program Development from the Interface Builder

The Interface Builder provides the software developer with a powerful set of tools for software development. These tools make it easy to develop a sophisticated and powerful user interface for a software system. In addition, much of the framework for other components in the software system can be generated by the Interface Builder. More specifically, it provides the following features for supporting software development in Objective-C.

- *Graphical construction of an interface*
  Using icons that are instances of the Application Kit classes, the software developer visually constructs an interface for a software system. The icons are dragged into a window, resized, labeled, and grouped as desired. Among the existing kit objects included in the palette of the Interface Builder are button, scroll view, custom view, form with form cell, text field, a box, sliders (vertical and horizontal), matrix of button cells, matrix of text field cells, panels, and menus. The user may add other icons to the Interface Builder to enhance its features even further.

- *Inspection of interface objects*
  Inspector windows are opened for the various interface objects to examine attributes[3] (outlets) and actions[4] (target messages). Descriptive attributes such as size, background, and resizability may be examined and easily changed.

- *Connection of objects to outlets and target messages*
  A simple procedure is used to connect any object in the software system to an

---

[3] In the Interface Builder, attributes are instance variables. These instance variables serve as outlets for receiving messages. For example a button that is part of a graphic user interface is established as an outlet with a name. Status of the button is then checked by sending messages to the outlet.

[4] Actions are messages that are invoked when a user-interface object is activated (such as what happens when a button is pressed). The Interface Builder allows connection of a user-interface object action to a target message. The target message may be in any appropriate class.

instance variable in another class or to connect target objects and messages. This is possible for existing objects in the Interface Builder and for objects added by the software developer.

- *Class browser*
  A class browser is available for examining the Application Kit classes. It opens an inspector for examining outlets (instance variables) and actions (messages) for any class. The software developer may use this browser to attach new classes to the hierarchy and to create an instance of a class for connection to other components in the software system.

- *Creation of new class templates*
  New classes added by the software developer are added to the software system by the Interface Builder. Templates are created for both the interface and implementation files for these new classes. The software developer only needs to add details for some methods.

- *Compilation*
  A make file is optionally created by the Interface Builder for compiling and linking the software system. Compilation may be invoked from within the Interface Builder or from a shell window, using the make file.

- *Other features*
  Other features in the Interface Builder include graphic tools for implementing design decisions about the resizability of a window and its views, a test mode for testing functions of the interface, tools for accessing the Sound Kit and Music Kit classes, tools for including icons in an application, and access to source files for easy editing.

This brief summary of features of the Interface Builder is not intended to be complete. A complete description is given in the NeXT reference manuals.[5]

7.4 USING THE APPLICATION KIT CLASS LIBRARY

In this section we present several examples that use the Objective-C classes of the Application Kit provided on the NeXT computer. Solutions to the examples can be developed with comparative ease in other languages or other environments that provide similar classes.

The first of these examples shows how to define applications, windows, scrollable views, and menus. In addition the example shows how to interact with text files and with the printer. Two versions of this first example are presented.

The first version of the scrollable text example is based on direct usage of the appropriate Application Kit classes. It requires that one obtain a minimum familiarity with the purpose and protocol of the selected classes. A simple main driver program encapsulates all code that directly uses the Application Kit classes. This development

---

[5] See in particular Chapter 8, "Interface Builder," of the *NeXT System Reference Manual*.

approach may use any text editor. Commands for compiling, linking, and executing may be given from a UNIX shell.

The second version of the scrollable text example uses the Interface Builder application provided with the NeXT computer. This version illustrates the concepts of visual programming as supported by the Interface Builder. One component of the solution is achieved through the use of capabilities in the Interface Builder. A second component performs operations not provided by the Interface Builder. The example shows how to connect the two components into a working software system.

The second major example shows how a matrix of active buttons is produced to provide user-selectable options. The buttons have titles that may be changed, and each may be selected by clicking on it with the mouse. An important application of a matrix of active buttons is to present the user with a list of selectable items.

Finally, we discuss bitmap displays and present two more examples that use classes provided in the Application Kit. The first example shows how to display bitmap images in a view in a window. The second example shows how to make bitmap images into active objects by displaying them as the icons for control objects.

Menus, Scrollable Views, Open Panels, Text, Files, and Printing

There are a number of operations that are usually considered to be part of a graphic user interface in any software system. These include

1. creating and manipulating applications and windows,
2. creating menus and attaching them to actions,
3. opening files and reading or displaying their contents,
4. using the printer, and
5. quitting an application gracefully. This section presents two versions of an example that shows how these operations are accomplished in Objective-C by using the Application Kit classes on the NeXT computer.

Brief specifications for this example include the following:

- The software system provides a scrollable window on the contents of a text file.
- The user may select the text file to be viewed as a menu option, Open file.
- The initial window has a specified size that can modify.
- Vertical scrolling with the use of a scroll bar is automatically added to the window when the contents of a selected text file do not fit within the window.
- A menu option, Print text, is provided to allow the user to print the contents of the text file being viewed.
- A menu option, Print window, is provided to show how a window and all its contents may be printed.
- A menu option, Quit, is provided to gracefully terminate the software system.

We offer one solution to the example that involves direct access to the Application Kit classes and another solution that uses the Interface Builder. First, we present a preliminary design for this scrollable file-viewer example.

Design for a Scrollable File Viewer with Menus. Using methods given in Chapter 2 for object-oriented design, we present a preliminary design for the scrollable file-viewer example. The design is only partially presented since the classes already exist as part of the NeXT environment. The reader is referred to NeXT documentation for a more complete description of the classes.

Primary Objects

- aFileViewer
  An instance of FileViewer. This object is created for this example.
- NXApp
  A predefined global instance of class Application. On the NeXT computer, any example that has windows and that must interact with the user through the mouse or keyboard should have an associated application object. It can then respond appropriately to user events.
- theWindow
  An instance of class Window created for this example. This object will be used to display the contents of a text file.
- theScrollView
  An instance of class ScrollView created for this example. This view allows display of its contentView which may be larger than the size of its display area. Scroll bars are automatically added so the user may view different parts of the contentView.
- filePanel
  An instance of OpenPanel created for this example. Objects of this class are used to get a file name from the directory on the system.
- myText
  An instance of class Text created for this example. This object represents a view of an object containing text. It is used to represent the contents of a text file to be viewed.
- mainMenu
  An instance of class Menu created for this example. This object is the primary menu. It is attached to an application.
- myStream
  This object (variable) has a type, NXStream, designed for handling streams. It is used to stream over an input file to be viewed. Since Objective-C is a hybrid language, myStream is not required to be a true object. Operations on myStream are governed by predefined functions for its type; messages are not sent to myStream. Variable myStream is declared to be of type NXStream for this example.

Attributes for the Primary Objects and Supporting Objects. All the attributes of aFile-Viewer are listed as primary objects and variables.[6] This emphasizes the fact that aFile-Viewer is established as a container object for accessing in a convenient way all the other objects. They could just as well have been defined in a main driver program.

Attributes for object aFileViewer

- NXApp
  This is a global variable, defined in the AppKit, that is typically assigned to the active application. It is not really an attribute of object aFileViewer. It is, however, assigned to a new Application within the details of one of the methods in class FileViewer.

- theWindow
  This attribute is also a primary object. It is the window for the file-viewer application.

- theScrollView
  The primary view in the file-viewer application is a scrollable view. It is used to display the contents of a file and allow scrolling over the file contents.

- filePanel
  This attribute is also a primary object. It allows the software to prompt the user for a file name to view.

- myText
  This object is a View that is installed as the content view of theScrollView. It is also a primary object.

- mainMenu
  This object is the main menu for the file-viewer application.

- myStream
  This parameter is a variable of predefined type NXStream. It is not accurately characterized as an object. Its purpose is to provide a stream over the contents of a selected text file. This attribute is used by the supporting objects filePanel and myText.

Partial list of attributes for object NXApp *(from class* Application*)*

- appName
  A variable of type char* that is the name of the application.

- currentEvent
  A variable of type NXEvent that is the event most recently received from the event queue.

- windowList
  An instance of List. This object is the list of all windows in the application.

---

[6] The Application Kit classes have many attributes. Only those that are to be manipulated by this example are included here.

- keyWindow
  The Window that receives keyboard events. This will be primary object theWindow.
- mainWindow
  The Window that receives Menu commands or action messages from a Panel.

Partial list of attributes for object theWindow *(from class* Window)

- frame
  A variable of type NXRect that gives a window's location and size on the display screen.
- contentView
  This object is an instance of one of the View classes. It represents the contents of the window.
- backgroundGray
  The background gray level in the window.
- winEventMask
  A variable of type int that specifies the kinds of events to which the window should respond.

Partial list of attributes for object theScrollView *(from class* ScrollView)

- vScroller
  An instance of class Scroller that controls vertical scrolling.
- hScroller
  An instance of class Scroller that controls horizontal scrolling.
- contentView
  An instance of a View class that is to be displayed in the ScrollView.

Partial list of attributes for object filePanel *(from class* OpenPanel)

- form
  An instance of class Form that allows the user to type in a file name.
- browser
  The NeXT browser.
- okButton
  An instance of Button used to click OK when a file name has been selected.
- filename
  The variable of type char* that is the selected file name.

Partial list of attributes for object myText *(from class* Text)

- horizResizable
  A variable of type int used as a Boolean to represent whether the contentView (Text is a subclass of View) of myText is resizable.

Figure 7.3 _____

Hierarchy of primary object classes for the File Viewer

Object
  FileViewer
  Responder
   Application
   Window
    Panel
     Menu
     SavePanel
      OpenPanel
  View
   Text
   ScrollView

_____

- vertResizable
  A variable of type int that is used as a Boolean to represent whether vertical resizing is possible.
- textStream
  A variable of type NXStream* that is used for reading and writing text.

Partial list of attributes for object mainMenu *(from class* Menu*)*

- superMenu
  The Menu for which this object is a submenu.
- matrix
  The Matrix object used to store the MenuCells that make up a menu.
- attachedMenu
  The submenu that is attached to this menu.

Partial list of classes for supporting objects

- Form, Scroller, Button, Matrix, MenuCell

Structure: A Hierarchy of Classes. The hierarchy of classes is determined largely by existing classes in the Application Kit that are used in this software system. The only user-defined class is FileViewer. The hierarchy of classes shown in Figure 7.3 is identified from the class structure of the primary objects. Actual classes of the primary objects are shown in boldface.

Key Messages and a Prototype Solution. As described in Chapter 2, a high-level prototype is first established with the most abstract messages. These messages are then broken down into lower levels by functional decomposition to find the key messages in a solution to a software system.

Level 1: Messages sent to object aFileViewer

```
aFileViewer = [ FileViewer new ]; // create the main object
[ aFileViewer initialize ];      // initialize all attributes
[ aFileViewer run ];             // display the window and run
[ aFileViewer free ];            // free the object
```

Level 2: Partitioning of messages initialize *and* run *sent to* aFileViewer

```
initialize
  NXApp = [ Application new ];
  filePanel = [ OpenPanel new ];
  [ self setTheWindow ];
  [ self setTheScrollView ];
  [ self setMyText ];
  [ self setMainMenu ];

run
  [ self startWindow ];
  [ NXApp run ];
  [ NXApp free ];
```

Level 3: Partitioning of messages setTheWindow, setTheScrollView, setMyText, setMainMenu, *and* startWindow

— setTheWindow (pseudocode operations)
  ◦ Create the frame rectangle for the window.
  ◦ Create the window with selected options.
  ◦ Set background gray.
  ◦ Set the title to "Textfile Viewer".

— setTheScrollView (pseudocode operations)
  ◦ Create scroll view with frame to match theWindow.
  ◦ Enable vertical scrolling.
  ◦ Disable horizontal scrolling.
  ◦ Install theScrollView as contentView of theWindow.

— setMyText (pseudocode operations)
  ◦ Get content rectangle of scroll view.
  ◦ Create text view to match content rectangle.
  ◦ Enable vertical resizing.
  ◦ Disable horizontal resizing.
  ◦ Enable resize notification to ancestor view.
  ◦ Set minimum size and maximum size.

— setMainMenu (pseudocode operations)
  ◦ Create mainMenu with title "File Viewer".
  ◦ Add option "Open file" with target message getFile and target object aFile-Viewer.

- ∘ Add option "Print text" with target message printText and target object aFile-Viewer.
- ∘ Add option "Print window" with target message smartPrintPSCode: and target object theWindow.
- ∘ Add option "Quit" with target message terminate: and target object NXApp.
— startWindow (pseudocode operations)
- ∘ Display theWindow.
- ∘ Make theWindow the front window.
- ∘ Make theWindow the key window.
- ∘ Display mainMenu.

Level 4: Partitioning of messages getFile *and* printText

— getFile (pseudocode operations)
- ∘ Run the filePanel (an OpenPanel object).
- ∘ Get the selected fileName.
- ∘ Open myStream on fileName.
- ∘ Read contents of myStream into myText.
- ∘ Close myStream.
- ∘ Install myText as contentView of theScrollView.
— printText
- ∘ Set page layout parameters.
- ∘ Set font in case it has been changed.
- ∘ Send message printPSCode: to myText.

The exact details of these methods will vary depending on whether the Interface Builder is used to develop the software system or whether a direct implementation is used. In the next two subsections we examine both approaches.

A Scrollable File Viewer with Menus, Using Direct Development. In this section we present a direct implementation of the file-viewer example without the aid of the Interface Builder. It is therefore the responsibility of the software developer to access and use several classes in the Application Kit to construct the interface objects and their connections. Specifically the software developer must do the following.

- Create an application object.
- Create a window object and attach it to the application.
- Create a scrollable view object.
- Create a menu with submenus, menu items, targets, and actions.
- Create a text view.
- Open a stream on a file using an open panel.
- Attach contents of file to text view.
- Install text view into scrollable view.

Figure 7.4 _____
Initial window for file-viewer example—direct implementation

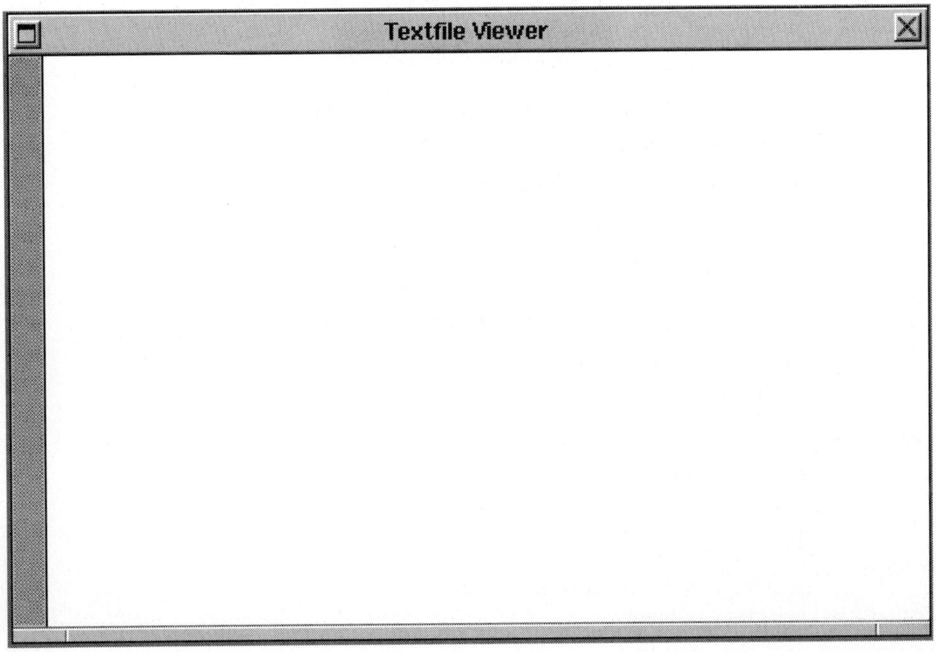

- Open a print panel.
- Print a window.
- Print a text view's contents.
- Quit gracefully.

Details of how these steps are implemented are given in the source code listings. We first look at the results and then reexamine some of the source code details. Figure 7.4 shows the interface developed for this example. It appears to consist only of a window with an area for viewing the contents of a file. As we know from the discussion in the preceding section, it is more than it appears. The window contains a scroll view that contains a text view.

Figure 7.5 shows the main menu for the file-viewer application. The single characters shown on the right side of each menu cell are the keyboard equivalents (to be pressed with the command key) for accomplishing the indicated actions. Alternately, the user may press any option by clicking on it with the mouse. Listing 7.1 gives the interface for the FileViewer class. Listing 7.2 gives details for the main driver program. It simply creates an instance of aFileViewer, sends it the messages initialize, run and free. Listing 7.3 gives the implementation details for class FileViewer.

Figure 7.5 _____

Menu for file-viewer example—direct implementation

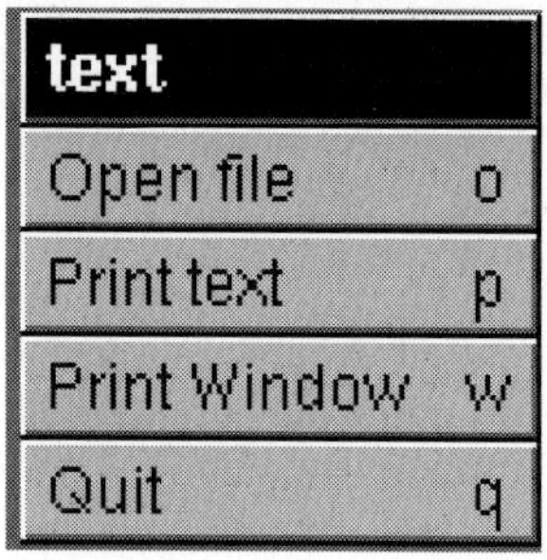

_____

Listing 7.1 _____

Source listing for class FileViewer interface—FileViewer.h

```
// FileViewer.h—Interface to class FileViewer

#import <appkit/appkit.h>

@interface FileViewer : Object
{
   id theWindow;
   id theScrollView;
   id filePanel;
   id myText;
   id mainMenu;
   NXStream *myStream;
}
// initialization methods
- initialize;

// run methods
- run;

// supporting and hidden methods not to be used externally
- setTheWindow;
- setTheScrollView;
- setMyText;

- setMainMenu;
- startWindow;

- getFile;
- printText;

@end
```

In Listing 7.3 the message addItem: action: keyEquivalent: used in method setMain-Menu is sent to object mainMenu. It returns a new MenuCell object that is next sent the message setTarget:, which attaches the action for that menu option to a particular object.

Listing 7.2

Source listing for *File Viewer* main driver—text.m

```
// A scrollable text view on a file with menu print capability

#import "FileViewer.h"

main(int argc, char *argv)
{
    id aFileViewer = [ FileViewer new ];

    [ aFileViewer initialize ];
    [ aFileViewer run ];
    [ aFileViewer free ];

}
```

Listing 7.3

Source listing for class FileViewer implementation—FileViewer.m

```
// FileViewer.m—Implementation for class FileViewer

#import "FileViewer.h"

@implementation FileViewer

NXSize aSize;
NXRect aRect, contentRect;
const char *fileName;

// initialization methods
- initialize
{
    NXApp = [ Application new ];
    filePanel = [ OpenPanel new ];
    [ self  setTheWindow ];
    [ self setTheScrollView ];
    [ self  setMyText ];
    [ self setMainMenu ];
}

// run methods
- run;
{
    [ self startWindow ];
    [ NXApp run ];
    [ NXApp free ];
}
```

(continues)

```
// supporting and hidden methods not in the interface
- setTheWindow    // support initialize
{
  NXSetRect ( &aRect, 100.0, 350.0, 500.0, 300.0 );
  theWindow = [ Window newContent: &aRect
          style: NX_TITLEDSTYLE
          backing: NX_BUFFERED
          buttonMask: NX_ALLBUTTONS
          defer: NO ];
  [ theWindow setBackgroundGray: NX_WHITE ];
  [ theWindow setTitle: "Textfile Viewer" ];
}

- setTheScrollView     // support initialize
{
  theScrollView = [ ScrollView  newFrame: &aRect ];
  [ [ theScrollView setVertScrollerRequired: YES ]
         setHorizScrollerRequired: NO ];
  [ theWindow setContentView: theScrollView ];
}

- setMyText      // support initialize
{
  contentRect = aRect;
  [ theScrollView getContentSize: &contentRect.size ];
  myText = [ Text newFrame: &contentRect
         text: NULL
         alignment: NX_LEFTALIGNED ];
  [ myText notifyAncestorWhenFrameChanged: YES ];
  [ myText setVertResizable: YES ];
  [ myText setHorizResizable: NO ];

  aSize.width = 0.0;
  aSize.height = contentRect.size.height;
  [ myText setMinSize: &aSize ];

  aSize.width = contentRect.size.width;
  aSize.height = 1000000;
  // a large number
  [ myText setMaxSize: &aSize ];
}

- setMainMenu     // support initialize
{
  mainMenu = [ Menu newTitle: "File Viewer" ];
  [ [ mainMenu addItem: "Open file"
      action: @selector ( getFile )
      keyEquivalent: 'o' ] setTarget: self ];
  [ [ mainMenu addItem: "Print text"
      action: @selector ( printText )
      keyEquivalent: 'p' ] setTarget: self ];
```

```
  [ [ mainMenu addItem: "Print window"
      action: @selector ( smartPrintPSCode: )
      keyEquivalent: 'w' ] setTarget: theWindow ];
  [ [ mainMenu addItem: "Quit"
      action: @selector ( terminate: )
      keyEquivalent: 'q' ] setTarget: NXApp ];
  [ NXApp setMainMenu: mainMenu ];
}

- startWindow     // support run
{
  [ theWindow display ];
  [ theWindow orderFront: nil ];
  [ theWindow makeKeyWindow ];
  [ mainMenu display ];
}

- getFile        // support menu
{
  [ filePanel runModalForDirectory: "/" file: "" ];
  fileName = [ filePanel filename ];
  myStream = NXMapFile ( fileName, NX_READONLY );
  [ [ myText readText: myStream ] sizeToFit ];
  NXCloseMemory ( myStream, NX_FREEBUFFER );
  [ theScrollView setDocView: myText ];

}

- printText       // support menu
{
  [ [ [ [ NXApp printInfo ]
    setOrientation: NX_PORTRAIT andAdjust: YES ]
    setHorizCentered: NO ]
    setVertCentered: NO ];
  [ Text setDefaultFont: [ Font
    newFont: "Helvetica"
    size: 12.0
    style: 0
    matrix: NX_FLIPPEDMATRIX ] ];
  [ myText printPSCode: nil ];
}

@end
```

Figure 7.6 shows the file-viewer window with the contents of file FileViewer.m displayed in its scroll view. Notice that scroll bars appear because the file is too large to fit within the window. These scroll bars are automatically added by class ScrollView when needed. The image in Figure 7.6 is printed by choosing the "Print window" menu option.

A Scrollable File Viewer with Menus, Using Interface Builder. In this section we present another solution to the file-viewer example, using the Interface Builder. The interface shown in Figure 7.7 was created using the Interface Builder (IB). It is a little different

Figure 7.6 _____

File-viewer window with a file displayed—direct implementation

```
┌─────────────────────────────────────────────────────────────┐
│ ▣                        Textfile Viewer                    ⊠ │
├─────────────────────────────────────────────────────────────┤
│ // FileViewer.m – Implementation for class FileViewer         │
│                                                               │
│                                                               │
│ #import "FileViewer.h"                                        │
│                                                               │
│ @implementation FileViewer                                    │
│                                                               │
│ NXSize aSize;                                                 │
│ NXRect aRect, contentRect;                                    │
│ const char *fileName;                                         │
│                                                               │
│ // initialization methods                                     │
│ - initialize                                                  │
│ {                                                             │
│     NXApp = [ Application new ];                               │
│     filePanel = [ OpenPanel new ];                            │
│     [ self setTheWindow ];                                    │
│     [ self setTheScrollView ];                                │
│     [ self setMyText ];                                       │
│     [ self setMainMenu ];                                     │
└─────────────────────────────────────────────────────────────┘
```

_____

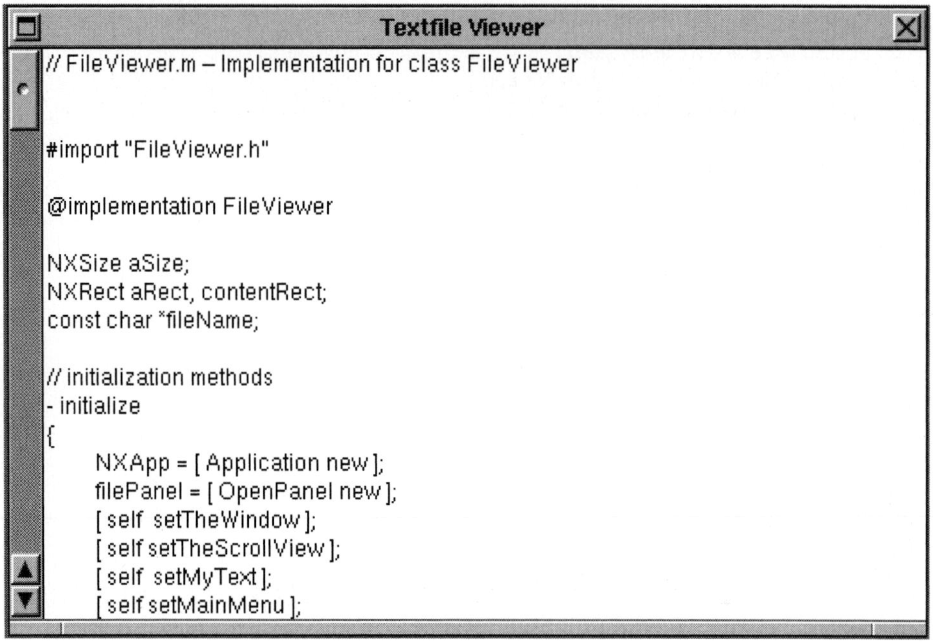

from the interface created using the direct approach in order to emphasize that it *is* different. In particular it is different in size and includes an enclosing box (an instance of Box) with a label to identify the scrollable view.

The menu for this implementation is shown in Figure 7.8. It is also a little different, with two additional menu options, "Info" and "Hide." The "Info" option opens an information panel that displays information about the application, as shown in Figure 7.9. This panel and its contents were created as shown and modified directly within the Interface Builder.

Listing 7.4 gives the interface description for class FileViewer as developed using the Interface Builder. It is clear from a comparison of this listing with that for the direct implementation that two attributes and several methods are missing in Listing 7.4. Specifically, attributes theWindow and mainMenu are missing from the class description. This does not mean they are not part of the software system; they are created and from part of the .nib file created by the Interface Builder.[7] The attribute theScrollView is included in

_____

[7] The Interface Builder allows the user to include interface objects as part of a software system through graphic manipulation. Instances of the AppKit classes and user-defined classes may be created within the Interface Builder and attached as outlets to specific objects. Instantiation of the user-interface objects (windows, buttons, etc.) as well as user-defined classes is accomplished at run time by loading a file called projectName.nib. This file contains code for all the instantiations, outlet connections, and target connections created by the Interface Builder.

Figure 7.7 _____

Initial window for the file-viewer example—IB implementation

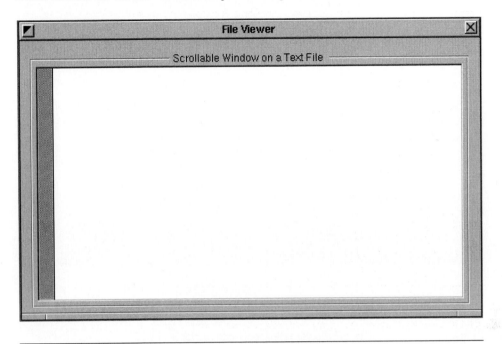

Figure 7.8 _____

Menu for the file-viewer example—IB implementation

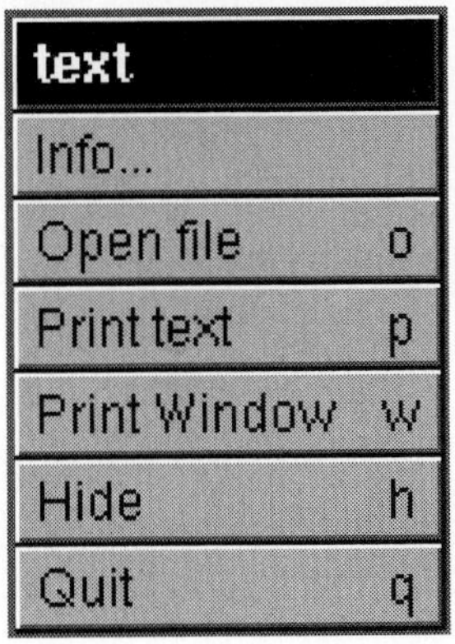

class FileViewer only because the software developer is still required to specifically attach myText as the contentView of theScrollView.

All the operations performed by startWindow in the direct implementation are also automatically handled by the Interface Builder. Methods setTheWindow and run are no longer needed.

Figure 7.9 _____

Info panel for the file-viewer example—IB implementation

Listing 7.4 _____

IB source listing for class FileViewer interface—FileViewer.h

```
// Interface to IB version of FileViewer.h
/* Generated by Interface Builder */
//    Modified by the authors

#import <appkit/appkit.h>

@interface FileViewer: Object
{
   id  theScrollView;

// attributes added by the authors
   id filePanel;
   id  myText;
   NXStream *myStream;
}

// added by interface builder
- setTheScrollView:anObject;
- initialize: sender;
- getFile:sender;
- printText:sender;

// added by the authors
- setMyText;

@end
```

Listing 7.5 _____

IB source listing for the *File Viewer* main driver—text_main.m

```
// IB version of the FileViewer test program
/*
 *    Generated by the NeXT Interface Builder.
 */
// Modified by the authors

#import <stdlib.h>
#import <appkit/Application.h>

void main(int argc, char *argv[])
{
    id fileViewerObject;
    NXApp = [Application new];
    [NXApp loadNibSection:"text.nib" owner:NXApp];
    fileViewerObject = NXGetNamedObject("FileViewerInstance", NXApp );
    [ fileViewerObject initialize: nil ];
    [NXApp run];
    [NXApp free];
    exit(0);
}
```
_____

The main driver source file, text_main.m, is given in Listing 7.5. Most of this file was generated automatically by the Interface Builder. The three lines shown in italics were added by the software developer to invoke an initialization sequence for theViewer-Object. The object FileViewerInstance is an instance of FileViewer created in the Interface Builder for forming connections. This example shows how to access such an existing object that was created in the Interface Builder.

Listing 7.6 gives the implementation details for the FileViewer class. Details for method setTheScrollView are automatically provided by the Interface Builder when the-ScrollView is established as an outlet and connected to the ScrollView image in the main window. The details for method initialize are also much simpler than they are for the direct implementation, requiring only that an OpenPanel object be created and attached to filePanel, and that myText be initialized.

The creation and connection of all Menu options is also achieved from the Interface Builder, resulting in additional savings of program development effort.

Figure 7.10 shows the file-viewer window with the file FileViewer.h opened and displayed.

This section has presented two implementations of an example that deals with windows, menus, files, and scrollable views. In comparing the direct implementation with the Interface Builder implementation, it is clear that the Interface Builder can significantly reduce the effort required to develop a first class interface.

Listing 7.6 _____

IB source listing for class FileViewer implementation—FileViewer.m

```objc
// Implementation for class FileViewer - FileViewer.m
/* Generated by Interface Builder */
/* Modified and implemented by the authors        */
/*===========================================================*/
#import "FileViewer.h"

@implementation FileViewer

  NXRect contentRect;
  const char *fileName;

- setTheScrollView:anObject
{
   theScrollView = anObject;
    return self;
}

- initialize: sender
{
   [ self setMyText ];
   filePanel = [ OpenPanel new ];
   return self;
}

- getFile:sender
{
  [ filePanel runModalForDirectory: "/" file: "" ];
  fileName = [ filePanel filename ];
  myStream = NXMapFile( fileName, NX_READONLY );
  [ [ myText readText: myStream ] sizeToFit ];
  NXCloseMemory ( myStream, NX_FREEBUFFER );
  [ theScrollView setDocView: myText ];
  return self;
}

- printText:sender
{
// Make sure we have the right page parameters
   [ [ [ [NXApp printInfo ]
     setOrientation: NX_PORTRAIT andAdjust: YES ]
   setHorizCentered: NO ]
   setVertCentered: NO ];
  [ Text setDefaultFont: [ Font
     newFont:"Helvetica"
     size:12.0
     style:0
     matrix:NX_FLIPPEDMATRIX ] ];      // In case it has been changed
   [ myText printPSCode: sender ];
   return self;
}
```

```
- setMyText
{
 // Create myText  and set its properties
  [ theScrollView getContentSize:&(contentRect.size) ];
  myText = [ Text newFrame:&contentRect
       text: NULL
       alignment: NX_LEFTALIGNED ];
  [ myText notifyAncestorWhenFrameChanged:YES ];
  [ myText setVertResizable: YES ];
  [ myText setHorizResizable: NO ];
}
@end
```

Figure 7.10 _____

File-viewer window with a file opened—IB implementation

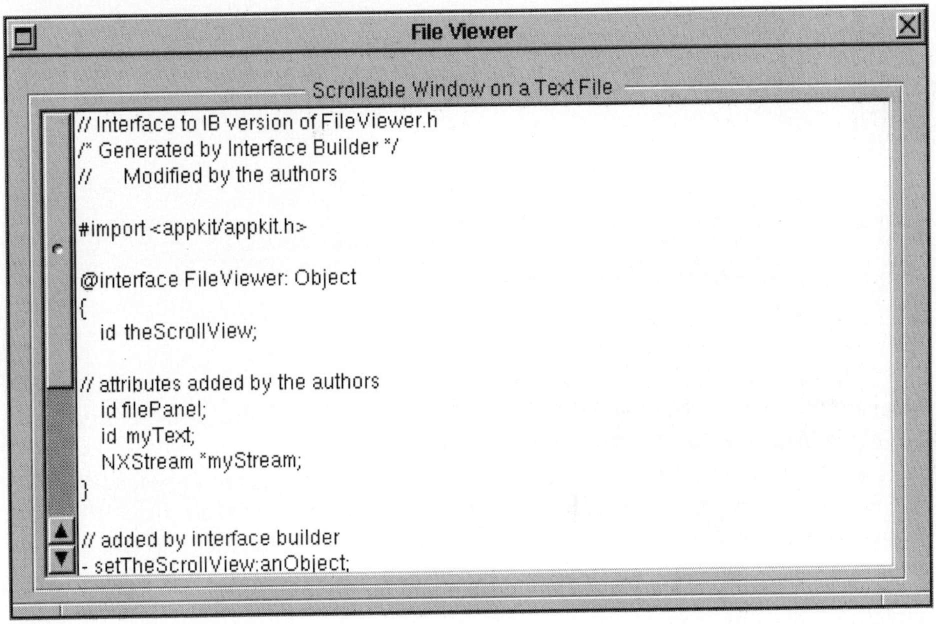

Matrices, Button Cells, and Scrollable, Selectable Lists

The major emphasis for the next example is on how to build a scrollable and selectable list with labels that can be changed. It has many potential applications, such as displaying a list of the messages in a class in a way that any message may be selected (clicked with the mouse) for further information or action. Adding to and deleting from the list are to be shown along with label changes. Of the available interface objects for representing a

Figure 7.11 _____

Initial window for the scrollable matrix of selectable cells

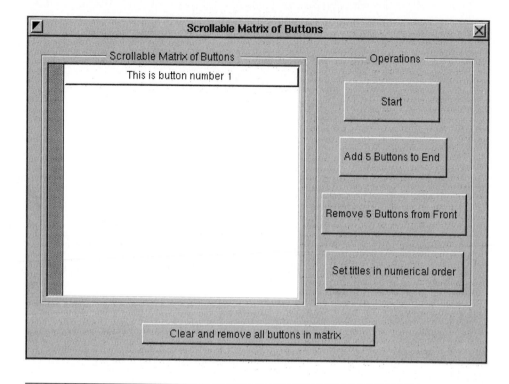

selectable list, the one chosen is a Matrix of ButtonCells. This matrix is to be installed as
the contentView of a ScrollView to make it scrollable.

Figure 7.11 shows the interface for this example, developed entirely within the Interface Builder. A new class, ScrollMatrix, is defined as a subclass of Object. Its only purpose
is to support this example. We first describe the components in the user interface and then
describe attributes and messages for class ScrollMatrix.

The interface shows a Matrix of ButtonCell objects in a ScrollView in a Box on the left
side. The right side shows four Button objects in a Box. A fifth Button is at the bottom.
Although it is desirable for the matrix to be empty initially, we have found no way to do
this operation graphically within the Interface Builder. The matrix thus has one button
cell in it, labeled This is button number 1. It is easily removed as the program is launched.
In this example, the Start button invokes a method that removes this button.

The objects in the interface have the following functions.

• Matrix of ButtonCells.
  This compound object is used for displaying a list of selectable titles. New titles
  (ButtonCells) may be added at any location, or existing titles may be selectively
  removed. The title of any ButtonCell can be changed.

Figure 7.12 _____
Menu for the scrollable matrix of selectable cells

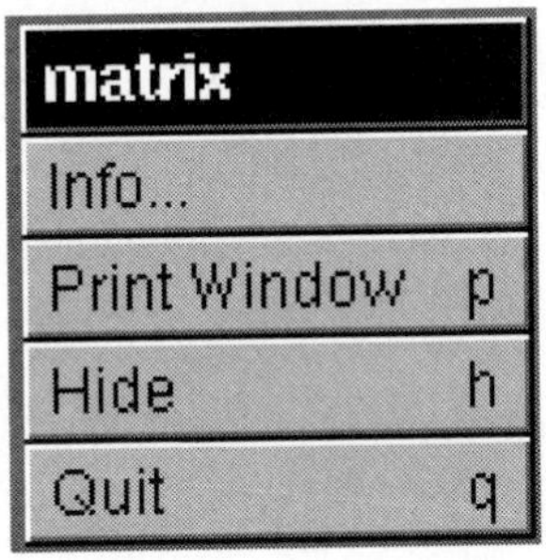

- Boxes labeled "Scrollable Matrix of Buttons" and "Operations".
  These objects are used to group and label other objects in the interface.
- Button labeled "Start".
  This is the first button to press on running the program. It performs some initialization, including

  1. establishing a prototype ButtonCell for the Matrix,

  2. removing the first button to give an empty list,

  3. setting the buttonMatrix as the contentView of the ScrollView, and

  4. redisplaying the empty list.

- Button labeled "Add 5 Buttons to End".
  Pressing this button causes five buttons to be added to the end of the existing list. Each has the initial label Added to end of matrix. The scroll view is large enough to show ten buttons before it must start scrolling.
- Button labeled "Remove 5 Buttons from Front".
  Pressing this button causes the first five buttons in the matrix to be removed. Any adjustments to the scroll view are automatically made.
- Button labeled "Set titles in numerical order".
  This button causes all existing buttons in the matrix to be retitled from button 1 to the actual number showing the order of each button in the list.
- Button labeled "Clear and remove all buttons in matrix".
  This button causes the matrix to be cleared of all buttons and redisplayed as empty.

Figure 7.12 shows the menu options implemented for this example. The option that is specific to this example is Print Window. It may be selected at any time during execution of the example to print the window and all its contents.

Listing 7.7 gives the interface for a class, ScrollMatrix, developed to support this example. To appreciate the support provided by Interface Builder in creating this example, note that the code shown in italics was the only code added by the software developer. Except for an import statement, addition of the new attribute count, and several comments, the entire interface was created by the Interface Builder. This class has the following attributes and key messages, as shown in Listing 7.7.

- scrollView
  This attribute of class ScrollMatrix is an instance of class ScrollView. It is created in the Interface Builder and attached to the scroll view image in the interface.
- buttonMatrix
  This attribute of class ScrollMatrix is an instance of Matrix. It is created in the Interface Builder and attached to a Matrix of ButtonCells.
- prototypeCell
  This attribute is an instance of ButtonCell. It specifies the initial properties of any new button cell added to the buttonMatrix.
- count
  This variable is an int used to store the current number of button cells in the buttonMatrix.
- setScrollView:
  This message is added to the interface for ScrollMatrix by the Interface Builder to support creation of the instance variable scrollView.
- setButtonMatrix:
  This message is added by the Interface Builder to support creation of the instance variable buttonMatrix.
- setPrototypeCell:
  This message is added by the Interface Builder to support creation of the instance variable prototypeCell.
- start:
  This message was added by the software developer to the list of actions for class ScrollMatrix. It is the target message attached to the Start Button.
- add:
  This message was added by the software developer to the list of action messages for class ScrollView and is attached as the target message for the Add 5... Button.
- setTitles:
  This message added by the software developer is attached as the target message for the Set titles in... Button.
- remove:
  This message added by the software developer is attached as the target message for the Remove 5... Button.
- clearButtons:
  This message added by the software developer is attached as the target message for the Clear... Button.
- select:
  This message added by the software developer is attached as the target message for any selected button in the buttonMatrix. When a button is selected, a message indicating its number and title is printed in a shell window.

Listing 7.7 _____

IB source listing for class ScrollMatrix interface—ScrollMatrix.h

```
/* Generated by Interface Builder */
/* Modified by the authors    */
#import <objc/Object.h>
#import <appkit/appkit.h>

@interface ScrollMatrix:Object
{
    id  scrollView;
    id  buttonMatrix;
    id  prototypeCell;
    int count; // number of cells in the buttonMatrix
}
// instance variable initializations, set by IB
- setScrollView:anObject;
- setButtonMatrix:anObject;
- setPrototypeCell:anObject;

// control button target messages
- add:sender;
- start:sender;
- setTitles:sender;
- remove:sender;
- clearButtons: sender;
// buttonMatrix target message
- select:sender;

@end
```

Listing 7.8 gives the source code for the main driver file for the scroll matrix example. It was created entirely by the Interface Builder. It shows how the user-interface objects and connections created within the Interface Builder are loaded into the software system by using the expression [NXApp loadNibSection:"matrix.nib" owner:NXApp];. Basically the code in Listing 7.8 creates a new application, tells it to load its .nib file, tells it to run, frees the application, and exits. This sequence of steps is automatically generated by the Interface Builder for any project as the main driver program.

Implementation details for the "List Selector" are given in Listing 7.9. A template for each method was created by the Interface Builder. Again, the code added by the software developer is shown in italics. Essentially we had to add details for all the action methods: add:, start:, setTitles:, remove:, clearButtons:, and select:.

Figure 7.13 shows the result of pressing the Add 5 Buttons to End button after having first pressed the Start button. Five new buttons are added to the list, each with the default label of Added to end of matrix.

Figure 7.14 shows the resulting window after we have added fifteen buttons to the matrix and pressed the Set titles in numerical order button. The view has been scrolled so that the first three buttons and the last two are not shown.

Listing 7.8 _____

IB source listing for List Selector main driver—matrix_main.m

```
/*
 *    Generated by the NeXT Interface Builder.
 */

#import <stdlib.h>
#import <appkit/Application.h>
void main(int argc, char *argv[])
{
    NXApp = [Application new];
    [NXApp loadNibSection:"matrix.nib" owner:NXApp];
    [NXApp run];
    [NXApp free];
    exit(0);
}
```

Listing 7.9 _____

IB source listing for class ScrollMatrix implementation—ScrollMatrix.m

```
/* Generated by Interface Builder */
/* Modified and implemented
    by the authors                    */
#import "ScrollMatrix.h"
#import <stdio.h>

@implementation ScrollMatrix

// A dummied up list of names for the buttons
static char * names[ 30 ] =
    { "button 1",
      "button 2",
      "button 3",
      "button 4",
      "button 5",
      "button 6",
      "button 7",
      "button 8",
      "button 9",
      "button 10",
      "button 11",
      "button 12",
      "button 13",
      "button 14",
      "button 15",
      "button 16",
      "button 17",
      "button 18",
      "button 19",
```

```
      "button 20",
      "button 21",
      "button 22",
      "button 23",
      "button 24",
      "button 25",
      "button 26",
      "button 27",
      "button 28",
      "button 29",
      "button 30"
   };
// instance variable initializations, set by IB
- setScrollView:anObject
{
    scrollView = anObject;
    return self;
}
- setButtonMatrix:anObject
{
    buttonMatrix = anObject;
    return self;
}
- setPrototypeCell:anObject
{
    prototypeCell = anObject;
    return self;
}
// control buttons target messages
- add:sender
{
  int i;

    [ [ prototypeCell setTitle: "Added to end of matrix" ]
     setType: NX_PUSHONPUSHOFF];
    [ buttonMatrix setPrototype: prototypeCell ];
    for ( i = 0; i < 5; i++ )
     [ buttonMatrix addRow ];
    [ [ buttonMatrix sizeToCells ] display ];
    count = [ buttonMatrix cellCount ];
    printf( "Cell count after add = %d \n", count );
    return self;
}

- start:sender
{
  int i;

// Set prototype and remove initial buttonCell from buttonMatrix
    prototypeCell = [ ButtonCell newTextCell: "Prototype" ];
    [ buttonMatrix removeRowAt: 0 andFree: YES ];
```

(continues)

```
[ scrollView setDocView: buttonMatrix ];
[ [ buttonMatrix superview ] setAutoresizeSubviews:YES ];
[ [ buttonMatrix superview ] setAutosizing:NX_HEIGHTSIZABLE |
  NX_WIDTHSIZABLE ];

count = [ buttonMatrix cellCount ];
[ [ buttonMatrix sizeToCells ] display ];
printf( "Initial cell count = %d\n", count );
return self;
    }

- setTitles:sender
{
   int i;

   count = [ buttonMatrix cellCount ];
   for ( i = 0; i < count; i++ )
   [ [ buttonMatrix cellAt: i : 0 ] setTitle: names[ i ] ];
   [ buttonMatrix sizeToCells ];
   return self;
}

- remove:sender
{
   int i;

   count = [ buttonMatrix cellCount ];
   if ( count >= 5 )
   {
    for ( i = 0; i < 5; i++ )
      [ buttonMatrix removeRowAt: 0 andFree: YES ];
    [ [ buttonMatrix sizeToCells ] display ];
   }
   count = [ buttonMatrix cellCount ];
   printf( "Cell count after removal = %d \n", count );
   return self;
}

- clearButtons: sender
{
   int i;

   for ( i = 0; i < count; i ++ )
       [ buttonMatrix removeRowAt: 0 andFree: YES ];
   [ [ buttonMatrix sizeToCells ] display ];

   count = [ buttonMatrix cellCount ];
   printf( "Cell count after clearing all buttons = %d \n", count );
   return self;
}
```

```
// buttonMatrix target message
- select:sender
{
    int row;

    row = [ buttonMatrix selectedRow ];
    printf( "Selected row %d  with title %s \n", row, [ [ buttonMatrix cellAt: row  : 0 ] title ] );
    return self;
}

@end
```

Figure 7.13 _____

The scrollable matrix after pressing the Add... button

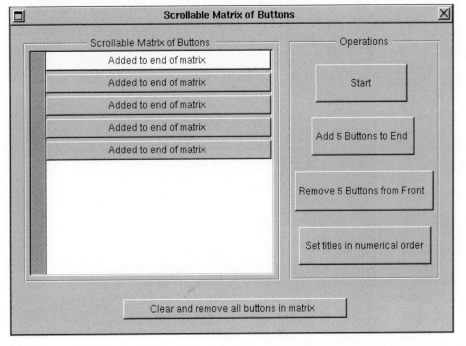

Figure 7.15 shows the display after removing the first five buttons from the matrix. Notice that the scroll bars have disappeared because all ten remaining buttons now fit within the scroll view.

Figure 7.16 shows the display after pressing the Clear and remove all buttons in matrix button.

Figure 7.14 _____

The scrollable matrix after pressing Set titles... button

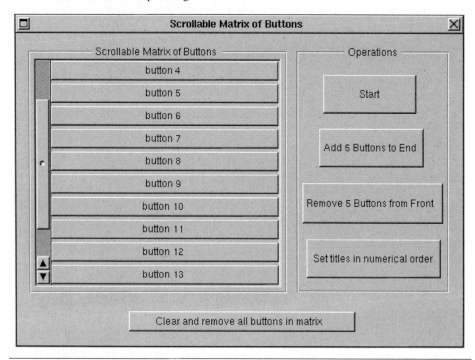

Displaying Graphic Images

Graphic images on the NeXT come in three flavors:

- Views
  Instances of View or its subclasses. A View is rectangular and has a drawing area that is specified by its frame. Each view can draw itself according to method drawSelf::.

- Controls
  Controls are instances of Control or subclasses of Control. Controls can do everything views can do (Control is a subclass of View), but they have the added feature of user interaction. A control also has an associated icon that may be created from a Bitmap instance. Control icons are automatically printed when the controls are printed.

- Bitmaps
  Instances of Bitmap or its subclasses. A bitmap has a rectangular frame, a name and an integer type. Bitmaps are drawn into the *focused* view using *composite* methods. Bitmaps may be displayed on the screen within a view using a variety of compositing rules. Key methods in Bitmap are composite: toPoint: and composite: fromRect: toPoint: .

Figure 7.15 _____
The scrollable matrix after pressing the Remove ... button

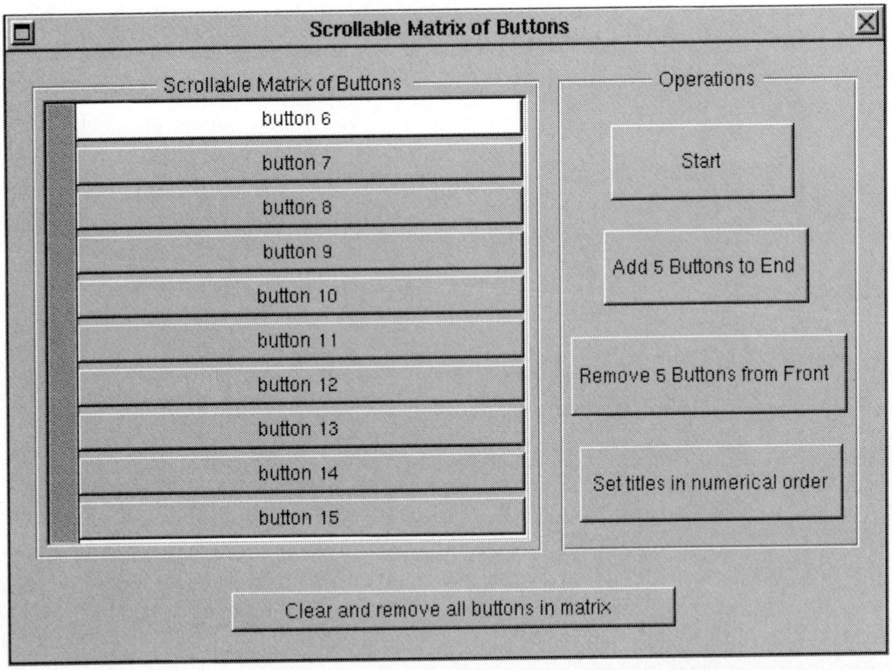

Figure 7.16 _____
The scrollable matrix after pressing the Clear... button

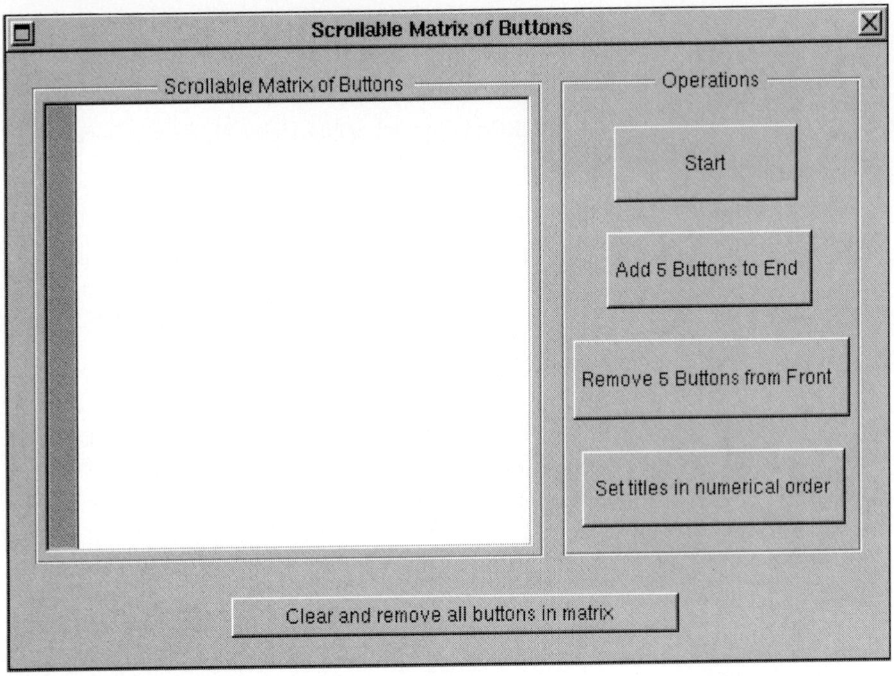

In this section we describe the properties of bitmaps and present two examples of their use. In the first example, the bitmap image is displayed within a view at a specified location with a specified compositing rule. The image is passive: it cannot respond to events. In the second example, bitmap images are displayed as the icons for controls. This makes them able to respond to events and to be automatically printed when the control is printed.

Bitmaps. Bitmaps are instances of class Bitmap, which is a subclass of Object. Bitmaps may be created and initialized in a number of ways, using methods in class Bitmap. In addition there are several supporting C functions for manipulating bitmap images and files. A summary is given below for the class Bitmap, followed by a list of the supporting C functions.

Summary of class **Bitmap**:

Attributes:

NXRect	frame;	// The rectangular frame of the bitmap
char	*iconName;	// The name of the bitmap
int	type;	// The type of the bitmap (there are 4 types)

Notice that the actual data for the bitmap is not an attribute. The image can, however, be accessed by using methods in class Bitmap. Factory methods exist for the creation of Bitmap objects either with name references or as objects with type id. The image for a bitmap may come from several sources, including the operating system or a TIFF file.

Methods exist for displaying, archiving, and accessing attributes of Bitmaps. A complete description is given in the NeXT documentation.

List of C functions supporting images:

Functions for copying an image:

void   NXCopyBits (int gstate, const NXRect *aRect,
                                        const NXPoint *dPoint)

Functions for dealing with bitmap images:

void   NXImageBitmap (const NXRect *rect, int pixelsWide,
                                        int pixelsHigh, int bps, int spp, int config,
                                        int mask, const void *data1, const void *data2,
                                        const void *data3, const void *data4,
                                        const void *data5)

void   NXReadBitmap (const NXRect *rect,int pixelsWide,
                                        int pixelsHigh, int bps, int spp, int config,
                                        int mask, void *data1, void *data2, void *data3,
                                        void *data4, void *data5)

void   NXSizeBitmap (const NXRect *rect, int *size,
                                        int *pixelsWide,   int *pixelsHigh, int *bps,
                                        int *spp, int *config, int *mask)

Functions for dealing with TIFF files:

void *   NXReadTIFF (int imageNumber, NXStream *stream,
                                       NXTIFFInfo *info, void *data)

void   NXWriteTIFF (NXStream *stream, NXImageInfo
                                       *image,   void *data)

int   NXGetTIFFInfo (int imageNumber, NXStream *stream,
                                       NXTIFFInfo *info)

Direct Display versus Icons on Cells. Bitmap images may be displayed as passive objects within a focused view. As passive objects, they do not respond to events, and they are not automatically printed when their enclosing view is printed. A bitmap image becomes an active object when attached to a Control object as its icon. Additionally, the image is automatically printed when the control is printed.

In this section we first present an example that represents passive bitmap images. A second example illustrates the attachment of images to controls. These examples were created with the assistance of the Interface Builder. Figure 7.17 shows the interface for the passive bitmap example. The interface contains the following objects.

Figure 7.17 _____
User interface for the passive bitmap example

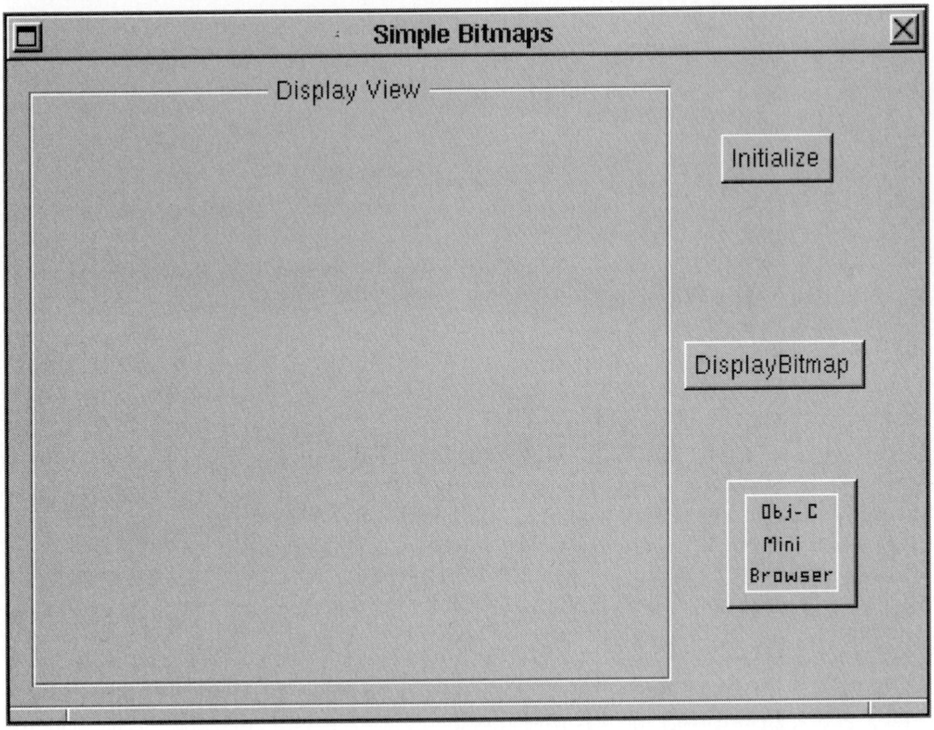

- Display View
  This object is an instance of Box. It is the focused view within which the bitmap images are to be displayed.
- Initialize Button
  The purpose of this Button is to create a Bitmap object from a TIFF file.
- DisplayBitmap Button
  The purpose of this Button is to display the Bitmap object at several locations within the focused view.
- Obj-C ... Button
  This button does nothing except show how a Bitmap image may be attached and displayed as the icon of a Button (a Button is a Control).

A simple class called Test is created to contain the attributes and messages related to this example. The components of class Test are listed in Listing 7.10 and described below.

- aBitmap
  This attribute is an instance of class Bitmap. It is instantiated from a TIFF file.
- displayView
  This attribute is an instance of class Box. It was created in the Interface Builder and attached to the image for a Box.
- setDisplayView:
  This message was added by the Interface Builder to initialize the attribute displayView.
- initialize:
  This message added by the software developer is attached as the target message for the Initialize Button. It creates aBitmap from the file browser2.tiff.
- displayBitmap:
  This message added by the software developer is attached to the DisplayBitmap Button as its target message. It causes aBitmap to be composited at nine different locations within displayView, using the compositing rule NX_SOVER (display the source over the background).

Listing 7.11 gives the main driver file source listing. It was created entirely by the Interface Builder.

Listing 7.12 gives the details for the implementation of class Test for this example. Much of the structure of this listing was also provided by the Interface Builder. Of particular interest are the following messages that deal with bitmaps; the first creates the bitmap, and the second displays it at aPoint within the focused view.

```
aBitmap = [ Bitmap newFromTIFF: "browser2.tiff" ];
[ aBitmap composite: NX_SOVER toPoint: &aPoint ];
```

Figure 7.18 shows the result of running the example after pressing the Initialize button and then pressing the DisplayBitmap button. The bitmap images stay with the window when it is moved; however, resizing the window in its current implementation

Listing 7.10 _____

Interface to class Test for passive bitmap example—Test.h

```
// Test class for passive display of bitmaps
/* Generated by Interface Builder */
// modified by the authors

#import <objc/Object.h>

@interface Test:Object
{
    id  aBitmap;
    id  displayView;
}

- setDisplayView: anObject;
// methods added by the authors
- displayBitmap:sender;
- initialize: sender;

@end
```
_____

Listing 7.11 _____

Listing for main driver for passive bitmap example—simple_main.m

```
/*
 *      Generated by the NeXT Interface Builder.
 */

#import <stdlib.h>
#import <appkit/Application.h>

void main(int argc, char *argv[])
{
    NXApp = [Application new];
    [NXApp loadNibSection:"simple.nib" owner:NXApp];
    [NXApp run];
    [NXApp free];
    exit(0);
}
```
_____

Listing 7.12 _____

Implementation for class Test for passive bitmap example—Test.m

```
// Implementation for Test class for passive display of bitmaps
/* Generated by Interface Builder */
// Modified by the authors

#import "Test.h"
#import <appkit/appkit.h>
```
(continues)

```
@implementation Test
- setDisplayView: anObject
{
  displayView = anObject;
  return self;
}

// methods added by the authors
- displayBitmap:sender
{
  int i,j;
  NXPoint aPoint;
  [ displayView  lockFocus ];
  for ( i = 0; i < 3; i++ )
   for ( j = 0; j < 3; j++ )
    {
      aPoint .x =  50 + 100 * i;
      aPoint .y = 10 + 100 * j;
      [ aBitmap composite: NX_SOVER toPoint:  &aPoint ];
    }
  [ displayView unlockFocus ];
    return self;
}

- initialize: sender
{
  aBitmap = [ Bitmap newFromTIFF: "browser2.tiff" ];
  return self;
}

@end
```

causes the bitmap images to be lost (they are redisplayed by pressing the DisplayBitmap button again). The image on the lower-right button is always redisplayed automatically since it is an icon for that button.

The next example illustrates in more detail how bitmap images may be attached as icons to control objects to give them active status. The border and background attributes of buttons are adjustable, so it is possible to have a button appear to be nothing more than a graphic image. The interface for the icon bitmap example is shown in Figure 7.19. It consists of the following components within its main window.

- Initialize Button
  This Button is pressed to create three bitmap objects. Two are used as icons to be displayed on selected buttons, and the third is displayed on the Initialize Button and SetIcons Button after they are pressed to show that they have already been used.
- SetIcons Button
  This Button when depressed causes one of two bitmap images to be attached as icons for the buttons in the matrix. They are also displayed.

Figure 7.18 _____

Result of pressing the Initialize and DisplayBitmap buttons—passive example

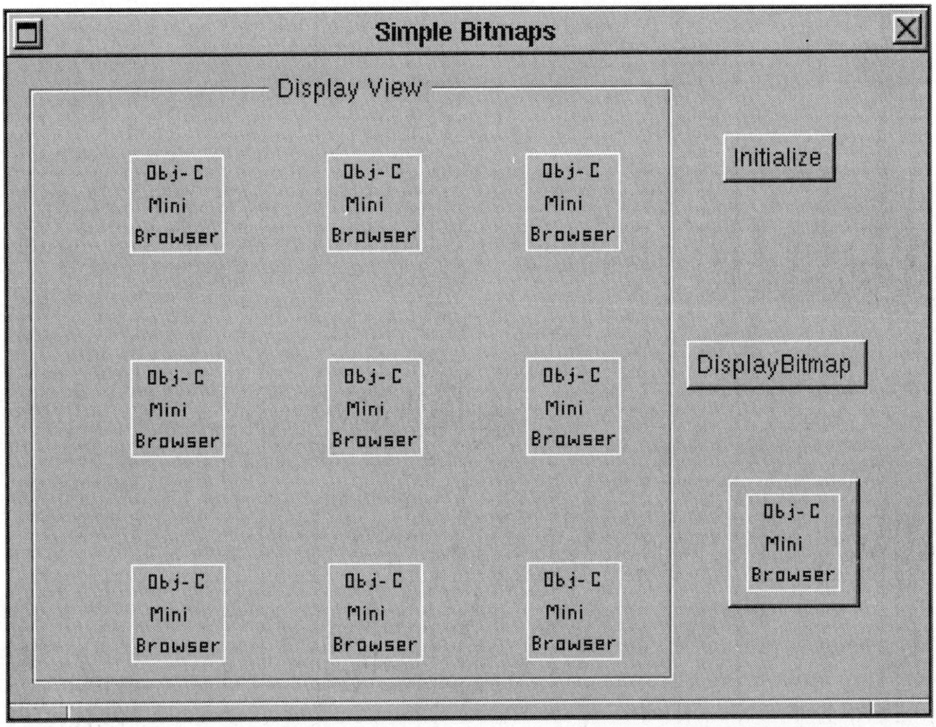

- Print Button

  This Button causes the window and its views to be printed.

- Matrix of ButtonCells

  This object is a 6-row by 7-column Matrix of ButtonCell objects. Initially, as shown in the figure, the ButtonCell objects are simply given the title Button. ButtonCell objects may have both an icon and a title. In this example the title disappears when the icon is displayed.

As in the previous example, a class called Test is created to support attributes and operations for this example. Listing 7.13 gives the interface source file for the example.

A description follows of the attributes and messages in Listing 7.13. All three attributes were added to the class using the Interface Builder and attached to the appropriate objects shown in Figure 7.19.

- matrix

  An instance of Matrix, this attribute is attached to the Matrix of ButtonCells in the user interface for this example.

Listing 7.13 _____
Interface to class Test for bitmap icon example—Test.h

```
// Interface to class Test for Control icons - Test.h
/* Generated by Interface Builder */
// Modified by the authors

#import <objc/Object.h>

@interface Test:Object
{
    id  matrix;
    id  initButton;
    id  setIconsButton;
}

- setMatrix:anObject;
- setInitButton: anObject;
- setSetIconsButton: anObject;
// methods added by the authors
- initialize:sender;
- setIcons:sender;

@end
```

- initButton
  This attribute is an instance of class Button and is attached to the Initialize Button.
- setIconsButton
  This attribute is an instance of class Button and is attached to the SetIcons Button in the user interface.

Messages setMatrix:, setInitButton: and setIconsButton: were automatically added by the Interface Builder and implemented completely in the implementation file. The last two messages were added by the software developer to class Test and attached as target messages to the appropriate buttons.

- setMatrix:
  This message initializes attribute matrix.
- setInitButton:
  This message initializes attribute initButton.
- setSetIconsButton:
  This message initializes attribute setIconsButton.
- initialize:
  This message is a target for the Initialize Button. It creates three Bitmap objects from three TIFF files. It then sets the icon for the Initialize Button to indicate that it has been pressed.

Figure 7.19 _____
User interface for icon bitmap example—from Interface Builder

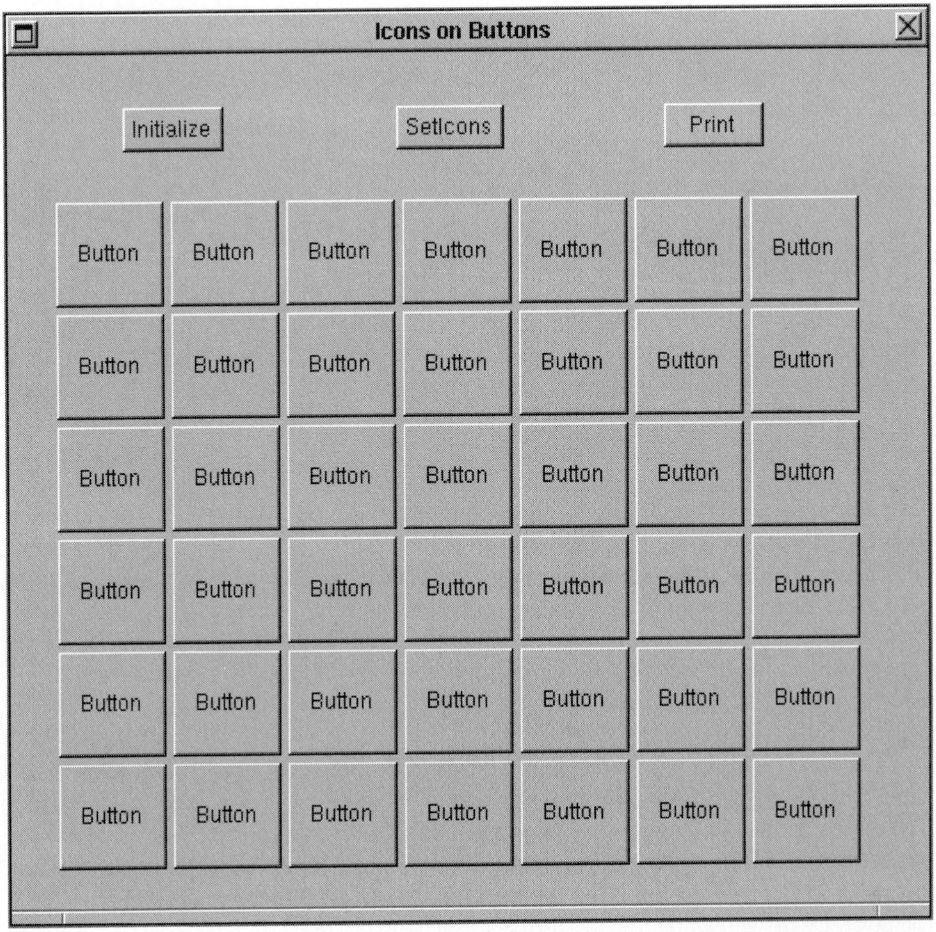

• setIcons:
  This message is a target for the SetIcons Button. It causes one of two bitmaps to
  be displayed on the button in matrix. It then sets the icon for the SetIcons Button
  to indicate that it has been pressed.

  Notice that no attribute exists in class Test for the button labeled Print. It is created as
part of the Interface Builder .nib file and is connected to the main window for the application with target message smartPrintPSCode:.
  The main drive file listing is given in Listing 7.14. It was created entirely by the
Interface Builder.

Listing 7.14 _____

Listing for main driver for bitmap icon example—bitmaps_main.m

```
/*
 *    Generated by the NeXT Interface Builder.
 */

#import <stdlib.h>
#import <appkit/Application.h>

void main(int argc, char *argv[])
{
    NXApp = [Application new];
    [NXApp loadNibSection:"bitmaps.nib" owner:NXApp];
    [NXApp run];
    [NXApp free];
    exit(0);
}
```

The implementation details for class Test are given in Listing 7.15 This example shows a different method for the creation of Bitmap objects than was used in the passive bitmap example. Factory method addName: fromTIFF: creates a new Bitmap object from a TIFF file that is referenced by a name string instead of an id object name.[8] This name string is then used as a parameter for manipulating the bitmap. Message setIcon: uses the bitmap name as a parameter to set the icon for the Button objects. Message setIcon: at: : uses the bitmap name to set the icon of a buttoncell at a specified coordinate location in matrix.

The final result of this example is shown in Figure 7.20. The Bitmap object with name browser created from TIFF file browser2.tiff is displayed as the icon for all Button-Cell objects in the first three rows of the matrix. The Bitmap object with name willy is created from TIFF file willy.tiff and displayed as the icon for all ButtonCell objects in the last three rows of the matrix.[9] The Bitmap object with name done is created from TIFF file done.tiff and shown on the Initialize and SetIcons buttons.

This chapter has presented several examples that show how the Interface Builder saves time in the development of a graphical user interface for any application and how it increases productivity by providing templates for developer-generated classes. Although it is possible to use the Application Kit classes directly, as was demonstrated for the file-viewer example, the Interface Builder greatly simplifies their use. Other kit classes, such as the Music Kit and Sound Kit classes, may be easily integrated into applications by using the Interface Builder also.

_____

[8] TIFF (tagged-image file format) images may be created by graphics editors or by scanners.

[9] File willy.tiff is provided on the NeXT computer. The other TIFF files were created by the authors.

Listing 7.15 _____

Implementation for class Test for bitmap icon example—Test.m

```
// Implementation for class Test for Control icons - Test.m
/* Generated by Interface Builder */
// Modified by the authors

#import "Test.h"
#import <appkit/appkit.h>

@implementation Test

- setMatrix:anObject
{
    matrix = anObject;
    return self;
}

- setInitButton:anObject
{
    initButton = anObject;
    return self;
}

- setSetIconsButton:anObject
{
    setIconsButton = anObject;
    return self;
}
// method details added by the authors
- initialize:sender
{  // Create three Bitmap objects with names

    [ Bitmap addName: "browser" fromTIFF: "browser2.tiff" ];
    [ Bitmap addName: "willy" fromTIFF: "willy.tiff" ];
    [ Bitmap addName: "done" fromTIFF: "done.tiff" ];
    [ initButton setIcon: "done" ];
    return self;
}

- setIcons:sender
{
    int i, j;
    for ( i = 0; i < 7; i++ )
    {
     for ( j = 0; j < 3; j++ )
     [ matrix setIcon: "browser" at: j : i ];
     for ( j = 3; j < 6; j++ )
     [ matrix setIcon: "willy" at: j : i ];
    }
```

(continues)

```
    [ setIconsButton setIcon: "done" ];
    return self;
}

@end
```

Figure 7.20 _____
Result of pressing Initialize and SetIcons buttons—icon bitmap example

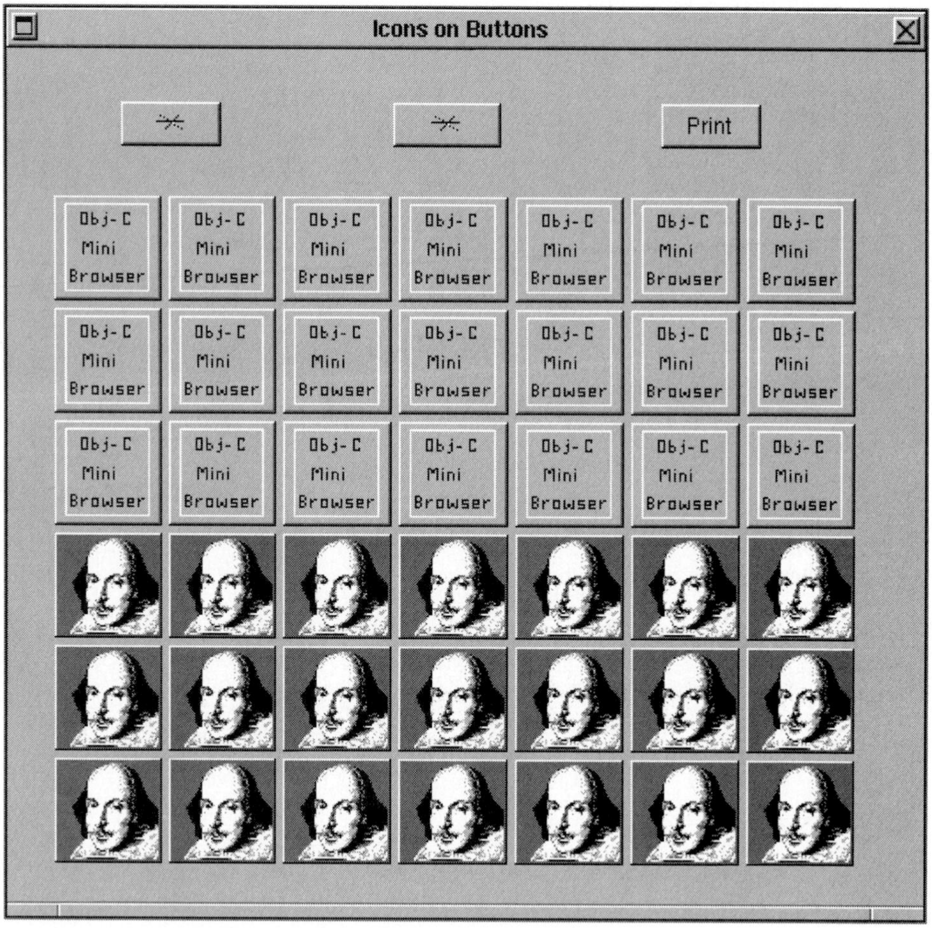

The Interface Builder is an excellent example of a true visual programming application. In the next chapter we present more features of this powerful tool through additional
examples of applications.

## CHAPTER 8

More Examples of Object-Oriented Problem Solving and Objective-C

In this chapter we present two more major examples of the object-oriented approach to problem solving using Objective-C and the NeXT environment. The first example shows how to use the Interface Builder to create a graphic interface for the *Swamp Runner* simulation discussed in earlier chapters. Only the user interface features of the *Swamp Runner* are presented since details of the design and the primary classes were presented earlier.

A second, new example presents the specification, design, and partial implementation of a new application called MiniBrowser, a window-oriented application for browsing Objective-C classes. Historically, it was one of the first applications we developed on the NeXT computer because of its utility for examining the details of class descriptions.

The user interface for the MiniBrowser was created with the Interface Builder. In addition it uses some of the concepts presented in Chapter 7 for dealing with text files, scrollable views, selectable lists, and the printer.

8.1 A GRAPHIC INTERFACE FOR SWAMP RUNNER, USING INTERFACE BUILDER

The Objective-C implementation of the *Swamp Runner* simulation presented in Chapter 5 was based on supporting classes in Stepstone's ICPak 101. It did not include the display of graphic images, only character images. In this chapter we show how to use the Interface Builder to create a graphic user interface for *Swamp Runner* that can display graphic images. In addition it shows how the user may select a path through the swamp by clicking on quicksand cells to make them path cells. Adaptation of selected ICpak 101 classes for use on the NeXT was also accomplished for the *Swamp Runner* simulation.[1]

---

[1] Partial implementations were accomplished for classes IdArray, OrdCltn, Point, Sequence, and Set.

One of the original objectives for *Swamp Runner* was to allow the user to select a path through the swamp, subject to constraints on the nature of the path. In Chapter 5 the path is generated automatically, subject to those same rules. We now show how easy it is to let the user select a path through the swamp by representing the swamp as a Matrix of ButtonCells with icons.

The following discussion does not present a complete solution. It only shows how to set up a graphic interface for the application and how to tie selection of a ButtonCell to modification of its icon.[2]

From the Interface Builder we develop a display of the swamp, as shown in Figure 8.1. In the box labeled The Swamp (containing a matrix of 15 x 20 button cells) there is a single button cell shown to indicate the size of the swamp cells. This is for illustrative purposes only. All other button cells in the 15 x 20 matrix have no borders, which is the desired mode. In the actual user interface, none of the button cells have visible borders, so that the matrix no longer appears to be a collection of individual buttons. This effect is desirable for this application.

Figure 8.2 shows the Inspector window for the ButtonCell objects from the Interface Builder. It shows how various options may be set for the button cells. Significant options for this example are that the button cell is to have a centered icon, is of type On/Off, is not disabled (it is therefore selectable), and is not bordered. The inspector also shows that a file called QuicksandImage.tiff contains the default icon for the button cell and that an alternate icon is given in file PathImage.tiff.

In Figure 8.3 we see an Inspector window for the Matrix object that is the swamp. The prototype is an instance of ButtonCell that is the prototype cell of which the matrix is composed. Its attributes are established by clicking on the inspect button for the prototype. Mode list means that multiple cells may be selected in the matrix.

Next we describe the interface objects shown in Figure 8.1 in more detail. The interface is divided into four major functional areas, with appropriate objects grouped within a separate Box for each area. The four areas are: Control, Swamp Runners, The Swamp, and Statistics, as indicated by the labels for the four boxes.

Control objects include two independent buttons that are instances of class Button.

- Initialize

  This button is pressed to initialize the *Swamp Runner* simulation. It displays a QuicksandImage for each button cell in the swamp and enters a mode where the user may create a path through the swamp by selectively clicking on swamp cells.

- Run

  This button is pressed to start the simulation. It uses the selected swamp traveler to traverse the swamp. The default is the Dimwit. Progress of the traveler is shown graphically by displaying its image on each path cell traversed for a given attempt. When the traveler steps in quicksand, the path is regenerated, and a new attempt begins. When the traveler has successfully traversed the swamp, its image will appear on each cell in the path.

---

[2] The icon for each button was created using a graphics editor provided on the NeXT, called *Icon*.

Figure 8.1 _____
User interface for the *Swamp Runner* simulation

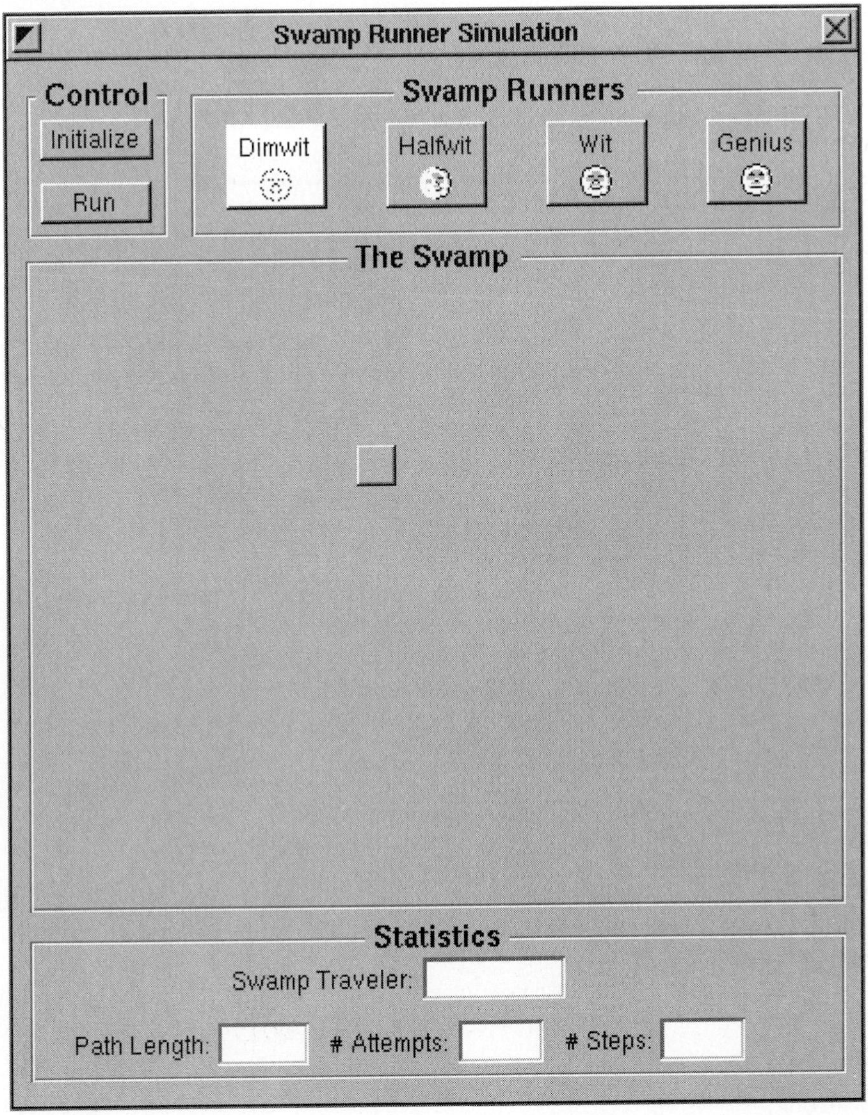

Swamp Runners objects consist of a matrix of button cells operating in the radio mode (only one may be selected at any time).

• The initial selection is for the Dimwit swamp traveler. The user may choose any of the four swamp travelers prior to pressing the Run button.

• The button cells in this matrix are initialized to have both a label and an icon. The icons represent the appropriate kind of swamp traveler and are the images for the traveler.

Figure 8.2 _____
ButtonCell inspector window in the Interface Builder

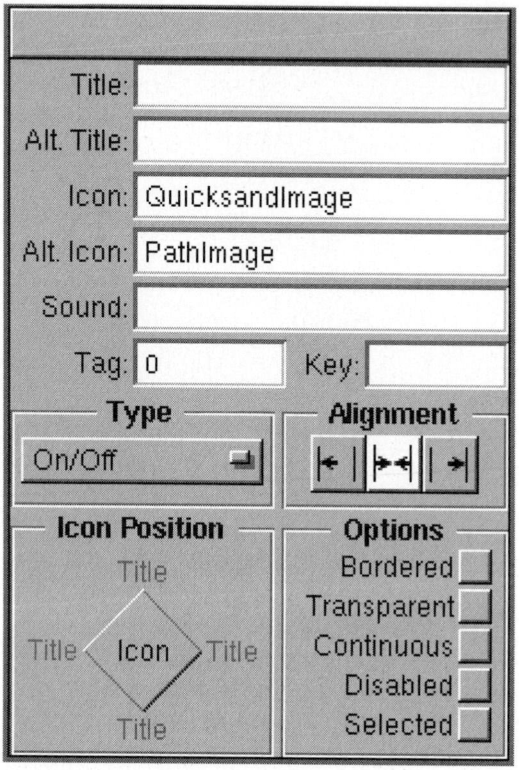

The Swamp consists of a 15×20 matrix of button cells as described earlier. Upon initialization, the default icon representing a quicksand cell is displayed on each button cell. The alternate icon, representing a path cell, is displayed on the cells that are part of the generated path.

Statistics consists of four instances of class Form. Each form includes a title and a FormCell that is the text area. These objects are used to display statistical parameters for a given run.

- Swamp Traveler:
  The window will display a text string indicating the kind of swamp traveler.
- Path Length:
  This window will display the number of path cells in the path.
- # Attempts:
  This window displays the number of attempts required by the swamp traveler to traverse the swamp.
- # Steps:
  This window displays the total number of moves required by a swamp traveler to traverse the swamp.

Figure 8.3 _____

Matrix inspector window, showing attribute selection for the swamp

Figure 8.4 _____

Menu options for *Swamp Runner*

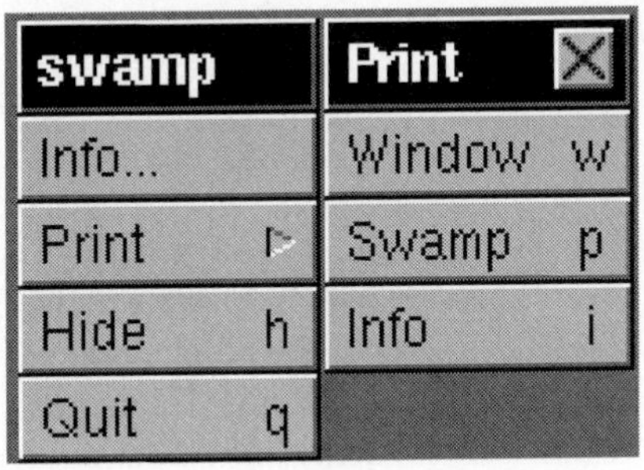

Figure 8.4 shows the menu options established for *Swamp Runner*. The print options allow the user to print the entire window or just the swamp. Both menu options are attached directly to target objects and target methods, using the Interface Builder. More specifically, the Print window option sends the message smartPrintPSCode: to the mainW-

Figure 8.5 _____
Example of a user-generated path through the swamp

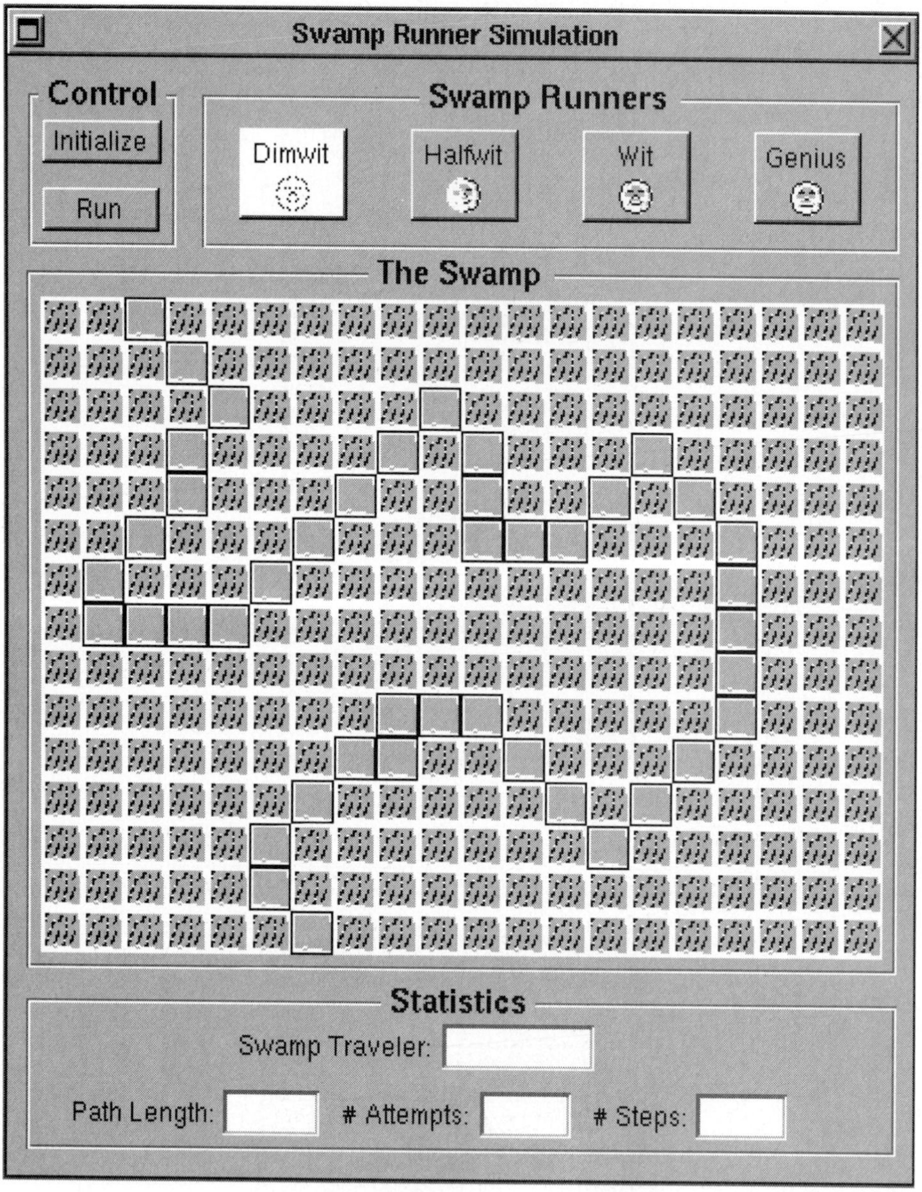

indow of the interface. Option Print swamp sends the message smartPrintPSCode: to the Matrix object that is the swamp.

An example of a path generated by the user is shown in Figure 8.5. The user creates the path by clicking on a swamp cell to change it from a quicksand cell to a path cell. The system enforces the same constraints as the automatic path-generation logic

Figure 8.6 _____

Resulting display after a traversal by a Wit

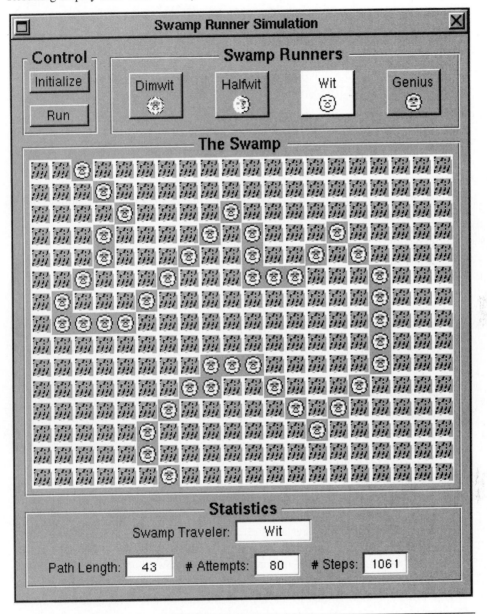

described in Chapter 2. If the user clicks on a cell that is not a valid choice for the next path cell, the cell image remains that of a quicksand cell. The images for quicksand cells and path cells were generated with a graphics editor application and saved as TIFF files.

Figure 8.6 shows the final result of running the simulation for a Wit swamp traveler. The Wit image is displayed along the path, and the statistical results are shown in the forms at the bottom of the window. During a simulation run, the swamp traveler image is displayed as the icon of a given swamp cell for each step taken. This gives a graphic depiction of the actual progress of the swamp traveler. When a traveler steps in quicksand, the path is cleared, and the graphic display is repeated for the next attempt.

A major goal in this section has been to show how graphic objects may be interactive and respond to events by attaching bitmap images to button cells. This example further illustrates the power of the Interface Builder for building graphical user interfaces. In the next section we describe the MiniBrowser application.

8.2 NEEDS STATEMENT FOR MiniBrowser— AN OBJECTIVE-C CLASS BROWSER

There is a need for a window-based, interactive browser to view Objective-C class hierarchies and individual class protocol. This browser may also serve as a learning tool to explore the functionality of Objective-C classes and as a demonstration of an object-oriented solution to a software system.

Initially, this software system provides only the ability to examine existing classes. It does not provide the ability to modify the protocol of an existing class or the ability to create new classes. The following is a list of the features that characterize additional properties and functionality for the MiniBrowser software system.

Paths

- The browser maintains a default list of paths to search for class descriptions.[3] The user may modify this default list as the first step in running the application.

Window and subwindows

- The main window has three subwindows, two of which have an associated two-choice radio button set. The three subwindows are *class window*, *message window*, and *display window*. (See figure 8.7 for a view of the main window.)
- The *class window* displays an alphabetical list of all classes in the working path list. This subwindow has a two-choice radio button set that selects either interface or implementation files. A class in this scrollable window may be selected with the mouse for additional information.
- The *message window* displays a list of message selectors for a selected class in the class window. A message selector in this scrollable window may be selected with the mouse for additional information. The window has a two-choice radio button set that toggles between factory and instance message selectors.
- The *display window* is used to display text information that is dependent on the status of selected items in the other two subwindows and on menu options available for selected items.

---

[3] Class descriptions are given in interface files and implementation files. These files may be located in several different directories. It is desirable to be able to examine both of these files for any class in any directory.

8.3 SPECIFICATION FOR MiniBrowser

In this section we present a more detailed specification of the performance parameters for the MiniBrowser. Specifications are presented in six categories:

1. system considerations,
2. directory paths,
3. display windows,
4. controls,
5. menu options, and
6. operations summary.

1. *System considerations.*
   The MiniBrowser software system is a window-based, graphics-oriented application that provides user interaction through selection by a mouse and keyboard. It is constrained to meet the following system requirements.

   - The hardware and software environment must support interactive windows.
   - The hardware and software system must support user interaction with a pointing device such as a mouse.
   - The software system is designed to work with UNIX-style directories and file handling.
   - Components in the user interface for this software system are dependent upon the existence of supporting classes or software that implements their functionality. If these classes do not exist, they must be implemented.

2. *Directory paths.*
   With the realization that classes in an Objective-C software system may be scattered in different directories on the storage medium, the MiniBrowser maintains a list of directories in which to search for class descriptions. This path list has the following properties, some of which are dependent on the organization of classes on the NeXT computer.

   - The path to the common classes, /usr/include/objc, is always included in the path list by default. It cannot be removed.
   - The path to the Application Kit classes, /usr/include/appkit, is always included in the path list by default. It cannot be removed.
   - A maximum of five additional directory paths may be added by the user to the path list. A prompter window is opened when the application is started that allows the user to modify the five additional paths.
   - User-modified directory paths are remembered between subsequent executions of the MiniBrowser application.

3. *Display windows.*
   The main window of the MiniBrowser has three subviews that group interface objects into three categories. These subviews are given the labels Class Window, Message Window, and Display Window. The purpose of each window is described below.

- The Class Window displays an alphabetical list of all classes (with extensions) in the working path list. Classes are identified by file names that begin with an uppercase letter and have either .h or .m as an extension. This convention for class files allows the system to distinguish between Objective-C class interface files and C header files. It requires consistent file-naming conventions for user-defined classes. The Class Window subview has a two-choice radio button set that selects either interface or implementation files.

  Many of the classes provided with an Objective-C system may not have an implementation source file. For this reason, the list of classes for the implementation option is often shorter than for the interface option. A class in this window may be selected with the mouse for additional information. This window is scrollable.

- The Message Window displays a list of message selectors for a selected class in the class window, including messages inherited from all classes in its hierarchy, in reverse hierarchical order (e.g., selected class followed by its parent followed by its parent all the way up to Object). If no class is selected in the class window, then the message window is empty. Message selectors are given without parameters to keep the list concise and easy to scan.

  A message selector in the Message Window may be selected with the mouse for additional information. If the implementation option is in effect for the class window, the list of message selectors for a selected class will be complete; however, those messages from parent classes whose implementation is not available will show up as light gray and not be selectable.

  This window is scrollable. It has a two-choice radio button set that toggles between factory and instance message selectors.

- The Display Window is used to display text information that is dependent on the status of selected items in the other two subviews and on menu options available for selected items. Additional details on the use of this window are given under item 5 (Menu options) below. It is a scrollable window.

4. *Controls.*

   The main window has two sets of controls for selection of options by the user. The two controls have the following functions.

   - The Class File Type control allows the user to select either interface or implementation files to be listed for all classes in the path list. When the Interface option is chosen, the Class Window displays an alphabetized list of all class interface files with an .h extension. When the Implementation option is chosen, the Class Window displays an alphabetized list of all class implementation files in the path list with an .m extension.

   - The Message Type control allows the user to select either factory or instance messages for a selected class in the Class Window. These messages are displayed alphabetically for the selected class and all its parent classes in reverse hierarchical order.

5. *Menu options.*

There are several menu options for the MiniBrowser, which are organized into six major menu options, three of which have submenus. The following options are available with the described functionalities.

∘ Info...

This menu option displays an information window.

∘ Edit

This menu option has a submenu with four options for editing text. Each option works as it should; however, no option for saving any changes to text is provided. This menu option does allow the user to cut and paste text from the MiniBrowser to another text application. The submenu options follow:

— Cut

Remove a selected block of text.

— Copy

Copy a selected block of text to a buffer without removing it.

— Paste

Copy the contents of a buffer into the text at the cursor location.

— Select All

Select all the text in the active view.

∘ Print

This menu option has a submenu with the following four options for printing.

— Browser Window

Print the main window with all its subviews.

— Class List

Print the contents of the Class Window. This gives an alphabetized printout of all classes in the directories of the path list. The printout lists either those classes for which interface files exist or those classes for which implementation files exist. The list is also displayed in the Display Window.

— Message List

Print the list of all message selectors for a chosen class, including all inherited messages, in reverse hierarchical order. Either factory messages or instance messages are printed, depending on the choice of the Message Type control. The list of messages is also displayed in the Display Window.

— Display Text

Print all the contents in the Display Window.

∘ Classes

This menu option has a submenu with the following options:

— Attributes

Show in the Display Window all the attributes for a selected class, including inherited attributes, in reverse hierarchical order. These attributes are
taken directly from the interface file for a class and its parent classes.
The list includes all comments for attributes embedded in the class
description.

— Class Listing

This option displays the contents of the class file in the Display Window
for a selected class. It displays either the interface file or implementation
file, depending on the state of the Class File Type control.

— Dependents

This menu option has a submenu that is currently empty of options. This
is a planned maintenance item that will provide options for examining
dependencies among classes and messages.

° Hide

This option is predefined on the NeXT Computer to hide the windows of an
application while keeping it active.

° Quit

This option gracefully quits the application.

6. *Operations.*

The following operations describe the functional requirements for the MiniBrowser.

° When the MiniBrowser application is started, it displays the main window and
its subviews. In addition it displays a window that allows the user to add/mod-
ify up to five additional directory paths. The window includes an acceptance
button that must be pressed before the application can continue.

° Once the user has accepted the directories for the path list, the application
displays an alphabetized list of all class interface file names in the Class
Window. The default control settings are Interface for the Class File Type
control and Factory for the Message Type control.

° Selection of a class name causes two things to happen:

1. the hierarchy for the selected class is shown in the Display Window, and

2. the list of message selectors for that class is displayed in the Message
Window.

Messages in all parent classes are shown in groups according to the reverse
hierarchy. A nonactive button is displayed between each class group to identify
it.

° Selection of a message name causes the details for the message to be displayed in the Display Window. Details are from the interface or implementation, depending on which option is chosen for the Class File Type control.

° All remaining operations are from menu selections. Menu functions are
described above.

○ It is desirable to have more than one browser open at any given time. This requires multiple access to open files by the active browser applications. This capability is supported by the NextStep/UNIX environment.

From this specification for the MiniBrowser application, we proceed to discuss some of the design issues.

8.4 DESIGN FOR MiniBrowser: THE USER INTERFACE

The first step in the design of the MiniBrowser application is to construct a user interface with all the required windows, views, controls, and menu options. This is easily achieved with the Interface Builder. The resulting interface is shown in Figure 8.7. Objects in the interface include the following.

- *Main window*
  The main window, labeled Objective-C MiniBrowser, consists of three major groupings of interface objects. These are Class Window, Message Window, and Display Window.

- *Initial Conditions window*
  This supporting window, labeled Initial Conditions, is used to add up to five new directory paths to the path list. It contains a TextField object with the title Enter directories to browse, five Form objects (each contains a FormCell) for entering directory paths, and a Button object labeled Directory Selections Completed for pressing when the selection is completed.

- *Class window*
  This subview consists of a Box with the label Class Window that groups several objects. The enclosed window is a ScrollView with a Matrix of ButtonCells as its contentView. The button cells are borderless and there is initially only one button in the matrix. The matrix operates in radio mode: only one button may be selected at any given time. This matrix and a similar matrix in the Message window operate like the scrollable matrix of selectable cells described in Chapter 7 under "Matrices, Button Cells, and Scrollable, Selectable Lists."

  This subview also contains a radio button set that is the control for selecting either interface or implementation files for the class list. The default mode is interface files. This object is also implemented as a Matrix of two ButtonCells. The button cells have both a title and an icon, whose relative positions may be changed as desired.

- *Message window*
  This subview consists of a Box with the label Message Window that groups several objects. The enclosed window is a ScrollView with a Matrix of Button-Cells as its contentView. The button cells are borderless, and there is initially only one button in the matrix. The matrix operates in radio mode.

  This subview also contains a radio button set that is the control for selecting either factory messages or instance messages for the message list. The default

Figure 8.7 _____

Interface for the MiniBrowser created with the Interface Builder

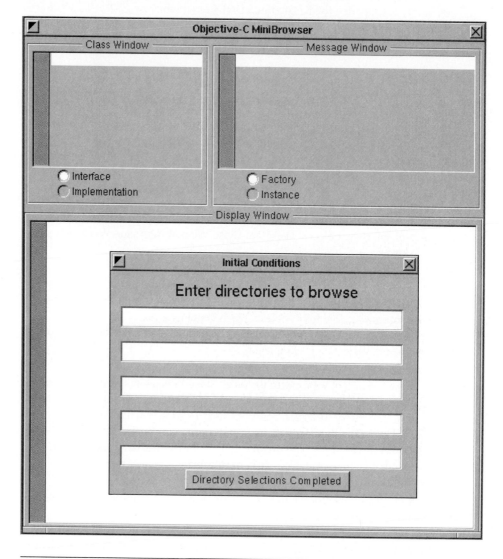

mode is factory messages. This object is also implemented as a Matrix of two ButtonCells. The button cells have both a title and an icon, whose relative positions may be changed as desired.

• *Display window*

This object is a Box with the label Display Window. It encloses a ScrollView that contains an instance of Text as its contentView. This window is used to display textual information.

Figure 8.8(a) and (b) _____
Menu options for the MiniBrowser application

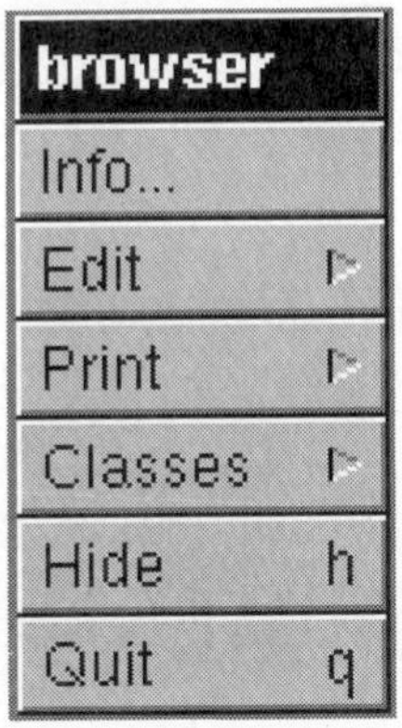

(a)

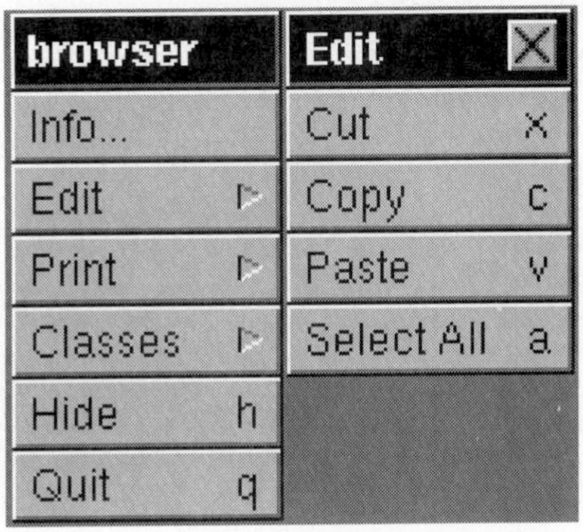

(b)

Menu options are shown in Figure 8.8. The main menu is shown in Figure 8.8*a*. Submenus are shown in Figure 8.8*b* for the Edit option, in Figure 8.8*c* for the Print option, and in Figure 8.8*d* for the Classes option. The Dependents submenu is a planned maintenance item.

Within the Interface Builder, several new classes were added to support this application. Instances were created and connections made between most of the interface objects and their appropriate outlets or target actions. These connections are described in more detail in the next sections.

Figure 8.8(c) and (d) _____

Menu options for the MiniBrowser application

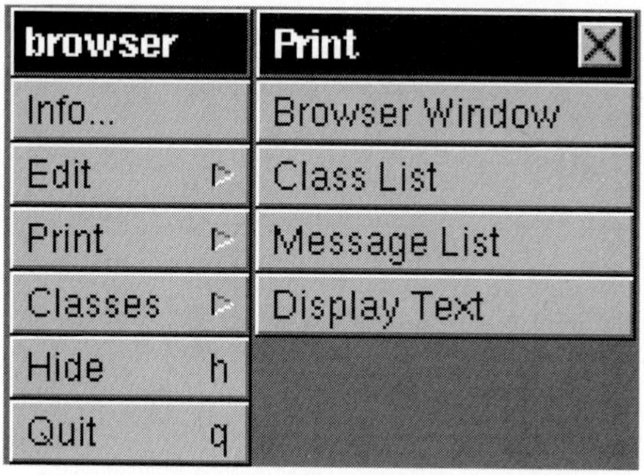

(c)

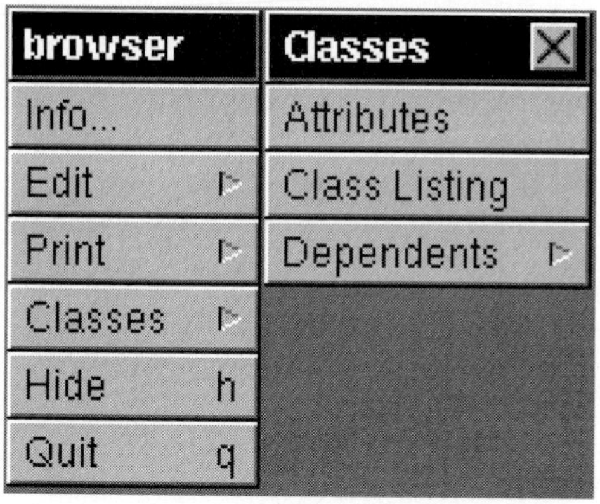

(d)

8.5 MiniBrowser APPLICATION: OBJECTS, ATTRIBUTES, AND STRUCTURE

In this section, additional design details are given, using methods described earlier. First, a description of the primary objects is presented, followed by a discussion of their attributes. Supporting objects are identified, and finally, a class structure is presented for the MiniBrowser application.

Primary Objects

There is one and only one primary object in this application; that object is the browser (primary object aMiniBrowser is an instance of class MiniBrowser). It has a number of supporting objects that it uses to perform its various functions. Many of these supporting objects are defined by interface classes in the Application Kit.

Since the browser must search file directories for class-description files and must access these text files to extract information, two supporting objects are defined to perform these operations. These objects are described by the new classes FileTable (for manipulating lists of files) and FileScanner (for scanning text files).

Attributes for the Primary Objects

The following attributes are listed and described for primary object aMiniBrowser.

- classWindow
  An instance of ScrollView, this attribute is the scrollable view in the Class Window group of interface objects.

- classList
  An instance of Matrix, this attribute is the matrix of button cells that represents a selectable list of classes in the Class Window. Titles of the button cells will be class names. This attribute is the contentView of classWindow.

- classWindowType
  This object is also a Matrix that is the radio button set for selecting interface or implementation files in the Class Window.

- messageWindow
  An instance of ScrollView, this attribute is the scrollable view in the Message Window group of interface objects.

- messageList
  This attribute is the list of message selectors in the Message Window. It is implemented as a Matrix of ButtonCells. Titles of the button cells will be message selectors. This attribute is the contentView of messageWindow.

- messageWindowType
  This attribute is the radio button set in the Message Window for selecting between factory and instance messages. It is a Matrix of ButtonCells.

- displayWindow
  An instance of ScrollView, this attribute is the scrollable view in the Display Window group of interface objects.

- displayText
  This attribute is an instance of Text. It is used for displaying textual information and is the contentView of displayWindow.

- fileTable

  This attribute is an instance of class FileTable. It maintains several lists of file names that represent classes in the active directory paths. It is implemented as a pointer to class FileTable to support dynamic binding.

- fileScanner

  This attribute is an instance of class FileScanner. It contains protocol for scanning text files to extract attributes, message selectors, or method details for class descriptions. It is implemented as a pointer to class FileScanner to support late binding.

- prototype

  This attribute is an instance of class ButtonCell. When adding new button cells to a matrix, the prototype is useful for establishing properties of that button cell. This attribute supports the addition of new button cells to classList and messageList.

- pathForm1, pathForm2, pathForm3, pathForm4, pathForm5

  These five attributes are the five Form objects in the Initial Conditions window. They are used for entering new path names.

- selected

  This int is used as a Boolean. It is set to 1 when a class name is selected in the classList.

All connections between interface objects and their appropriate attributes for the primary objects were made using the Interface Builder, with the exception of displayText. It is created by a startup message that is sent to aMiniBrowser when the application is launched. Other initializations are also performed by this message. They are described in more detail in Section 8.6.

Supporting Objects

In addition to the interface objects, supporting objects for the MiniBrowser consist of the contained objects fileTable and fileScanner. A brief description of their major attributes and operations is given below.

Summary for supporting object fileTable:

Purpose:

- Keep tables of directory paths and class file names.
- Keep path names for message selectors for rapid access.
- Maintain storage for up to 400 strings representing either class names or message selectors.
- Used by both the classList and messageList to support their operations.

Selected attributes:

- fileTable1[50]

  Holds file names for the common classes

- fileTable2[100]
  Holds file names for the Application Kit classes
- fileTable3[300], fileTable4[300], fileTable5[300], fileTable6[300], fileTable7[300]
  Hold file names for the five user-defined directory paths
- table[400]
  Intermediate storage for elements to be displayed in either classList or message-
  List windows

Primary operations:

- Methods for creating the tables of file names
- Methods for accessing selected file names
- Methods for sorting file names alphabetically for display

  Summary for supporting object fileScanner:

Purpose:

- Open selected class files for processing.
- Provide logic for scanning a file to select and display message lists.
- Provide logic for finding and displaying the details for a selected method.

Selected attributes:

- f
  A pointer to FILE, this attribute provides access to a file.
- ch
  This char is the last character read from the file.
- index
  This int is an index into the file.

Primary operations:

- Methods for getting the next message selector from a class file
- Methods for extracting the list of attributes from a class file
- Methods for getting the entire contents of a class file
- Methods for extracting details of a method from a class file

Supporting objects fileTable and fileScanner provide much of the low-level detail for
file handling and string manipulation.

Class Structure for MiniBrowser

The structure of the MiniBrowser software system is given by its hierarchy of classes, as
shown in Figure 8.9. In addition to the interface classes in the Application Kit, there are
three new classes added to represent the browser, the file table, and the file scanner.

Figure 8.9 _____

Hierarchy of classes for the MiniBrowser application

Object

--- Primary classes (created for this application) ---

  MiniBrowser
  FileTable
  FileScanner

--- Supporting classes (part of NextStep) ---

  Responder
   Application
   View
     Box
     Text
     ScrollView
     ClipView
     Control
       Scroller
       Matrix
         Form
  Cell
    ButtonCell
    MenuCell
    SliderCell
  Window
    Panel
    Menu

Note: Additional support classes are used as part of the NextStep environment.

_____

8.6 *KEY METHODS FOR MiniBrowser*

There are a number of methods in class MiniBrowser for initializing the instance variables. The following key methods are also part of this class. Many are attached as target actions to interface objects.

- startup2
  This method was added to support the new feature of allowing a user to select up to five additional directory paths for finding class descriptions. This feature was added as a maintenance item after the software system was working. The method is invoked in the main driver program. It sets up the table of directories in FileTable.

- startup
  This method is also invoked on start-up of the software system. It is now

invoked as the last step in the details of method startup2. Its purpose is to perform the following operations:

- ∘ Create an instance of Text and assign to displayText.
- ∘ Set parameters for prototype.
- ∘ Set the classList and messageList matrices to allow no selection.
- ∘ Remove the existing single button cell from classList and messageList.
- ∘ Make classList the contentView of classWindow.
- ∘ Make messageList the contentView of messageWindow.
- ∘ Create the initial class list from all class file names in the path list.
- ∘ Display the alphabetized list of class interface files in classList.

- selectClassFileType:
  This method is the target of the Class File Type control in the Class Window. It clears the message window, checks the state of the control, and sends message headerClassWindow (if interface was selected) or implementationClassWindow (if implementation was selected).

- headerClassWindow
  This message is sent by message selectClassFileType:. It searches the directory paths to find all interface files representing class descriptions, sorts them alphabetically, installs their names as titles on the classList matrix, and redisplays the matrix in the Class Window.

- implementationClassWindow
  This message is sent by message selectClassFileType:. It searches the directory paths to find all implementation files representing class descriptions, sorts them alphabetically, installs their names as titles on the classList matrix, and redisplays the matrix in the Class Window.

- selectMsgType:
  This message is the target message for the Message Type control. It causes the message window to be cleared and redisplayed for the factory or instance messages of a selected class. It invokes the message setClass: that does all the work.

- selectClass:
  This message is the target for the classList matrix; it is also invoked by message selectMsgType:. It starts a chain of events that causes the appropriate files to be searched for messages to which a selected class can respond. These include those in the class file plus all the files of its parent classes. It then invokes message display: hierarchyDisplay, which causes the hierarchy of the selected class to be displayed in displayWindow. Finally it invokes message message-Window.

- messageWindow
  This message is invoked by message selectClass:. It uses the list of messages for a selected class to modify titles for the matrix messageList. It then displays the matrix with its new titles.

- selectMessage

  This message is the target for the matrix messageList. When a message is selected in the list, it invokes this method. It then uses the fileScanner to locate details of the selected message and displays those details in the displayWindow.

- clearCellsIn: aMatrix

  This supporting message is used by several others. Its purpose is to clear all button cells in aMatrix. It is used to clear either classList or messageList by various operations.

- display: aString

  This supporting message is sent by several other methods to display aString in displayWindow.

- displaySelClassHier:

  This message is the target for menu option Classes—Attributes. It uses the file scanner and file table objects to get the attributes of a selected class, including attributes inherited from all superclasses of the selected class. These attributes are then displayed in displayWindow.

- displayClassFile:

  This message is the target for menu option Classes—Class Listing. It opens the file for the selected class and displays its entire contents in the displayWindow.

- printClassList:

  This message is the target for menu option Print—Class List. It displays the entire list of classes from classList in the displayWindow and then invokes the printer to print the list of classes.

- printMessageList:

  This message is the target for menu option Print—Message List. It displays the complete list of messages given by messageList for a selected class in the displayWindow and then invokes the printer to print a complete list of all messages for the selected class.

- printDisplayText:

  This message is the target for menu option Print—Display Text. It invokes the printer and prints the contents of displayWindow.

There are several other messages in the protocol for class MiniBrowser that play a supporting role. A complete list is given in the following section.

8.7 SELECTED IMPLEMENTATION DETAILS FOR MiniBrowser

In this section we present the interface file and main driver program for the MiniBrowser application.

Listing 8.1 shows details for the interface to class MiniBrowser.

Listing 8.2 shows details of the main driver program for the MiniBrowser application. It was generated by the Interface Builder and modified to include the initialization of the system using message startup2.

Listing 8.1 _____
Source code for the interface to class MiniBrowser

```
-------------------------
// File: MiniBrowser.h
// Interface to MiniBrowser class

#import <objc/Object.h>
#import "FileTable.h"
#import "FileScanner.h"

@interface MiniBrowser : Object
{
// Outlets generated for interface builder
    id displayText;
    id classList;
    id messageWindow;
    id displayWindow;
    id classWindow;
    id messageList;
    id classWindowType;
    id messageWindowType;
    id pathForm1;
    id pathForm2;
    id pathForm3;
    id pathForm4;
    id pathForm5;

// Other instance variables
    FileTable *fileTable;        // Used to hold and manipulate tables of files
    FileScanner *fileScanner;    // Used to scan files
    int selected;                // Set to 1 when file selected in Class Window
    id prototype;                // ButtonCell prototype
}

// Startup methods
- startup: sender;
- startup2;

// Methods to support interface builder
- setPathForm1: anObject;
- setPathForm2: anObject;
- setPathForm3: anObject;
- setPathForm4: anObject;
- setPathForm5: anObject;
- setClassList:anObject;
- setMessageWindow:anObject;
- setDisplayWindow:anObject;
- setClassWindow:anObject;
- setMessageList:anObject;
- setClassWindowType:anObject;
- setMessageWindowType:anObject;                          (continues)
```

```
- displaySelClassDeps:sender;
- displaySelClassHier:sender;
- selectMsgType:sender;
- selectClassFileType:sender;
- displayClassFile:sender;
- selectClass:sender;
- selectMessage:sender;

// Window methods
- clearCellsIn: aMatrix;
- implementationClassWindow;
- headerClassWindow;
- messageWindow;
- display: (char*) aString;

// Printing methods
- printClassList: sender;
- printMessageList: sender;
- printDisplayText: sender;

@end
```

Listing 8.2 _____
Source code for the main driver file for the MiniBrowser application

```
/* File:  browser_main.m
 *     Generated by the NeXT Interface Builder.
   Modified by the authors
 */

#import <stdlib.h>
#import <appkit/Application.h>
#import "MiniBrowser.h"

void main(int argc, char *argv[])
{
    id miniBrowserObject;
    NXApp = [Application new];
    [NXApp loadNibSection:"browser.nib" owner:NXApp];

    // Added by the authors
    miniBrowserObject = NXGetNamedObject("MiniBrowserInstance", NXApp );
    [ miniBrowserObject startup2 ];

    [NXApp run];
    [NXApp free];
    exit(0);
}
```

8.8 EXAMPLE OPERATION FOR MiniBrowser

This section illustrates with figures the operational details for the MiniBrowser software system. Figure 8.10 shows the initial display on launching the #application. The Initial Conditions window has been edited to include a path to the classes for the MiniBrowser, so that we may view those classes as well as the Application Kit and common classes.

Figure 8.10 _____
Initial display of the MiniBrowser application

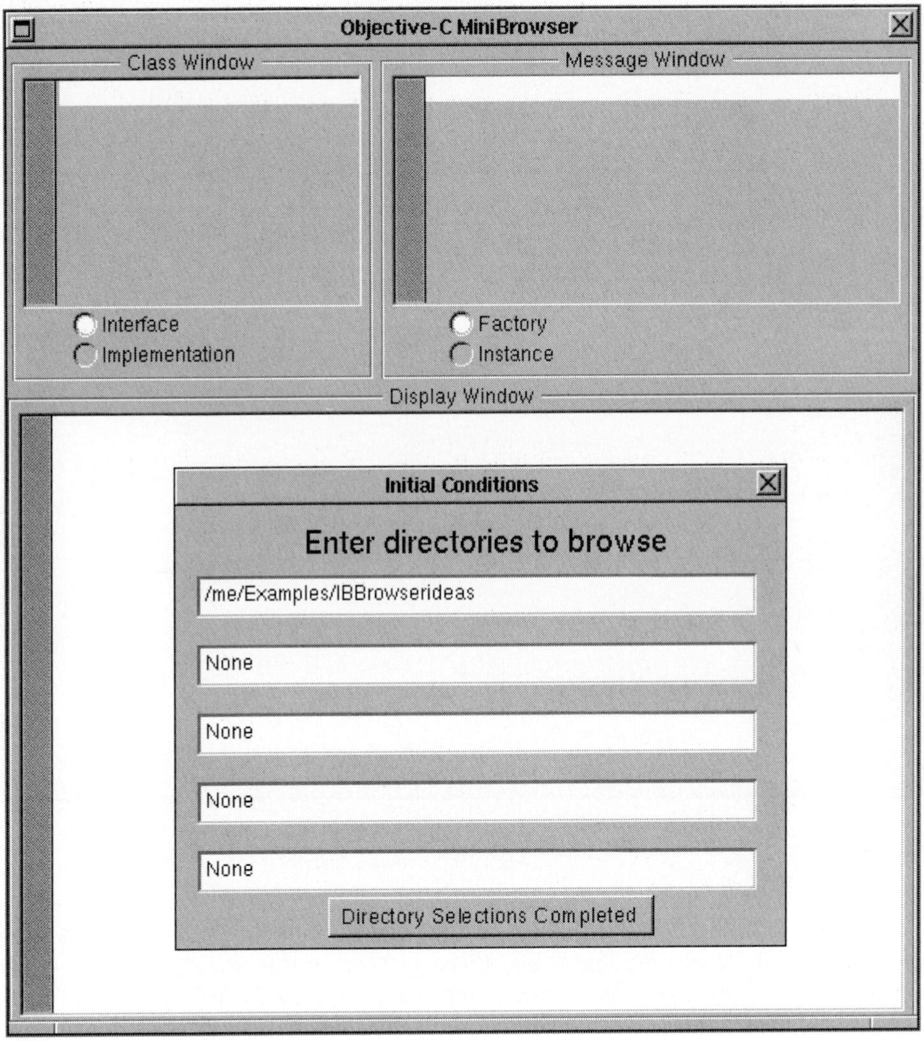

Figure 8.11 _____

Result of selecting a class for display of its factory messages

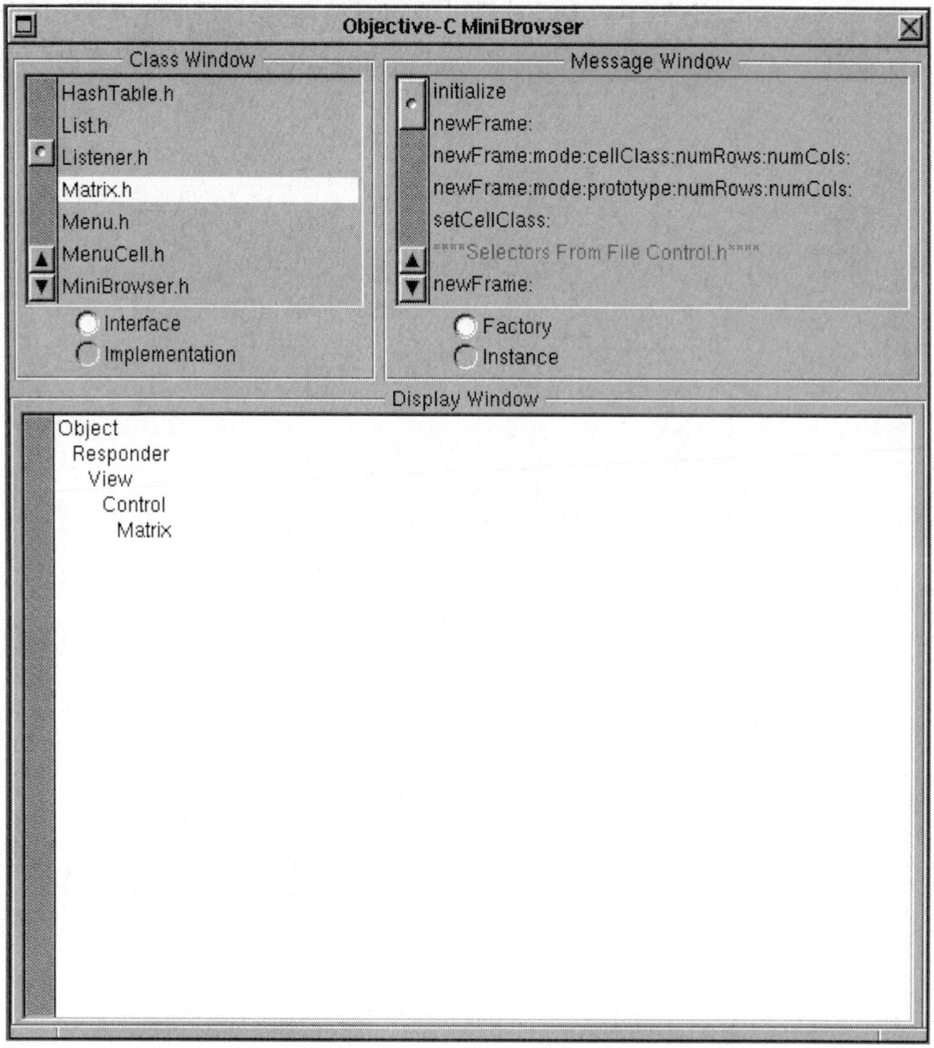

Figure 8.11 shows how the browser displays the list of messages for a selected class and its hierarchy. Notice the line in the Message Window that says ****Selectors From File Control.h****. Message selectors below this line are those inherited by Matrix from its parent class, Control. Further scrolling of the window shows messages inherited from the

Figure 8.12
Result of selecting a message of a selected class

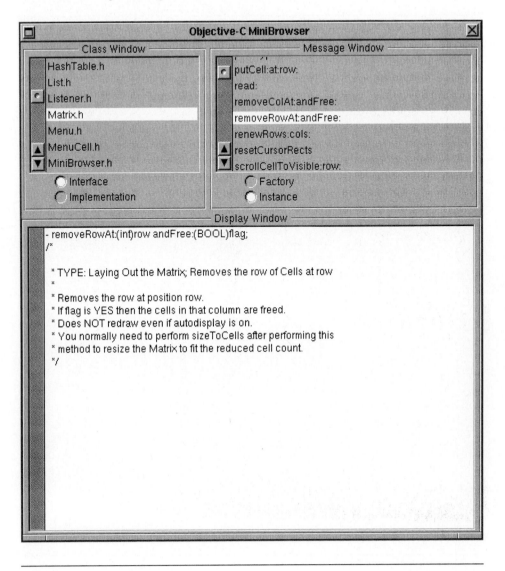

other parent classes, View, Responder, and Object, in reverse hierarchical order. The messages are factory messages.

Figure 8.12 shows the result of selecting a message for class Matrix. The interface for the selected message, including any comments, is displayed in the displayWindow.

Figure 8.13
Initial list of implementation files

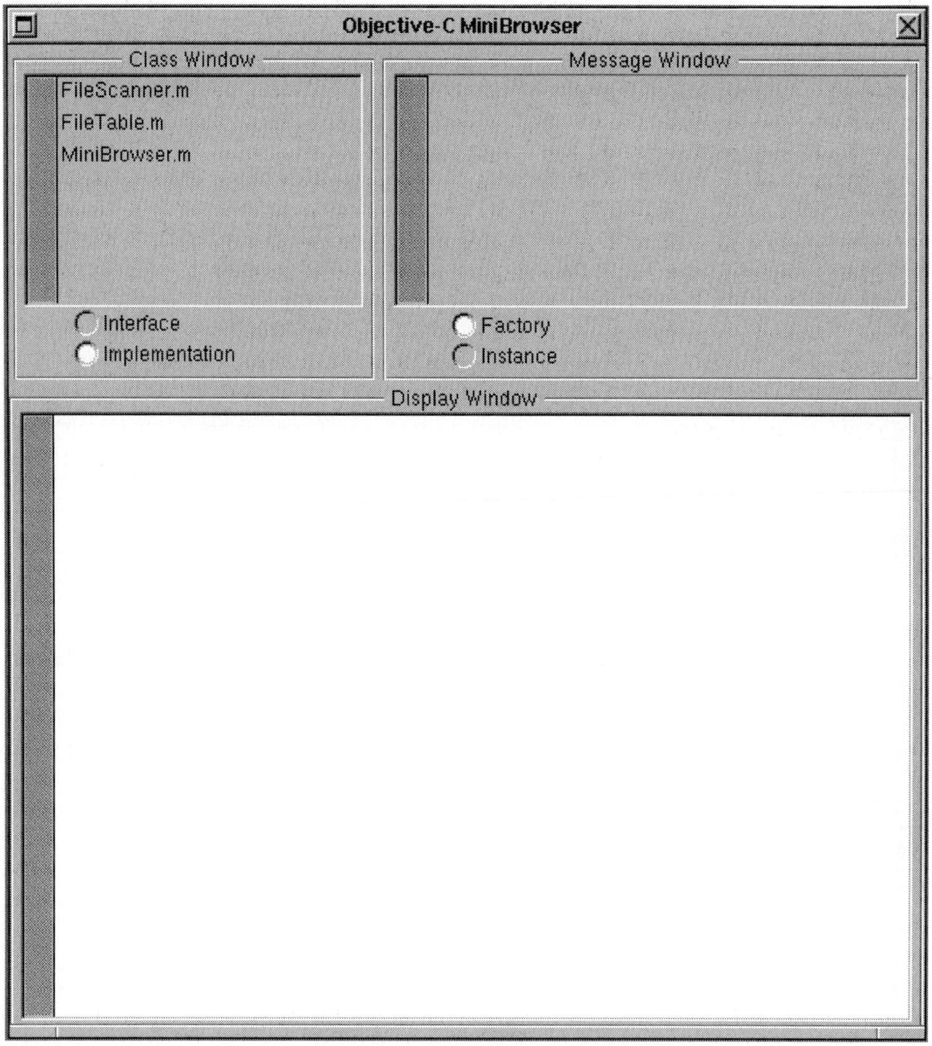

Objective-C MiniBrowser		

Class Window
FileScanner.m
FileTable.m
MiniBrowser.m

○ Interface
○ Implementation

Message Window

○ Factory
○ Instance

Display Window

Figure 8.13 shows an initial list of classes for which implementation files are available. Notice that none of the Application Kit classes appear in this list since their implementation files are not present. When no class name is selected, as shown, the messageList window is empty, as is the displayWindow.

Figure 8.14 _____

Implementation details for a selected message

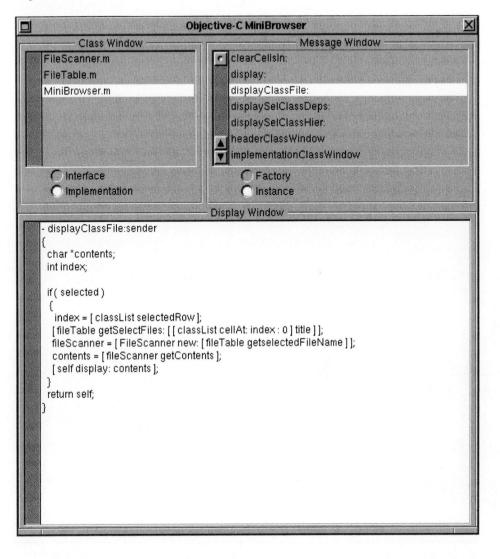

Figure 8.14 illustrates how the method details may be viewed for a selected instance message in the implementation file.

Figure 8.15 shows a list of attributes, including all inherited attributes, for a selected class. This is the result of a menu option. The attributes are shown in the displayWindow in groups according to the reverse hierarchy of the class.

Figure 8.15 _____

List of attributes for a selected class

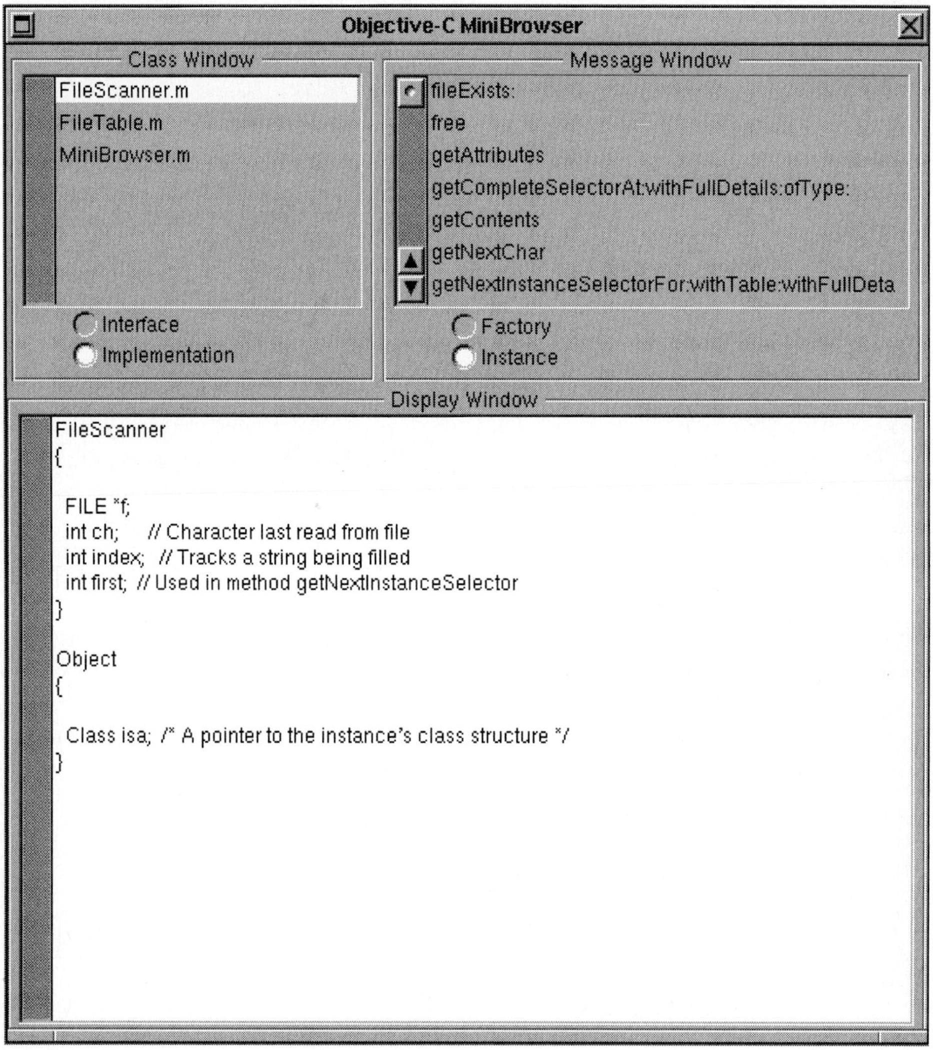

This chapter has presented additional details for two medium-sized applications that use graphic interface objects. The interface objects shown in the examples are part of the Application Kit classes on the NeXT computer and were assembled using the Interface Builder.

Interface File Listings
for Class Object

This appendix presents listings for the interface files for class Object for both the NeXT and Stepstone implementations of Objective-C.

Listing A.1 _____
Interface file for Object—NeXT version

```
/*
Object.h
Copyright 1988, 1989 NeXT, Inc.
DEFINED AS:  A common class
HEADER FILES: <objc/Object.h>
*/

#import "objc.h"
#import "objc-class.h"
#import "typedstream.h"

@interface Object
{
 Class isa;  /* A pointer to the instance's class structure */
}

+ initialize;
+ new;
- free;
- copy;
+ free;
- (const char *) name;
- (unsigned int) hash;
- (BOOL) isEqual:anObject;
- self;
+ class;
+ superClass;
```

```
- class;
- superClass;
- (BOOL) isKindOf: aClassObject;
- (BOOL) isMemberOf: aClassObject;
- (BOOL) isKindOfGivenName: (STR)aClassName;
- (BOOL) isMemberOfGivenName: (STR)aClassName;
+ (int) version;
+ setVersion: (int) aVersion;
+ (BOOL) instancesRespondTo:(SEL)aSelector;
- (BOOL) respondsTo:(SEL)aSelector;
- (IMP) methodFor:(SEL)aSelector;
+ (IMP) instanceMethodFor:(SEL)aSelector;
- perform:(SEL)aSelector;
- perform:(SEL)aSelector with:anObject;
- perform:(SEL)aSelector with:object1 with:object2;
+ poseAs: aClassObject;
- findClass:(STR)aClassName;
- subclassResponsibility:(SEL)aSelector;
- shouldNotImplement:(SEL)aSelector;
- notImplemented:(SEL)aSelector;
- doesNotRecognize:(SEL)aSelector;
- error:(STR)aString, ...;
- awake;
- write:(NXTypedStream *) stream;
- read:(NXTypedStream *) stream;
- finishUnarchiving;

id object_dispose(Object *anObject);
id object_copy(Object *anObject, unsigned nBytes);
id object_realloc(Object *anObject, unsigned nBytes);
Ivar object_setInstanceVariable(id, STR name, void *);
Ivar object_getInstanceVariable(id, STR name, void **);

@end
```

Listing A.2 _____

Interface file for Object—Stepstone version

```
//
//      Runtime Library Class Interface
//      (c) Stepstone 1988. All rights reserved.
//      $Source: d:/objc40/src/runtime/rcs/object.h $
//      $Revision: 2.2 $
//      $Date: 89/07/15 23:56:42 $
//      $State: Exp $
//
#import "objc.h"
#import "mivarargs.h"

@interface Object
{
```

```
@public
 struct _SHARED *isa;
 unsigned short attr;
 unsigned short objID;
}
+  initialize;
+  poseAs: aFactoryId;
+  (unsigned ) ndxVarSize;
+  new;
+  new: (unsigned) arg;
+  free;
+  readFrom:(STR )aFileName;
+  (SHR ) class;
+  (SHR ) self;
+  (SHR ) superClass;
+  (BOOL) isSubclassOf: aClass;
+  (BOOL ) instancesRespondTo:(STR )aSelector;
+  (IMP ) instanceMethodFor:(SEL )aSelector;
-  (STR ) elements;
-  (STR ) describe;
-  (unsigned ) capacity;
-  (BOOL) isStaticInstance;
-  (BOOL) isDynamicInstance;
-  (BOOL) isIndexable;
-  (BOOL) isMarked;
-  awake;
-  initialize;
-  initialize: (unsigned) arg;
-  (unsigned short) identity;
-  release;
-  findClass:(STR )aClassName;
-  idOfSTR:(STR )aClassName;
-  findClass:(STR )aClass requestor:(STR )requestor;
-  (STR ) name;
-  (STR ) str;
-  (unsigned ) size;
-  (unsigned ) hash;
-  (BOOL ) isEqual:anObject;
-  (BOOL ) notEqual:anObject;
-  (int ) compare:anObject;
-  (int ) invertCompare:anObject;
-  (BOOL ) isSame:anObject;
-  (BOOL ) notSame:anObject;
-  free;
-  (BOOL ) storeOn:(STR )aFileName;
-  asGraph:(BOOL )unique;
-  show;
-  print;
-  printString:(STR )aBuf;
-  printOn:(IOD )anIOD;
-  self;
```

(continues)

- (SHR) class;
- (SHR) superClass;
- (BOOL) isKindOf:aClass;
- (BOOL) isMemberOf:aClass;
- (BOOL) respondsTo:(STR)aSelector;
- shallowCopy;
- deepCopy;
- copy;
- (IMP) methodFor:(SEL)aSelector;
- perform:(STR)aSelector;
- perform:(STR)aSelector with:anObject;
- perform:(STR)aSelector with:obj1 with:obj2;
- perform:(STR)aSelector with:obj1 with:obj2 with: obj3;
- subclassResponsibility;
- subclassResponsibility:(SEL)aSelector;
- shouldNotImplement;
- shouldNotImplement:(SEL)aSelector from:superclass;
- notImplemented;
- notImplemented:(SEL)aSelector;
- doesNotRecognize:(STR)aMessage;
- error:(STR)aCStr, ...;
- sys$awake;

@end

An Overview of Stepstone's
ICpak 101 Libraries

Stepstone's version of Objective-C includes a rich set of foundation classes that are described in this appendix. The hierarchy of these 16 ICpak 101 classes is shown in Figure B.1.

The Stepstone foundation classes described in this appendix offer the Objective-C software developer a coherent, Smalltalk-like set of reusable software components that may be used as an initial framework for building applications. The application developer can add to any of these classes using categories or the technique of posing (described in Chapter 3), may create subclasses of any particular class, or build customized classes that inherit directly from Object. Before making such decisions, the developer should become familiar with the behaviors provided in this useful set of foundation classes.

Each of the ICpak 101 foundation classes is described.[1] The reader should consult the Stepstone user's manual for more details concerning any of the classes described.

B.1 ICpak 101 SPECIFICATION SHEET

Each class in ICpak 101 is specified by its properties in the following categories.

— Inherits from:	A list of parent classes from which the class inherits, given with immediate superclass listed first.
— Classes used:	A list of classes upon which the current class depends.
— Interface file:	A listing of the interface file for the class.

---

[1] The descriptions are patterned after those in the Stepstone manual. They are abstracted here by permission. In particular, the interface files are exactly those provided by Stepstone. Descriptions of the actions of methods are closely patterned after the Stepstone manual for accuracy.

Figure B.1 _____

ICpak 101 hierarchy of foundation classes

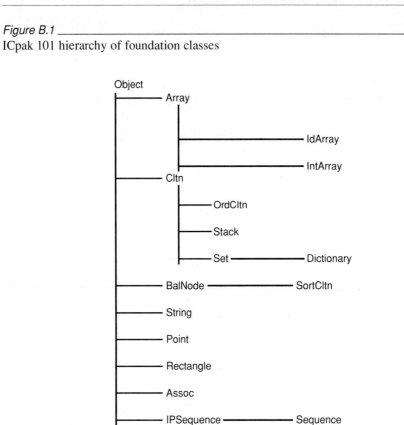

— General comments:	Hints on using the class appropriately.
— Instance variables:	A list and explanation of all instance variables.
— Factory method selectors:	List and description of factory methods.
— Instance method selectors:	List and description of instance methods.

A specification sheet should provide a potential user with sufficient information to intelligently use the software component that is described. In our view it is often desirable to examine the source code of the implementation file for a particular class. This code displays the algorithms that are used to implement key features of the class. Although Stepstone provides this source code, we are not at liberty to reproduce it in this book. Our specifications for each component are limited to the interface file only.

Most of ICpak 101's components are described in great detail; for a few components, only the source code of the interface file is presented.

B.2 ARRAY CLASS

Inherits from: Object

Classes used: None

Interface file:

```
//
//    ICpak 101 Foundation Library Class Interface
//    (c) Stepstone 1988. All rights reserved.
//
//    $Source: d:/objc40/src/icpak101/RCS/array.h $
//    $Revision: 2.1 $
//    $Date: 89/04/30 22:34:31 $
//    $State: Exp $
//
//    Title:  Array - Abstract Superclass of all Array classes
//

#import "ICpak101.h"
#import "Object.h"
@interface Array : Object
{
 unsigned capacity;
 void *elements;
}
+ (unsigned ) ndxVarSize;
+  with:(unsigned )nArgs;
+ new;
+ new: (unsigned) nElements;
- (STR ) describe;
- (unsigned ) capacity;
- (STR ) elements;
- initialize;
- initialize: (unsigned) nElements;
- (unsigned ) size;
-  sys$awake;
-  copy: (unsigned ) varSize;
-  copy;
-  shallowCopy;
-  capacity:(unsigned )nSlots;
-  printOn:(IOD )anIOD;
-  printContentsOn:(IOD )anIOD;
- (BOOL ) isEqual:anObject;
- (unsigned ) hash;
-  sort;
-  free;
-  boundsViolation:(unsigned )anOffset;

@end
```

General comments: This is an abstract superclass that provides protocol for all array subclasses. It supports indexed access to any set of objects.

Instance variables:
— capacity:
   Maintains a count of the number of objects contained within an object
— elements:
   A pointer to the indexed storage that an object contains

Factory method selectors:
with: (unsigned) nArgs; va_declare(va_alist) ;
   — Creates and returns an instance of Array with capacity for nArgs elements. The initial elements are separated by commas.

+ new;
   — Creates an instance of Array with no initialization.

+ new: (unsigned) nElements;
   — Creates an instance of Array with capacity nElements.

+ (unsigned) ndxVarSize;
   — Returns the size of an individual indexed instance variable. Implementation is a subclass responsibility.

Instance method selectors:
- initialize;
   — Initializes an instance by providing a default value for capacity and allocating storage for the indexed elements. The implementation is dependent on the ndxVarSize method implemented in subclasses.

- initialize: (unsigned) nElements;
   — Initializes an instance with capacity equal to nElements.

- (unsigned) size;
   — Returns the number of items in the receiver.

-copy;
   — Returns a copy of the receiver, including all of its indexed instance variables.

-shallowCopy;
   — Returns a copy of the receiver, including all of its indexed instance variables. The user should be cautious of potential aliasing effects that will occur if any of the instance variables of the source are modified.

- capacity: (unsigned) nSlots;

> — Returns a new instance of Array with nSlots allocated for indexed instance variables. If nSlots is larger than the current capacity, the excess memory is zero-filled. If nSlots is smaller than the current capacity, the contents copied from the receiver are truncated.

-printOn: (IOD) anIOD; // IOD is a typedef for FILE*

> — Prints the name of the class and, in parentheses, the result of the print-ContentsOn: method of the receiver, and the value of anIOD. Returns the receiver. Subclasses need only to redefine the printContentsOn: method.

- printContentsOn: (IOD) anIOD;

> — Prints the contents of the Array on anIOD. Implementation is a subclass responsibility.

-(BOOL) isEqual: anObject;

> — Returns YES (1) if the receiver is equal to anObject; otherwise returns NO (0). The implementation is a subclass responsibility.

- (unsigned) hash;

> — Returns an unsigned integer, which is the same for two objects that are equal according to the isEqual: method. Implementation is a subclass responsibility.

-sort;

> — Sorts an instance in place and returns the sorted instance. Implementation is a subclass responsibility.

- free;

> — Deallocates storage for the receiver.

- boundsViolation: (unsigned) anOffset;

> — Prints an error message and exits if anOffset is used to access an Array instance beyond its capacity.

- (STR) describe;

> — Returns the AsciiFiler type encoding for indexed instance variables. Implementation is a subclass responsibility.

- (unsigned) capacity;

> — Returns the number of indexed instance variables in the receiver.

- elements;

> — Returns the receiver's elements as a (char*).

B.3 IdArray CLASS

Inherits from: Array, Object

Classes used: None

Interface file:

```
//
//    ICpak 101 Foundation Library Class Interface
//    (c) Stepstone 1988. All rights reserved.
//
//    $Source: d:/objc40/src/icpak101/RCS/idarray.h $
//    $Revision: 2.2 $
//    $Date: 89/07/16 00:14:00 $
//    $State: Exp $
//

#import "ICpak101.h"
#import "Array.h"

@interface IdArray : Array

+ (unsigned ) ndxVarSize;
+ with:(unsigned )nArgs, ...;
- (STR ) describe;
- at:(unsigned )anOffset;
- at:(unsigned )n put:anObject;
- (unsigned ) size;
- copy;
- shallowCopy;
- capacity:(unsigned )nSlots;
- printContentsOn:(IOD )anIOD;
- (BOOL ) isEqual:anObject;
- (unsigned ) hash;
- sort;
- sortBy:(SEL )aComparisonSelector;
- add:anObject;
- addContentsTo:aCollection;
- addContentsOf:aCollection;
- remove:anObject;
- removeContentsFrom:aCltn;
- packContents;
- eachElement;
- eachElementInPlace;
- elementsPerform:(SEL )aSelector;
- elementsPerform:(SEL )aSelector with:obj1;
- elementsPerform:(SEL )aSelector with:obj1 with:obj2;
- elementsPerform:(SEL )aSelector with:obj1 with:obj2 with:obj3;
- asIdArray;
- contents;
- freeContents;
- (BOOL ) contains:anObject;
- find:anObject;
```

- findMatching:anObject;
- (unsigned) offsetOf:anObject;
- (unsigned) offsetMatching:anObject;
- (unsigned) offsetMatchingSTR:(STR)aCString;

@end

General comments: IdArrays hold arbitrary objects as their elements. The collection classes use IdArray to hold their members. Unlike other subclasses of Array, IdArray implements size to return the number of occupied slots as determined by the number of non-nil entries.

Instance variables: None.

Factory method selectors:
+with: (unsigned) nArgs; va_declare(va_alist);

    — Creates and returns a new instance of IdArray with the first nArgs slots initialized.

+ (unsigned) ndxVarSize;

    — Returns the size of an id.

Instance method selectors:
- at: (unsigned) anOffset;

    — Returns the object at Offset.

- at: (unsigned) anOffset put: anObject;

    — Replaces the object at anOffset with anObject and returns the receiver.

- (unsigned) size;

    — Returns the number of non-nil slots in the IdArray.

- copy;

    — Returns a new copy of the receiver.

- shallowCopy;

    — Returns a new copy of the receiver.

- capacity: (unsigned) nSlots;

    — Changes the capacity to nSlots. Zero-fills memory if nSlots is larger than the current capacity, and truncates if nSlots is smaller than current capacity.

- printContentsOn: (IOD) anIOD;

    — Prints the members of this IdArray on anIOD by sending the message print-On: to each element in the IdArray. Returns the receiver.

- (BOOL) isEqual: anObject;

    — Returns YES if all the following conditions are met:

1. Both the receiver and anObject are IdArrays or subclasses.
2. Both have the same capacity.
3. For each array offset, the receiver's element isEqual: to the corresponding element in anObject.

- (unsigned) hash;

— Returns a hash value based upon "bitwise exclusive or" of the class of the receiver, its capacity, and the results of sending the hash message to each of its elements.

- sort;

— Sorts the receiver with compare: as the selector to be used for ordering.

- sortBy: (SEL) aComparisonSelector;

— Enables the user to supply a comparison method using aComparisonSelector to perform the comparison.

- add: anObject;

— Adds anObject at the first empty slot (first location containing nil). IdArrays cannot expand automatically, so adding to a full IdArray produces an error.

- addContentsTo: aCollection;

— Adds each non-nil member of this IdArray to aCollection (an instance of one of the collection classes). This method will fail if aCollection does not have the capacity to hold the IdArray instance.

- addContentsOf: aCollection;

— Adds the contents of aCollection (an instance of one of the collection classes) to the IdArray. This method will fail if the IdArray instance does not have the capacity to hold aCollection. This method uses the eachElement method from class Sequence. Therefore, Sequence must be linked into the application if this method is used.

- remove: anObject;

— If anObject is found in the receiver, it is replaced by nil and returned. Otherwise nil is returned. The comparison is done with the C operator, ==.

- removeContentsFrom: aCltn;

— Removes all the members of the receiver from aCltn(an instance of one of the collection classes).

- packContents;

— Removes the nil slots while preserving the order of elements in the IdArray. This method is used primarily by the collection classes to eliminate holes left by the remove: methods.

- eachElement;

— Returns a Sequence over the receiver. It makes a copy of the array so that modification can be made to the sequence. The code for Sequence must be linked into the application.

- elementsInPlace;

— Returns an IPSequence over the receiver.

- elementsPerform: (SEL) aSelector;

— Sends a message to each element of the receiver with the selector aSelector.

- elementsPerform: (SEL) aSelector with: obj1;

— Same as elementsPerform and the parameter obj1.

- elementsPerform: (SEL) aSelector with: obj1 with: obj2;

— Same as elementsPerform with two parameters.

- elementsPerform: (SEL) aSelector with: obj1 with: obj2 with: obj3;

— Same as elementsPerform with three parameters.

- freeContents;

— Frees all members of the receiver, but not the receiver itself.

- (BOOL) contains: anObject;

— Returns YES if anObject is a member of the receiver. The find: method is used to determine membership.

- find: anObject;

— Searches for anObject in the receiver and returns anObject if found. Otherwise, returns nil. Find uses the C operator, ==.

- findMatching: anObject;

— Searches for an element in the receiver that matches anObject. Uses the isEqual: method.

- (unsigned) offsetOf: anObject;

— Returns the offset of the first object in the receiver that is the same as anObject. If the object is not present, the function returns -1. Uses the C operator, ==.

- (unsigned) offsetMatching: anObject;

— Returns the offset of the first object in the receiver that isEqual: to the receiver. Returns -1 if a match is not found.

- (unsigned) offsetMatchingSTR: (STR) aCString;

— Searches in the receiver for an object whose representation as a C string is equal to aCString. It assumes that all members respond to the isEqualSTR: message. Returns -1 if a match is not found.

- (STR) describe;

— Returns the AsciiFiler encoding for type id.

B.4 IntArray CLASS

Inherits from: Array, Object

Classes used: None

Interface file:

```
//
//    ICpak 101 Foundation Library Class Interface
//    (c) Stepstone 1988. All rights reserved.
//
//    $Source: d:/objc40/src/icpak101/RCS/intarray.h $
//    $Revision: 2.1 $
//    $Date: 89/04/30 22:34:38 $
//    $State: Exp $
//
#import "ICpak101.h"
#import "Array.h"

@interface IntArray : Array

+ (unsigned ) ndxVarSize;
+ with:(unsigned )nArgs, ...;
- (STR ) describe;
- (int ) intAt:(unsigned )anOffset;
- (int ) intAt:(unsigned )anOffset put:(int )anInt;
- copy;
- shallowCopy;
- capacity:(unsigned )nSlots;
- printContentsOn:(IOD )anIOD;
- sort;
- (BOOL ) isEqual:anObject;
- (unsigned ) hash;

@end
```

General comments: This class provides indexed access to an array of integers.

Instance variables: None.

Factory method selectors:

+ with: (unsigned) nArgs; va_declare (va_alist);

— Creates and returns a new instance of IntArray with the first nArgs slots initialized using a variable number of arguments.

+ *(unsigned) ndxVarSize;*

> — Returns the size of an int.

Instance method selectors:

- *(int) intAt: (unsigned) anOffset;*

> — Returns the integer (int) at anOffset. Generates an error if anOffset is greater than or equal to the capacity of the array.

- *(int) intAt: (unsigned) anOffset put: (int) anInt;*

> — Puts anInt into the index location at anOffset and returns the integer previously stored at anOffset. Generates an error if anOffset is greater than or equal to the capacity of the array.

- *copy;*

> — Returns a new copy of the receiver. Redefines the method in class Array for the purpose of speed.

- *shallowCopy;*

> — Returns a new copy of the IntArray. Redefines the method in class Array for the purpose of speed. Performs exactly as method copy for this subclass.

- *capacity: (unsigned) nSlots;*

> — Creates a new instance of IntArray with nSlots for its capacity. Zero-fills memory locations if nSlots is greater than the current capacity, and truncates if nSlots is smaller than the current capacity.

- *sort;*

> — Uses the C library function qsort() to sort the receiver in place.

- *(BOOL) isEqual: anObject;*

> — Returns YES if:

> 1. anObject is an IntArray
> 2. If the receiver has the same capacity as anObject
> 3. If all of the corresponding integers are the same

- *(unsigned) hash;*

> — Returns a hash value based on the capacity and the values of the individual integers.

- *(STR) describe;*

> — Returns the AsciiFiler encoding for an int.

B.5 Cltn CLASS

Inherits from: Object

Classes used: IdArray

Interface file:

```
//    ICpak 101 Foundation Library Class Interface
//    (c) Stepstone 1988. All rights reserved.
//
//    $Source: d:/objc40/src/icpak101/RCS/cltn.h $
//    $Revision: 2.2 $
//    $Date: 89/07/16 00:13:59 $
//    $State: Exp $

#import "ICpak101.h"
#import "Object.h"
#import "IdArray.h"
#import "IPSequence.h"
#import "Sequence.h"
#import "Set.h"
#import "OrdCltn.h"

@interface Cltn : Object
{
 id contents;
 unsigned capacity;
}
+ add:anObject;
+ with:(unsigned )nArgs, ...;
+ new;
+ new: (unsigned) nElements;
- initialize;
- initialize: (unsigned) nElements;
- add:newObject;
- addContentsTo:aCltn;
- addContentsOf:aCltn;
- remove:anObject;
- removeContentsOf:aCltn;
- removeContentsFrom:aCltn;
- emptyYourself;
- eachElement;
- eachElementInPlace;
- elementsPerform:(SEL )aSelector;
- elementsPerform:(SEL )aSelector with:obj1;
- elementsPerform:(SEL )aSelector with:obj1 with:obj2;
- elementsPerform:(SEL )aSelector with:obj1 with:obj2 with:obj3;
- asSet;
- asOrdCltn;
```

- asIdArray;
- as:aClass;
- printOn:(IOD)anIOD;
- printContentsOn:(IOD)anIOD;
- free;
- freeContents;
- copy;
- (unsigned) size;
- (BOOL) isEmpty;
- (BOOL) contains:anObject;
- find:anObject;
- (unsigned) offsetOf:anObject;
- (unsigned) hash;
- (BOOL) isEqual:aCltn;
- expand;
- contents;

@end

General comments: This is an abstract superclass of several collection subclasses. Each subclass has a specialized way to store objects, access them, handle the creation of duplicates, and so on. Protocol is established in this class and implemented in the various subclasses.

In addition to instance variables, a global variable (class variable), cltnDefault-Capacity, is used to determine the amount of space allocated for subclasses that are sent the new message. It is initialized to 10 but may easily be changed. Its value should never be set to 0.

Sequence is a class that is closely tied to Cltn and designed to work with all its subclasses.

Instance variables:
— *contents*: Points to an instance of IdArray that actually contains the contents of the collection.
— *capacity*: Contains the total number of slots in the IdArray pointed to by contents.

Factory method selectors:
+ *add: anObject;*
— Creates a new instance of Cltn and sends it the message [newInstance add: anObject]. This method is useful in cases where the user does not want to allocate storage for a collection unless it is actually used.

+ *with: (unsigned) nArgs va_declare(va_alist);*
— Creates a new instance of Cltn with the first nArgs slots initialized.

Instance method selectors:

- initialize;

    — Initializes an instance by setting the capacity to the default value and creating an IdArray instance of the proper size.

- initialize: (unsigned) nElements;

    — Initializes an instance with capacity set to nElements and creates an IdArray of the proper size.

- add: newObject;

    — Adds newObject to the collection. In those subclasses like Set, which may not choose to actually add the object, the effect may be null. Implementation is a subclass responsibility.

- addContentsTo: aCltn;

    — Adds every element of the receiver to aCltn and returns aCltn. If aCltn is nil, nil is returned. The argument aCltn need not be a subclass of Cltn, so long as it responds to add: in the same manner as all collection subclasses.

- addContentsOf: aCltn;

    — Adds each member of aCtln to the receiver. Returns the receiver. If aCltn is nil, no action is taken. The argument aCltn need not be a subclass of Cltn so long as it responds to the message eachElement in the same as the collection subclasses.

- remove:: anObject;

    — Removes anObject from the collection and returns anObject if found. Otherwise nil is returned. The object removed is the first one encountered. The implementation is a subclass responsibility.

- removeContentsOf: aCltn;

    — Removes each of the elements of aCltn from the receiver. Returns the receiver. The argument must be able to respond to the message eachElement and therefore does not need to be a subclass of Cltn.

- removeContentsFrom: aCltn;

    — Removes each of the members of the receiver from aCltn and returns the receiver. The argument aCltn must be able to respond to remove:.

- emptyYourself;

    — Removes all the members of the receiver and resets itself to the default size.

- eachElement;

    — Returns a Sequence over all the members of the receiver. It is necessary to link the Sequence class into the executable image.

- eachElementInPlace;

    — Returns an IPSequence over all the members of the receiver. The IPSequence class must be linked into the executable image.

- *elementsPerform: (SEL) aSelector;*
    — Sends the message aSelector to each element of the receiver. Returns the receiver.

- *elementsPerform: (SEL) aSelector with: obj1;*
    — Sends a one-parameter message to each element of the receiver.

- *elementsPerform: (SEL) aSelector with: obj1 with: obj2;*
    — Sends a two-parameter message to each element of the receiver.

- *elementsPerform: (SEL) aSelector with: obj1 with: obj2 with: obj3;*
    — Sends a three-parameter message to each element of the receiver.

- *asSet;*
    — Returns an instance of class Set containing all elements of the receiver.

- *asOrdCltn;*
    — Returns an instance of class OrdCltn containing all elements of the receiver.

- *asIdArray;*
    — Returns an instance of class IdArray containing all elements of the receiver.

- *as: aClass;*
    — Returns an instance of class aClass containing all the members of the receiver. The argument aClass must respond to new: and its instances must recognize the message add:.

- *printOn: (IOD) anIOD;*
    — Prints the contents of the receiver on anIOD.

- *printContentsOn: (IOD) anIOD;*
    — Sends the message [object printOn: anIOD] to each object in the receiver.

- *release;*
    — Frees the IdArray that holds the contents of the receiver. Returns nil.

- *freeContents;*
    — Frees all the members of the receiver, but not the receiver itself. Returns the receiver.

- *copy;*
    — Returns a new copy of the collection. The new collection has its own copy of the contents, the IdArray.

- *(unsigned) size;*
    — Returns the number of objects contained in the receiver. Implementation is a subclass responsibility.

- *(BOOL) isEmpty;*
    — Returns YES if the receiver is empty; otherwise returns NO.

- (BOOL) contains: anObject;

— Returns YES if the receiver contains anObject; otherwise returns NO. Implementation is in terms of the receiver's find: method.

- find: anObject;

— Searches for an object in the receiver. Returns anObject, if found; otherwise returns nil. Implementation is a subclass responsibility.

- (unsigned) offsetOf: anObject;

— Returns the offset within the receiver of anObject. Returns -1 if anObject cannot be found.

- (unsigned) hash;

— Returns a value based on the receiver's address and the result of sending the hash message to the contents.

- (BOOL) isEqual: aCltn;

— Returns YES if aCltn is a kind of Cltn, and if each member of its contents responds affirmatively to the message isEqual: when compared to the receiver's contents.

- expand;

— Expands the IdArray to twice its current size. Returns the expanded collection.

- contents;

— Returns a pointer to the instance of IdArray.

B.6   OrdCltn CLASS

Inherits from: Cltn, Object

Classes used: IdArray

Interface file:

```
//    ICpak 101 Foundation Library Class Interface
//    (c) Stepstone 1988. All rights reserved.
//
//    $Source: d:/objc40/src/icpak101/RCS/ordcltn.h $
//    $Revision: 2.2 $
//    $Date: 89/07/16 00:14:02 $
//    $State: Exp $

#import "ICpak101.h"
#import "Cltn.h"
#ifdef MSDOS
#import "StringCl.h"
#else
#import "String.h"
#endif
```

```
@interface OrdCltn : Cltn
{
 unsigned firstEmptySlot;
}
- (unsigned ) size;
- (unsigned ) lastOffset;
-  firstElement;
-  lastElement;
-  emptyYourself;
- (unsigned ) offsetOf:anObject;
-  addFirst:newObject;
-  addLast:newObject;
-  add:anObject;
-  addIfAbsent:anObject;
-  addIfAbsentMatching:anObject;
-  at:(unsigned )anOffset insert:anObject;
-  insert:newObject after:oldObject;
-  insert:newObject before:oldObject;
-  after:anObject;
-  before:anObject;
-  at:(unsigned )n;
-  at:(unsigned )anOffset put:anObject;
-  removeAt:(unsigned )anOffset;
-  removeFirst;
-  removeLast;
-  remove:oldObject;
-  find:anObject;
-  findMatching:anObject;
-  findSTR:(STR )aStr;
-  freeContents;
-  boundsError:(unsigned )anOffset in:(SEL )aSelector;
-  couldntFind:anObject in:(SEL )aSelector;

@end
```

General comments: This subclass of Cltn enjoys the property that its elements are ordered. Subclasses such as queues and stacks can be created as subclasses of OrdCltn. No nil entries are allowed between the first and last entries (from slot 0 to firstEmptySlot -1). All methods that add objects do not add nils. When entries are added or removed, the contents are packed, and the offsets of the entries change.

Instance variables:
— firstEmptySlot: Tracks the empty slot where the next element is to be added.

Factory method selectors: None.

Instance method selectors:
- *(unsigned) size;*
— Returns the number of objects in the collection.

- (unsigned) lastOffset;

> — Returns the offset of the last element. If there are no elements, returns -1.

- firstElement;

> — Returns the first element in the collection. If there are no elements, returns nil.

- lastElement;

> — Returns the last element in the collection. If there are no elements, returns nil.

- (unsigned) offsetOf: anObject;

> — Returns the offset of anObject, if not present, returns -1.

- addFirst: newObject;

> — Adds newObject as the first (index location 0 in IdArray) element of the collection. Returns the receiver.

- addLast: newObject;

> — Adds newObject as the last element of the collection and returns the receiver. This method is the same as method add:

- add: anObject;

> — Adds anObject to the collection as the last element and returns the receiver.

- addIfAbsent: anObject;

> — Adds anObject to the collection only if the collection does not have the same object (i.e., one that isSame:).

- addIfAbsentMatching: anObject;

> — Adds an object to the collection only if the collection does not have a matching object according to the method isEqual:. Returns the receiver.

- at: (unsigned) anOffset insert: anObject;

> — Inserts anObject at anOffset and returns the receiver. If anOffset is greater than firstEmptyState, an error is generated.

- insert: newObject before: oldObject;

> — Searches for oldObject and inserts newObject before oldObject. If oldObject is not found, an error is generated. Returns the receiver.

- insert: newObject after: oldObject;

> — Searches for oldObject and inserts newObject after oldObject. If oldObject is not found, an error is generated. Returns the receiver.

- after: anObject

> — Searches for anObject and, if found, returns the next object. If anObject is the last in the receiver, returns nil. An error is generated if anObject cannot be found.

- before: anObject

— Searches for anObject and, if found, returns the previous object. If anObject is the first in the receiver, returns nil and generates an error. An error is generated if anObject cannot be found.

- at: (unsigned) anOffset;

— Returns the object at anOffset. Generates an error if anOffset is greater than the size of the collection.

- at: (unsigned) anOffset put: anObject;

— Replaces the object at anOffset with anObject and returns the old member at anOffset. Generates an error if anOffset is greater than the size of the collection.

- removeAt: (unsigned) anOffset;

— Removes the object at anOffset. Returns the object removed.

- removeFirst;

— Removes the first element; returns nil if there are no elements.

- removeLast;

— Removes the last element; returns nil if there are no elements.

- remove: oldObject;

— Removes the oldObject and returns oldObject; otherwise returns nil.

- find: anObject;

— Returns the first member which satisfies isSame:. Returns nil if none is found.

- findMatching: anObject;

— Returns the first element which satisfies isEqual:. Returns nil if none is found.

- findSTR: (STR) aStr;

— Returns the first member whose string content matches aStr using isEqualStr:. If none is found, returns nil.

- freeContents;

— Frees all the members of the receiver, but not the receiver itself, which is returned.

B.7 Stack CLASS

Inherits from: Cltn, Object

Classes used: None

Interface file:

```
//      ICpak 101 Foundation Library Class Interface
//      (c) Stepstone 1988. All rights reserved.
//
//      $Source: d:/objc40/src/icpak101/RCS/stack.h $
//      $Revision: 2.1 $
//      $Date: 89/04/30 22:34:46 $
//      $State: Exp $

#import "ICpak101.h"
#import "Cltn.h"

@interface Stack : Cltn
{
 unsigned depth;
}
- (unsigned ) size;
- (unsigned ) depth;
- push:anObject;
- add:anObject;
- pop;
- swap;
- topElement;
- lastElement;
- emptyYourself;
- asIdArray;
- at:(unsigned )anOffset;
- removeAt:(unsigned )anOffset;

@end
```

General comments: A stack is a collection that maintains its elements in a last-in, first-out order. The methods push: and pop are the two key methods used for insertion and deletion. The methods at: and removeAt: (relative to the top position in the stack) may also be used to access information from a stack.

Instance variables:
— depth: Indicates the number of elements stored in a stack object.

Factory method selectors: None.

Instance method selectors:
- *(unsigned) size;*
 — Returns the number of elements contained in the stack.
- *add: anObject;*
 — Pushes anObject onto the stack. This method is equivalent to push:.
- *swap;*
 — Exchanges the top two elements and returns the receiver. An error is generated if the stack does not contain at least two elements.

- topElement;

— Returns the top element on a stack without removing it. Returns nil if the stack is empty.

- lastElement;

— This method is equivalent to topElement.

- at: (unsigned) anOffset;

— Returns the element at anOffset deep into the stack. An error is generated if anOffset is greater than or equal to the stack depth.

- removeAt: (unsigned) anOffset;

— Removes the element at anOffset deep into the stack and returns the element. The hole produced is closed up. An error is generated if anOffset is greater than or equal to the stack depth.

- asIdArray;

— Creates and returns a new instance of IdArray containing a copy of the stack. The first element of the IdArray is the top of the stack, and the last element of the IdArray is the last element pushed onto the stack.

B.8 Set CLASS

Inherits from: Cltn, Object

Classes used: IdArray

Interface file:

```
//    ICpak 101 Foundation Library Class Interface
//    (c) Stepstone 1988. All rights reserved.
//
//    $Source: d:/objc40/src/icpak101/RCS/set.h $
//    $Revision: 2.1 $
//    $Date: 89/04/30 22:34:44 $
//    $State: Exp $

#import "ICpak101.h"
#import "Cltn.h"

@interface Set : Cltn
{
 unsigned tally;
}

+ new;
+ new: (unsigned) nSlots;
- (id * ) findElementOrNil:anElement;
- remove:anObject;
- shrink;
- intersection:aCltn;
```

- union:aCltn;
- difference:aCltn;
- (unsigned) size;
- find:anObject;
- (BOOL) contains:anObject;
- (unsigned) occurrencesOf:anObject;
- add:newObject;
- addNTest:newObject;
- filter:newObject;
- replace:anObject;
- addContentsTo:aCollection;
- freeContents;
- emptyYourself;
- expand;

@end

General comments: A Set represents a collection that does not allow duplicate elements. A duplicate is determined by the method isEqual:. Sets expect that every element responds to two comparison methods which must behave in a coordinated way (i.e., the method hash is expected to return integers that are equal for all objects for which is-Equal: is true. Sets deal appropriately with collisions on this unsigned integer.

The implementation of class Set places objects added to them into a hash table based on the results of sending each object the hash message. It is assumed that an object will not be changed after being added to a Set. Sets are therefore not designed to hold dynamic objects such as collections.

To iterate through a Set, use Sequence.

Instance variables:
— tally: The number of elements in a Set.

Factory method selectors:
+ new;
— Returns an instance of Set with default size.

+ new: (unsigned) nSlots;
— Returns an instance of Set with size equal to nSlots.

Instance method selectors:
- initialize;
— Initializes a new instance of Set. It augments the implementation in class Cltn to allocate enough storage to avoid expansion.

- initialize: (unsigned) nSlots;
— Initializes a new instance of Set with enough storage to hold nSlots elements without having to expand.

- add: newObject;

— Adds newObject if it is not already in the Set and returns the receiver.

- addNTest: newObject;

— Adds newObject to the Set only if there is no matching object. Returns new-Object if the addition takes place; otherwise returns nil.

- filter: newObject;

— If there is a matching object in the Set, the new object is freed, and the matching object is returned. Otherwise, the new object is added and returned.

- replace: anObject;

— If a matching object is found, newObject replaces that object, and the matching object is returned. If there is no matching object, newObject is added to the receiver, and nil is returned.

- addContentsTo: aCollection;

— Adds the contents of the receiver's collection to aCollection and returns aCollection.

- (unsigned) size;

— Returns the number of elements in the Set.

- find: anObject;

— Returns any element in the receiver which isEqual: to anObject; otherwise returns nil.

- (BOOL) contains: anObject;

— Returns YES if anObject matches any object (using find:) in the receiver; otherwise returns NO.

- (unsigned) occurrencesOf: anObject;

— Returns 1 if anObject is in the receiver; otherwise returns 0 (using find:).

- remove: anObject;

— Removes anObject (using isEqual: to find matchup). Returns the removed element or nil if no matching entry can be found.

- intersection: aCltn;

— Returns a new Set that is the intersection of the receiver and aCltn. The new Set contains only the elements that are in both the receiver and aCltn.

- union: aCltn;

— Returns a new Set that is the union of the receiver and aCltn. The new Set contains all the elements from both the receiver and aCltn. The argument aCltn need not be a subclass of Cltn as long as it responds to find:.

- difference: aCltn;

> — Returns a new Set that is the difference of the receiver and aCltn. The new Set contains only the elements in the receiver that are not in aCltn.

- freeContents;

> — Frees all the elements in the Set, but not the Set itself. Returns the receiver.

B.9 Assoc CLASS

Inherits from: Object

Classes used: None

Interface file:

```
//    ICpak 101 Foundation Library Class Interface
//    (c) Stepstone 1988. All rights reserved.
//
//    $Source: d:/objc40/src/icpak101/RCS/assoc.h $
//    $Revision: 2.1 $
//    $Date: 89/04/30 22:34:32 $
//    $State: Exp $

#import "ICpak101.h"
#import "Object.h"

@interface Assoc : Object
{
 id key,value;
}

+ key:aKey;
+ key:aKey value:anObject;
- key;
- key:aKey;
- value;
- value:aValue;
- (int ) compare:anAssoc;
- (unsigned ) hash;
- (STR ) str;
- (BOOL ) isEqual:anAssoc;
- printOn:(IOD )anIOD;

@end
```

General comments: An association, **Assoc**, links a pair of objects: a key and a value. This is most useful in implementing a Dictionary.

Instance variables:

> — key: An object constituting the key of an Assoc.
> — value: An object that is associated with the key and returned when the key is looked up.

Factory method selectors:

+ key: aKey;

> — Returns a new instance of Assoc with its key equal to aKey and its value equal to nil.

+ key: aKey value: anObject;

> — Returns a new instance of Assoc with its key equal to aKey and its value equal to anObject.

Instance method selectors:

- key;

> — Returns the receiver's key.

- key: aKey;

> — Changes the receiver's key to aKey and returns the old key.

- value;

> — Returns the receiver's value.

- value: aValue;

> — Changes the receiver's value to aValue and returns the old value.

- (int) compare: anAssoc;

> — Returns a negative, zero, or positive number according to whether the receiver's key is less than, equal to, or greater than the key of anAssoc. It uses the compare: method to compare the keys.

- (unsigned) hash;

> — Returns the key's hash value.

- (BOOL) isEqual: anAssoc;

> — Returns YES if key isEqual: to anAssoc key; otherwise returns NO.

- (STR) str;

> — Returns the C-string representation of the key of the receiver. This method is only appropriate when the key of the receiver responds to the message str.

- printOn: (IOD) anIOD;

> — Prints an association on anIOD. (e.g., Assoc (<key> = <value>).

B.10 Dictionary CLASS

Inherits from: Set, Cltn, Object

Classes used: Assoc

Interface file:

```
//      ICpak 101 Foundation Library Class Interface
//      (c) Stepstone 1988. All rights reserved.
//
//      $Source: d:/objc40/src/icpak101/RCS/dictiona.h $
//      $Revision: 2.1 $
//      $Date: 89/04/30 22:34:35 $
//      $State: Exp $

#import "ICpak101.h"
#import "Assoc.h"

#import "Set.h"

@interface Dictionary : Set

+ with:(unsigned )nArgs, ...;
- atKey:aKey;
- atKey:aKey put:anObject;
- associationAt:aKey;
- keys;
- values;
- (BOOL ) includesAssociation:anAssociation;
- (BOOL ) includesKey:aKey;

@end
```

General comments: The class Dictionary implements a set of associations.

Instance variables: None

Factory method selectors:
+ with: (unsigned) nArgs; va_declare(va_alist);

> — Creates and returns a new Dictionary with contents initialized from its arguments. The parameter nArgs is the number of arguments, not the number of pairs (e.g., myDictionary = [Dictionary with: 4; key0, value0, key1, value1]).

Instance method selectors:
- atKey: aKey;

> — Returns the value of the association with aKey. Returns nil if the association is not found.

- atKey: aKey put: anObject;

> — Creates a new association with key aKey.

- values;

> — Returns an ordered collection (OrdCltn) of all the values.

- (BOOL) includesAssociation: anAssociation;

> — Returns YES if anAssociation is in the dictionary; otherwise returns NO.

- *(BOOL) includesKey: aKey;*
    — Returns YES if there is an association in the dictionary whose key equals aKey; otherwise returns NO.

- *associationAt: aKey;*
    — Returns the association whose key is equal to aKey. Returns nil if the association is not found.

B.11 BalNode CLASS

Inherits from: Object

Classes used: None

Interface file:

```
//     ICpak 101 Foundation Library Class Interface
//     (c) Stepstone 1988. All rights reserved.
//
//     $Source: d:/objc40/src/icpak101/RCS/balnode.h $
//     $Revision: 2.1 $
//     $Date: 89/04/30 22:34:33 $
//     $State: Exp $

#import "ICpak101.h"
#import "Object.h"

@interface BalNode : Object
{
 id key,left,right;
}
+ new;
- free;
- printOn:(IOD )anIOD;
- showNodesOn:(IOD )anIOD;
- showStructureOn:(IOD )anIOD nameLength:(int )nameLength;
- treeFree;
- treeFreeContents;
- freeExceptFor:lastFreed;
- copy;

@end
```

General comments: BalNode is an abstract superclass that provides protocol for creating any type of binary tree. BalNode allows the user to display or print a tree of nodes and free the subtrees.

BalNode puts all freed nodes into a cache. When a new node is requested, BalNode retrieves one from the cache, if available. Otherwise a new node is created by using the normal allocation function.

Instance variables:
- — key: The object that is referenced by a node
- — left: The left subtree of a node
- — right: The right subtree of a node

Factory method selectors:

+ new;
- — Returns a new node.

Instance method selectors:

- free;
- — Frees a node and returns nil.

- printOn: (IOD) anIOD;
- — Prints the contents of the tree rooted at the receiver on the specified IOD.

- showNodesOn: (IOD) anIOD;
- — Prints the contents of the tree rooted at the receiver by printing one line for each node in the following format: <leftEntry> <myEntry> <rightEntry>.

- treeFree;
- — Frees the receiver node and all subnodes of this node, but does not free the entries of the nodes. Returns nil.

- copy;
- — Makes a copy of this node and its subnodes. Returns the new copy of the tree.

B.12 SortCltn CLASS

Inherits from: BalNode, Object

Classes used: LHNode, RHNode, IdArray

Interface file:

```
//    ICpak 101 Foundation Library Class Interface
//    (c) Stepstone 1988. All rights reserved.
//
//    $Source: d:/objc40/src/icpak101/RCS/sortcltn.h $
//    $Revision: 2.2 $
//    $Date: 89/07/16 00:14:04 $
//    $State: Exp $

#import "ICpak101.h"
#import "Cltn.h"
#import "RHNode.h"
#import "LHNode.h"
```

```
#import "IdArray.h"
#import "BalNode.h"

#define ADD     0
#define REJECT  1
#define MERGE   2
#define REPLACE 3
#define VALDUPACTION(x) ((x) >= ADD && (x) <= REPLACE)

#ifdef SORTCLTN
static char * dupActionName[] =
{ "ADD", "REJECT", "MERGE", "REPLACE" };
#endif
@interface SortCltn : BalNode
{
 unsigned tally;
 SEL cmpSel;
 int addDupAction;
 int nameLength;
}

+ new;
+ new: (unsigned) nElements;
- initialize;
+ orderedBy:(SEL )aComparisonSelector;
+ orderedBy:(SEL )aComparisonSelector onDups:(int )action;
+ onDups:(int )action;
- addDupAction:(int )newDupAction;
- (int ) addDupAction;
- orderedBy:(SEL )aComparisonSelector;
- (SEL ) orderedBy;
- add:anObject;
- filter:anObject;
- addNTest:anObject;
- addContentsTo:aCltn;
- addContentsOf:aCltn;
- replace:newObject;
- merge:anObject;
- mergeFilter:anObject;
- remove:anEntry;
- removeContentsOf:aCltn;
- removeContentsFrom:aCltn;
- eachElement;
- elementsPerform:(SEL )aSelector;
- elementsPerform:(SEL )aSelector with:obj1;
- elementsPerform:(SEL )aSelector with:obj1 with:obj2;
- elementsPerform:(SEL )aSelector with:obj1 with:obj2 with:obj3;
- asIdArray;
- asSet;
- asOrdCltn;
- as:aClass;
```

- find:anObject;
- (BOOL) contains:anObject;
- (unsigned) size;
- (BOOL) isEmpty;
- printOn:(IOD)anIOD;
- showNodes;
- showNodesOn:(IOD)anIOD;
- showStructure;
- showStructureOn:(IOD)anIOD;
- (int) nameLength:(int)newNameLength;
- free;
- freeContents;

@end

General comments: The elements in a sorted collection, SortCltn, remain sorted at all times as elements are added and removed. The ordering is based on a comparison selector that is kept in the instance variable cmpSel. To determine the relative order of two objects, the comparison selector is sent to one object, with the other object as its argument. The default for this comparison selector is the method compare:.

Instance variables:
— tally: The number of elements in the sorted collection.
— cmpSel: The comparison selector used to determine the ordering between any two members of the collection.
— addDupAction: The action to be taken when the object being added to the collection is a duplicate.
— nameLength: The maximum number of letters used for printing each node when using the methods showStructure or showStructureOn:. The default is three.

Factory method selectors:
+ *orderedBy: (SEL) aComparisonSelector;*
— Creates a new instance of SortCltn whose method for comparing two elements is given by aComparisonSelector.

+ *orderedBy: (SEL) aComparisonSelector onDups: (int) action;*
— Creates a new instance of SortCltn whose method for comparing two elements is given by aComparisonSelector. Duplicate elements are handled according to the value of action, which may be ADD, REJECT, MERGE, or REPLACE, these are macros provided in SortCltn.h. The new collection is returned.
— ADD: Duplicates are allowed. A duplicate becomes the successor of the existing object.
— REJECT: Duplicates are not allowed. The method add: does nothing if a duplicate is encountered.

— MERGE: Duplicates are merged using the member's merge: method.

— REPLACE: Duplicates replace the corresponding members in the collection.

+ onDups: (int) action;

— Creates a new SortCltn. Duplicate elements are handled according to ADD, REJECT, MERGE, or REPLACE.

Instance method selectors:

- initialize;

— Initializes a new instance of SortCltn. By default, it uses compare: to compare two elements in the collection.

- new: (unsigned) nElements;

— Initializes a new instance of SortCltn with size nElements.

- addDupAction: (int) newDupAction;

— Changes the action that the collection uses for duplicating to newDupAction (ADD, REJECT, MERGE, or REPLACE). Returns the receiver.

- (int) addDupAction;

— Returns the dupAction instance variable of the receiver.

- orderedby: (SEL) aComparisonSelector;

— Changes the comparison selector used for ordering the collection to aComparisonSelector. If the collection is not empty and the new comparison selector is not the same as the previous one, unexpected results could occur. An error is generated under these circumstances. Returns the receiver.

- (SEL) orderedBy;

— Returns the comparison selector currently used to order the collection.

- add: anObject;

— Adds anObject to the collection, with the semantics being determined by the value of the instance variable addDupAction. Returns the receiver.

- filter: anObject;

— Adds anObject to the collection if it is not a duplicate and returns anObject. If it is a duplicate and it is not the same object as the one already in the collection, anObject is sent the free message. Returns the matching member from the collection.

- addNTest: anObject;

— Adds anObject based on the action of dupAction. If it's a duplicate, it returns anObject; otherwise it returns nil. The effect is to provide an atomic method that conditionally adds anObject while giving feedback concerning the outcome.

- addContentsTo: aCltn;

    — Adds every element of the receiver to aCltn and returns aCltn. The argument aCltn must only respond to the method add: and therefore need not be a subclass of Cltn.

- addContentsOf: aCltn;

    — Adds each member of aCltn to the receiver and returns the receiver. The argument aCltn need not be a subclass of Cltn as long as it responds to the method eachElement. Adding is based on the add: method.

- replace: newObject;

    — Replaces the first occurrence in the collection that matches newObject, using the comparison selector. If there is no matching entry, the newObject is added. Returns the original entry.

- merge: anObject;

    — Merges anObject into the receiver. If anObject is not in the collection, it is added. If it is in the collection, the entry in the collection is sent the message merge: with anObject as its argument. Returns the entry in the collection.

- mergeFilter: anObject;

    — Merges anObject into the receiver. If anObject is not in the collection, it is added. If it is in the collection, the entry in the collection is sent the merge: message with anObject as its argument. If anObject was not actually added to the collection, it is freed. Returns the entry in the collection.

- remove: anEntry;

    — Removes anEntry from the collection. Returns anEntry if found; otherwise returns nil.

- removeContentsOf: aCltn;

    — Removes each of the elements of aCltn from the receiver's collection. Returns the receiver.

- removeContentsFrom: aCltn;

    — Removes each member of the receiver from aCltn. Returns the receiver.

- eachElement;

    — Returns a Sequence over all the members of the receiver. This method requires the Sequence class to be linked into the executable image.

- elementsPerform: (SEL) aSelector with: obj1;

    — Sends a message to each element of the collection with aSelector and the argument obj1. Returns the receiver.

- elementsPerform: (SEL) aSelector with: obj1 with: obj2;

    — Sends a message to each element of the collection with aSelector and the arguments obj1 and obj2. Returns the receiver.

- elementsPerform: (SEL) aSelector with: obj1 with: obj2 with: obj3;

— Sends a message to each element of the collection with aSelector and the arguments obj1, obj2, and obj3. Returns the receiver.

- asIdArray;

— Returns the members of the collection stored in an instance of IdArray.

·- asSet;

— Returns an instance of class Set containing all the members of the receiver. It uses the method addContentsTo: to create the new set.

- asOrdCltn;

— Returns an instance of class OrdCltn containing all the members of the receiver. It uses the method addContentsTo: to create the new set.

- as: aClass;

— Returns an instance of class aClass containing all the members of the receiver. This method works only if the argument aClass recognizes new: and its instances recognize add:.

- find: anObject;

— Returns the first member in the collection which matches anObject; otherwise returns nil.

- (BOOL) contains: anObject;

— Returns YES if anObject is in the receiver; otherwise returns NO. The find: method is used in the implementation.

- (unsigned) size;

— Returns the number of objects in the collection.

- (BOOL) isEmpty;

— Returns YES if the receiver is empty; otherwise returns NO. Implemented in terms of the receiver's size method.

- printOn: (IOD) anIOD;

— Prints the collection in the sorted order. Each element in the collection is sent the method printOn:.

- showNodes;

— The sorted collection is stored as an AVL tree. The nodes are displayed on the stdout. Text output is provided.

- showNodesOn: (IOD) anIOD;

— Same as showNodes, except that the output is directed to anIOD.

- showStructure;

— Shows the structure of the internal AVL tree graphically on stdout.

- showStructureOn: (IOD) anIOD;

    — Same as showStructure, except that the output is directed to anIOD.

- (int) nameLength: (int) newNameLength;

    — Sets the name length used by showStructure and showStructureOn: to new-NameLength. Returns the old name length.

- free;

    — Frees the entire collection, but not its contents. Returns nil.

- freeContents;

    — Frees the entire collection, and all its contents. Returns nil.

B.13   String CLASS

Inherits from: Object

Classes used: None

Interface file:

```
//    ICpak 101 Foundation Library Class Interface
//    (c) Stepstone 1988. All rights reserved.
//
//    $Source: d:/objc40/src/icpak101/RCS/stringcl.h $
//    $Revision: 2.1 $
//    $Date: 89/04/30 22:34:46 $
//    $State: Exp $

#define STREQ(S1,S2) (scmp(S1,S2)==0)
#define isMemberOf(o, c) (((id)o)->isa == ((SHR)c))
#define LENSTR(o) (((BOOL)(isMemberOf(o, String)))?((id)o)->length:[o size])
#define STRSTR(o) (((BOOL)(isMemberOf(o, String)))?((id)o)->string:[o str])

#define NULLTERMINATOR '\0'

#import "ICpak101.h"
#import "Object.h"

@interface String : Object
{
   unsigned   size;
   unsigned   length;
   STR   string;
}

+ new;
+ new: (unsigned) nChars;
+ str:(STR )aString;
+ sprintf:(STR )fmt, ...;
- (STR) elements;
- assign:aString;
```

- assignSTR:(STR)aString;
- assignSTR:(STR)aString length:(unsigned)nChars;
- (char) charAt:(unsigned)anOffset;
- (char) charAt:(unsigned)anOffset put:(char)aChar;
- (STR) str;
- (int) asInt;
- (long) asLong;
- (double) asFloat;
- (double) asDouble;
- toLower;
- toUpper;
- (STR) strcat:(STR)aBuf;
- concat:aString;
- concatSTR:(STR)aCString;
- (int) compare:aString;
- (int) compareSTR:(STR)aCString;
- (BOOL) isEqual:aString;
- (BOOL) isEqualSTR:(STR)aCString;
- (int) dictCompare:aString;
- (int) dictCompareSTR:(STR)aCString;
- (unsigned) hash;
- printOn:(IOD)anIOD;
- copy;
- shallowCopy;
- asSTR:(STR)aString maxSize:(int)aSize;
- (unsigned) size;
- (unsigned) capacity;
- capacity:(unsigned)nChars;
- free;

@end

General comments: The String class holds null-terminated arrays of ASCII characters (i.e., C strings). Support for random access is provided. Support is provided for string conversion and comparison. String instances grow dynamically.

Instance variables:
— length: The current length of the null-terminated string contained by the instance
— size: The current size of the buffer used to store the null-terminated string contained by the instance
— string: A pointer to the storage buffer that contains the null-terminated string

Factory method selectors:
+ str: (STR) aCString;
— Creates an instance whose indexed variables contain the value of aCString. Returns the new instance.

+ sprintf: (STR) fmt; va_declare(va_alist);

 — Returns a new instance of String initialized just as the standard C library
function sprintf() is.

Instance method selectors:

- initialize;

 — Initializes a new instance of String with one indexed instance variable containing the null terminating character.

- initialize: (unsigned) nBytes;

 — Initializes a new String with room for nBytes plus a terminating null.

- (STR) str;

 — Returns a pointer to the null-terminated C string stored in the receiver.

- (int) asInt;

 — Returns the integer value of the C string, using the standard C function atoi().

- (long) asLong;

 — Returns the long value of the C string, using the standard C function atol().

- (double) asFloat;

 — Returns the double value of the C string, using the standard C function atof().

- (double) asDouble;

 — Same as asFloat.

- (STR) strcat: (STR) aBuf;

 — Concatenates the receiver's C string to aBuf. No length checking is done to
ensure that aBuf is large enough. Returns aBuf.

- concat: aStr;

 — Concatenates aStr, an instance of String or a subclass of String, to the end of
the receiver. Returns the receiver.

- (int) compare: aStr;

 — Compares the receiver's string to an instance of String or its subclasses.
Returns the comparison value. This value is negative if the receiver is
smaller than aStr, zero if they are the same, and positive if the receiver is
greater than aStr. Lexical comparisons are performed.

- (int) compareSTR: (STR) aCString;

 — Compares the receiver's string to aCString. Returns the comparison value.

- (int) dictCompare: aStr;

 — Compares the receiver's string to another instance of String or its subclasses
according to dictionary ordering (i.e., all characters other than letters and
numbers are ignored, and case is ignored). Returns the comparison value.

- *(int) dictCompareSTR: (STR) aCString;*
    — Compares the receiver's string to aCString according to dictionary ordering. Returns the comparison value.

- *(BOOL) isEqual: aStr;*
    — Returns YES if the value contained by aStr is equal to the contents of the receiver; otherwise returns NO.

- *(BOOL) isEqualSTR: (STR) aCString;*
    — Returns YES if the ordinary C string aCString is equal to the contents of the receiver; otherwise returns NO.

- *(unsigned) hash;*
    — Returns a hash value based upon the contents of the string contained by the receiver.

- *printOn: (IOD) anIOD;*
    — Prints the contents of the receiver using the standard C function fprintf() and returns the receiver.

- *copy;*
    — Returns a copy of the receiver with its internal C string copied as well.

- *shallowCopy;*
    — Same as copy for this class.

- *(char) charAt: (unsigned) anOffset;*
    — Returns the character at anOffset or zero if anOffset is greater than the length of the C string.

- *(char) charAt: (unsigned) anOffset put: (char) aChar;*
    — Replaces the character at anOffset with aChar and returns the old character that was in that location. Returns null if anOffset is greater than the length of the C string.

- *(unsigned) size;*
    — Returns the number of actual characters in the contained C string, excluding the null terminator.

- *capacity: (unsigned) nBytes;*
    — Changes the amount of space available for characters to nBytes. The original string contained by the receiver will be truncated if it is longer than nBytes.

- *(unsigned) size;*
    — Returns the number of characters this instance can currently hold.

B.14 Point CLASS

Inherits from: Object

Classes used: None

Interface file:

```
//      ICpak 101 Foundation Library Class Interface
//      (c) Stepstone 1988. All rights reserved.
//
//      $Source: d:/objc40/src/icpak101/RCS/point.h $
//      $Revision: 2.1 $
//      $Date: 89/04/30 22:34:41 $
//      $State: Exp $

#import "ICpak101.h"
#import "Object.h"

@interface Point : Object
{
 int xLoc,yLoc;
}

+  x:(int )x y:(int )y;
- (int ) x;
- (int ) y;
-  x:(int )x y:(int )y;
-  x:(int )x;
-  y:(int )y;
-  moveBy:aPoint;
-  moveBy:(int )x :(int )y;
-  moveTo:aPoint;
-  plus:aPoint;
-  minus:aPoint;
-  times:(int )aScalar;
- (BOOL ) isBelow:aPoint;
- (BOOL ) isAbove:aPoint;
- (BOOL ) isLeft:aPoint;
- (BOOL ) isRight:aPoint;
- (unsigned ) hash;
- (BOOL ) isEqual:anObject;
-  printOn:(IOD )anIOD;

@end
```

General comments: The Point class treats points as pixel representations for use with screen graphics and is intended for use with the Rectangle class. The origin, (0,0), is in the upper-left corner of the screen. The *x*-axis increases to the right; the *y*-axis increases downwards.

B.15 Rectangle CLASS

Inherits from: Object

Classes used: Point

Interface file:

```
//    ICpak 101 Foundation Library Class Interface
//    (c) Stepstone 1988. All rights reserved.
//
//    $Source: d:/objc40/src/icpak101/RCS/rectangl.h $
//    $Revision: 2.1 $
//    $Date: 89/04/30 22:34:42 $
//    $State: Exp $

#import "ICpak101.h"
#import "Object.h"
#import "Point.h"

#ifndef DEF_RECT
#define DEF_RECT

 typedef struct _PNT { @defs(Point) } PNT;

# define LEFT(rect) ((RECT*)rect)->origin.xLoc
# define RIGHT(rect) ((RECT*)rect)->corner.xLoc
# define TOP(rect) ((RECT*)rect)->origin.yLoc
# define BOTTOM(rect) ((RECT*)rect)->corner.yLoc
# define HEIGHT(rect) (BOTTOM(rect)-TOP(rect))
# define WIDTH(rect) (RIGHT(rect)-LEFT(rect))
#endif

@interface Rectangle : Object
{
 PNT origin,corner;
}

+ new;
+ origin:(PNT *)p corner:(PNT *)q;
+ origin:(PNT *)p extent:(PNT *)q;
+ origin:(int )x1 :(int )y1 extent:(int )x2 :(int )y2;
+ origin:(int )x1 :(int )y1 corner:(int )x2 :(int )y2;
+ fromUser;
- (int ) left;
- (int ) right;
- (int ) top;
- (int ) bottom;
- (int ) width;
- (int ) height;
- (int ) area;
- (int ) centerX;
- (int ) centerY;
```

```
-  moveBy:(PNT *)p;
-  moveBy:(int )x :(int )y;
-  top:(int )anInt;
-  bottom:(int )anInt;
-  left:(int )anInt;
-  right:(int )anInt;
-  moveTo:(PNT *)p;
-  moveTo:(int )x :(int )y;
-  origin:(PNT *)p corner:(PNT *)q;
-  origin:(PNT *)p extent:(PNT *)q;
-  origin:(PNT *)p;
-  corner:(PNT *)p;
-  extent:(PNT *)p;
-  origin;
-  corner;
-  extent;
-  center;
-  topLeft;
-  topCenter;
-  topRight;
-  bottomLeft;
-  bottomCenter;
-  bottomRight;
-  leftCenter;
-  rightCenter;
-  width:(int )anInt;
-  height:(int )anInt;
-  insetBy:(int )x :(int )y;
-  (BOOL ) intersects:aRectangle;
-  intersection:aRectangle;
-  union:aRectangle;
-  (BOOL ) contains:(PNT *)aPoint;
-  (unsigned ) hash;
-  (BOOL ) isEqual:aRect;
-  printOn:(IOD )anIOD;

@end
```

General comments: The Rectangle class in conjunction with the Point class forms the basis for user-interface graphics.

B.16 *IPSequence CLASS*

Inherits from: Object

Classes used: IdArray

Interface file:

```
//    ICpak 101 Foundation Library Class Interface
//    (c) Stepstone 1988. All rights reserved.
```

```
//
//     $Source: d:/objc40/src/icpak101/RCS/ipsequen.h $
//     $Revision: 2.1 $
//     $Date: 89/04/30 22:34:38 $
//     $State: Exp $

#import "ICpak101.h"
#import "Object.h"
#import "IdArray.h"
#import "Cltn.h"

@interface IPSequence : Object
{
 id contents;
 unsigned offset;
}
+ over:aCltn;
- over:aCltn;
- rewind;
- next;
- peek;
- previous;
- last;
- first;
- (unsigned ) size;
- printOn:(IOD )anIOD;
- printContentsOn:(IOD )anIOD;
- nonIdArray:objReturned returnedBy:returner method:(STR )method;

@end
```

General comments: The IPSequence class enables users to sequence through the Cltn subclasses by scanning a collection's contents in place. Typically, an IPSequence is generated for a collection. Within a loop, the next message is sent to the sequence until it reaches the end.

IPSequence may be used on any class that implements a contents method, which returns an IdArray containing the members of the collection.

The IPSequence is provided for backwards compatibility. The more reliable Sequence class is recommended for most applications.

B.17 Sequence CLASS

Inherits from: IPSequence, Object

Classes used: IdArray

Interface file:
```
//     ICpak 101 Foundation Library Class Interface
//     (c) Stepstone 1988. All rights reserved.
//
```

```
//    $Source: d:/objc40/src/icpak101/RCS/sequence.h $
//    $Revision: 2.2 $
//    $Date: 89/07/16 00:14:03 $
//    $State: Exp $

#import "ICpak101.h"
#import "Cltn.h"
#import "IdArray.h"
#import "IPSequence.h"

@interface Sequence : IPSequence

+ over:aCltn;
- over:aCltn;
- sort;
- sortBy:(SEL )aCmpSelector;
- free;
- copy;

@end
```

General comments: The Sequence class enables the user to reliably iterate through any type of collection. The only requirement for the collection is that it implement an asIdArray method, which returns an instance of IdArray containing the members of the collection. If the collection uses an IdArray, it is expected that sending the message asIdArray returns a copy of the internal IdArray and not the original.

The Sequence class works reliably under all circumstances, including those where the activities done while iterating modify the original collection. Sequences are preferred to IPSequences where the collection cannot be modified.

Instance variables: None

Factory method selectors:
+ over: aCltn;

— Returns a new sequence over the indicated collection.

Instance method selectors:
- over: aCltn;

— (Re)initializes a sequence over aCltn by deallocating the old contents and creating the new contents by sending the asIdArray message to aCltn.

- sort;

— Sorts the sequence by sending the sort message to its contents. Returns the sorted receiver.

- sortBy: (SEL) aCmpSelector;

— Sorts the sequence by sending the message sortBy: aCmpSelector to its contents. Returns the sorted receiver.

- release;

— Frees the IdArray that holds the contents of the collection and frees the sequence itself. Returns nil.

- copy;

— Makes a copy of the contents and the sequence and returns the new copy of the sequence.